Bad Scarlett

THE EXTRAORDINARY LIFE OF THE NOTORIOUS SOUTHERN BEAUTY MARIE BOOZER

DEBORAH C. POLLACK

the Peppertree Press
Sarasota, Florida

ISBN: 978-1-61493-494-3

Library of Congress Number: 2016919523

Printed January 2017

To the heroes and heroines of the North and the South, and in memory of my father, Capt. Joe, and my beloved Uncle Sammy, who always encouraged me.

Contents

List of Illustrations

Acknowledgments

I would like to first thank Penny Park, owner of the Wilson-Battle-Connell-Park Papers, who trusted me to borrow her family documents and gave me the permission to quote from them as well as to reproduce photographs. Her kindness and generosity are appreciated more than words can express. I also thank J. Reed Bradford, great-grandson of Julia C. Feaster Field, who scanned and photocopied his family archives, sent them to me, and granted permission for their use.

Alexander Moore, historian and former acquisitions editor of the University of South Carolina Press, should be mentioned in gratitude as well. I was fortunate to receive his advice, graciousness, and knowledge. He edited the manuscript and believes in the project with enthusiasm.

I am also very grateful to Julie Ann James, Teri Lynn Franco, and Rebecca Barbier of the Peppertree Press; and to DAR genealogist, Henrietta Rosson Morton.

Merci boucoup to Malik Benmiloud, *Responsable du Patrimoine Audiovisuel, Service de la Mémoire et des Affaires Culturelles, Cabinet du Préfet, Paris;* and Nathalie Minart, *Responsable Pôle Numérique, Direction du Cabinet du Préfet, Service de la Mémoire et des Affaires Culturelles, Préfecture de police;* and Corinne Priet, owner of the Hotel Villa Glamour, Paris, where Marie once lived. Annie Lise and Philippe Glardon, proprietors of the beautiful Château la Corbière in Switzerland, where Marie often stayed with her mother-in-law, were gracious to me as well, and provided an image of their chateau.

I am indebted to the readers of the first draft— my mom, P. J.; Audrey Peters; and Katie Dooley. They all shared their insights and opinions and gave me the confidence to pursue this. Other people and organizations to whom I owe gratitude include: Susanna Graydon Ardis; Sara Borden, Rights and Reproductions, Historical Society of Pennsylvania; Wallace Bradford; Debbie and Tom Brady; Louis P. Brady; Philippe Brian; Robert Buck; Roby Buckalew; Halley Cella, archives assistant, South Carolina Historical Society; Brianna Cregle, special collections assistant, Public Services Division, Department of Rare Books and Special Collections, Princeton University Library; Christopher Damiani, research assistant, Historical Society of Pennsylvania; Daughters of the American Revolution; Ben DiBiase, educational resources coordinator, Florida Historical Society; Wade Dorsey, archivist, South Carolina Department of Archives and History; Graham Duncan, manuscript specialist, South Caroliniana Library, University of South Carolina; Florida Atlantic University Library, John D. McArthur Campus; Carol Foe; Rosalie Foster, historian and president, North Brevard Heritage Foundation; Joel Fry, curator, Historic Bartram's Garden; Gloria Goldblatt; Anne M. Graham, CA, digital collections archivist, Museums, Archives and Rare Books, Kennesaw State University; Joan Harper, North Brevard Historical Society; David Haugaard, director of research services, Historical Society of Pennsylvania; Mark Hia, library technician, Palm Beach State College; Stephen Hoffius; Sarah Hood, user services librarian, J. Drake Edens Library, Columbia College, South Carolina; Gabrielle Houbre; Ajeya Kapadia, records, Brevard County Clerk; Brady Kerr; Lyle and Steve Kielley; Kathleen Krizek, librarian III, Special Collections, Jacksonville Public Library; Alana Lewis, Interlibrary Loan Lending, Addlestone Library, College of Charleston; Martha J. Loss, librarian, Central Brevard Library and Reference Center, Genealogy and Archives; Crystal Loyst, museum collections and research coordinator, Strathroy Museum, Ontario, Canada; Magazines and Newspapers Center, San Francisco Public Library; Leo Mavrovitis; Lorrey McClure, Published Materials, South Caroliniana Library; Eva and Daniel McDonald; Jena Meyer, archivist, South Carolina Historical Society; Patrick Morvan; New York county clerk; New York Public Library; Jayne Parker; Perkins Library, Duke University; Kathy Petersen, archives assistant, George J. Mitchell

2

Department of Special Collections and Archives, Bowdoin College Library; Jim Pinson, researcher, South Carolina Families; Charles Edwin Reed; Catherine Carson Ricciardi, archivist, Rare Book and Manuscript Library, Columbia University, Butler Library; Mary Ritch; Research and Instructional Services Department, Louis Round Wilson Special Collections Library, University of North Carolina at Chapel Hill, Wilson Library; Pat Schaefer, Collections Access and Research, Mystic Seaport, the Museum of America and the Sea; Lynsey Sczechowicz, audiovisual reference archivist, Hagley Museum and Library; Manju Sharma, reference/ILL librarian, Mandel Public Library of West Palm Beach; Kajette Solomon, administrator and Bridgeman education assistant, Bridgeman Art Library; Craig Stein, Esq., Stein & Stein, PA; Madelin Terrazas, archives assistant, Churchill Archives Centre, Churchill College; Jane Tuttle, archivist, J. Drake Edens Library, Columbia College, South Carolina; Steve Tuttle, South Carolina Department of Archives and History; Malea Walker, reference librarian, Newspaper and Current Periodical Reading Room, Library of Congress; Dwight S. Walsh Jr., archives and museum supervisor, the Citadel Archives and Museum; Susan Warren; Geoff Wexler, library director, Oregon Historical Society; Janis M. Whipple; Woodlands Trust for Historic Preservation; Kelly Wooten, research services and collection development librarian, Sallie Bingham Center for Women's History and Culture, Duke University; and Lauren Ziarko, archivist, Manhattanville College.

Preface

I first encountered Marie Boozer's name in a spurious 1878 pamphlet entitled *A Checkered Life: Being a Brief History of the Countess Pourtales, Formerly Miss Marie Boozer, of Columbia, S.C.*, republished in 1915 as *The Countess Pourtales* with an introduction by University of South Carolina history professor, Yates Snowden (1858–1933). The pamphlet was so libelous that the original author, former Confederate-era newspaperman Julian A. Selby, assumed the pseudonym "One Who Knows." After reading about Marie's supposed adventures, I became determined to learn more about her, and by the end of 2012 Marie's story had been copyrighted in a dual-biographic manuscript entitled *Rebelles*, which also explored another young woman who left the South. Because most of the manuscript concerned Marie, Alexander Moore suggested concentrating on her only, and aside from acquiring additional, largely period documentation, I essentially completed her biography by the end of 2013, but subsequently revised and polished the manuscript.

Manly Wade Wellman (1903–86), a popular North Carolina historian and novelist, denoted Marie's life as more exciting than the notorious celebrities Adah Isaacs Menken and Lola Montez. He also asserted that Marie was the basis for the characters of Scarlett O'Hara in *Gone with the Wind* and Amber St. Clare in *Forever Amber*.[1] While in many ways Marie resembled Scarlett O'Hara and was somewhat like Amber St. Clare, other characters reflecting the real Marie should be added to that list—Anna Karenina and that lively woman named Mame Dennis, Auntie Mame, in Patrick Dennis's novel.

Author, historian, and professor emeritus at Emory University, Bell Irvin Wiley (1906–80) deemed Marie "one of the four most famous southern women of the Civil War." This list included the first lady of the Confederacy—Mrs. Jefferson Davis.[2] Marie's true-life role in the Civil War was remarkable, but her most sensational episodes occurred following the war after escaping from South Carolina to New York City. There she fell in love with the wrong man, who almost destroyed her. Despite her callous treatment, Marie fought against ruination by cleverly suppressing it, adopting a laissez-faire attitude, and enduring in Paris the only way she knew. To avoid shame to her family, Marie adopted aliases *de rigueur* for any fallen woman in the nineteenth century. She was a realistic survivor, and by the time she was in her late twenties, saved herself from a sad fate by entering her second marriage. This union became her salvation. Redemption through marriage allowed her to re-invent her life and exceed expectations beyond the realm of imagination. Although she established this positive path far from the Palmetto State, South Carolinians and misogynistic northerners created and perpetuated demeaning legends about her. Unfortunately, some have been accepted as true by reputable writers.

In the 1930s Columbia, South Carolina, book dealer James Thornton Gittman promised Yates Snowden before he died that Gittman would "see to it that someday someone vindicated Marie Boozer of the false accusations" in print against her. And as Professor Snowden penned in 1915, it was a "pity" that Marie's "whole life story could not be procured and published."[3] Over one hundred years later, this is Marie's first full-length biography.

Introduction

Marie Boozer was a beautiful, brilliant, and notorious South Carolina strawberry blonde who lived an extraordinary life. A complex woman, she inhabited an antiquated age that defined her but could not constrain her. She was trained in deportment but driven by passion. She was warm and affectionate but could also be aloof. Above all, she was human—complete with foibles and attributes beyond the stereotypical perception held by the public. Her life was replete with adventure, travel, public scrutiny, and outlandish rumors.

Marie's experiences, life choices, and lessons are the crux of this biography, which has two themes: to record Marie's entire life as accurately as possible and to reveal why so many myths have surrounded her. Although her actual scandalous behavior lasted for around four years, any other notoriety is pure fiction. Of equal importance is the derogatory manner in which the national printed media responded to this southern belle. She was a celebrity who paid the dues of fame—elevated to a pinnacle of adulation followed by the slanders of a gossip-hungry public.

Marie and her mother, Amelia Harned Burton Boozer Feaster, also bore the brunt of southern resentment coupled with a widespread antifeminist attitude that has lasted for generations. The rise of feminine power in the late nineteenth century was concurrent with the Lost Cause movement, the post–Civil War devotion to ennobling the Confederacy. Southern women who raised money for veterans, widows, and monuments were seen not only as guardians of Confederate identity but also propagators of it in their roles as mothers. Yates Snowden's mother, Mary Amarinthia Yates Snowden (1819–98), who organized the Ladies

Memorial Association, epitomized this kind of heroine. The United Daughters of the Confederacy were also archetypes of southern womanhood, a status perpetuated by males who lauded the women and created tributes to them. However, men restricted southern women's power to keep them as willing allies and nurturers, and some ladies opposed suffrage and behaved according to men's commands. Any feminism within later generations carried a caveat—elitism. In 1914 Charleston, South Carolina, residents Louisa Bouknight Poppenheim, a prominent member of women's Lost Cause groups, and Mary Barnett Poppenheim, an editor of South Carolina Women of the Confederacy, favored "limited woman suffrage," in other words, only for the elite.[1]

Marie Boozer has taken her place in Civil War and post–Civil War lore as the antithesis of those venerated southern women. She has been vilified as a stereotypical hussy, complete with authentic and fabricated perils of a fallen feminine renegade. She is a bad Scarlett O'Hara who relinquished her love of the South, abandoned her homeland, and could never give birth to a supporter of Confederate heritage. Marie and her mother have also been scapegoats for frustration in some southerners stemming from the unfulfilled promise of the Confederate States of America.

As a sexual fixation and/or object of disdain, Marie has remained notorious for 150 years. She has been called a vixen, trollop, sorceress, adventuress, and worse. A legacy of rumor, innuendo, and misinformation from 1865 until the present day has held her story captive. To add infamy, for the past sixty or so years, novelists have done their best to inflate Marie's myth. For instance, E. L. Doctorow noted her fame in his historical novel *The March* and included an apocryphal sex story about Marie and General Hugh Judson Kilpatrick.

Marie and her mother played starring roles in two mid-twentieth-century historical novels written by women. The talented novelists responsible for these entertaining yet defamatory books, Nell Saunders Graydon and Elizabeth Boatwright Coker, were thorough researchers, but it was the late 1950s and some obscure information was not obtainable through the resources of that time. The authors also lacked Marie's family documents. Nevertheless, they listened to anecdotes and diligently combed through other people's family archives, church records, literature, and a few newspaper articles. Making up descriptions and events to fill in for the absence of facts, they did the best they could for their time. Nell Graydon's 1958 book was entitled *Another Jezebel: A Yankee Spy in South Carolina* and Mrs. Coker's 1959 national best-selling novel was *La Belle: A Novel Based on the Life of the Notorious Southern Belle, Marie Boozer.* Coker based it primarily on Julian A. Selby's imaginative and libelous *A Checkered Life* (reprinted as *The Countess Pourtales*) and an 1876 *San Francisco Chronicle* article partly reprinted in it.

After Coker's novel was published, both authors received the shocking news that Marie had given birth to a son and had living half nieces armed with family history, photographs, and several of Marie's letters. The nieces provided Graydon and Coker with copies of some letters, photos, and a few other papers from the family collection, but also knew that both writers had been complicit in spreading the old slanders against their grandmother and aunt. Therefore, they did not permit the novelists to reference or quote from the family collection or publish photographs in subsequent editions.

Filled with guilt and remorse over *Another Jezebel,* Nell Graydon donated copies of Marie's archives to important repositories, including the Southern Historical Collection at the University of North Carolina Libraries and Duke University. She, with permission from Marie's nieces, published some of Marie's letters in Columbia's newspaper, the *State,* on February 23, 1960.

Years later Coker penned two brief essays concerning what "actually happened" to Marie, yet the author did not have all the family documents, did not nearly know the entire truth about Marie, and again, as a veteran novelist, slipped into creatively inspired paragraphs. She also arrived at inaccurate conclusions. For example, Coker quoted a memoir, *The Puppet Show of Memory* by Maurice Baring, and assumed that the author had described Marie in his relating seeing Madame de Pourtalès in Paris during the 1890s. In truth, he had described Melanie de Bussiere, Comtesse Edmond de Pourtalès, a star of the Second Empire. However,

Coker included, largely from her friend Julian Bolick's research, salient recollections of Marie from persons whose ancestors had known her in Columbia. These interesting essays are located in Coker's papers at the South Caroliniana Library of the University of South Carolina.

This biography of Marie primarily rests on the archives in her nieces' estate and two other groups of family papers belonging to heirs. Marie expresses her own thoughts in two interviews published in 1876 and several descriptive letters from 1878–1905. Amelia's petition to Abraham Lincoln reveals who actually burned Columbia, South Carolina. Other private and public archives including Marie's adoption, marriage, and divorce records; sworn statements before Congress; attorneys' and military letters and memoirs; secret files of the Paris Préfecture de Police; notes from the demimonde of Paris; historical society papers; disclosures and diaries from Yankees and Rebels during and after the Civil War; witnesses at London's courthouses; and recollections from international diplomats serve to rebuild a truthful foundation of Marie Boozer's life.

CHAPTER ONE:

Introducing Marie and Her Mother, Amelia

*There was a girl in Columbia regarded as the prettiest girl in town,
named Mary Boozer. She was a notorious character, and her mother was
equally as bad. They were both beautiful women, but that does not go
very far if it has not the character to back it up.*

—J. F. Williams, *Old and New Columbia*, 1929[1]

Marie Boozer, also known as Mary, especially liked coaching by the
parade grounds of the Columbia, South Carolina, Arsenal precisely
when the military students were dismissed from their classes. In the early
1860s the young men often took notice and referred to her carriage as the
"beauty box." One admirer described her years later as sort of a teenage
vamp: "She loved to display her charm to the masculine eye and when
most of the men were away in the Confederate army, Mary drove out to
flirt with the boys of the old school." Most of the boys were too bashful to
call on her, but at least two took on the challenge. Those who were brave
enough to become her callers thought she possessed the style and allure
of Cleopatra with the perfect combination of vivacity and haughtiness.[2]

Well-groomed in the roles society expected of her, Marie nevertheless had an affinity for the outdoors, loved nature, and after a day filled
with coaching, socializing, and studying, she could enjoy a hearty supper.
After she evolved from southern maiden to southern belle, she was still
known as vivacious, beautiful, and witty and became an even more powerful male magnet. As soon as she made an appearance on the front step

of her house, "it was a signal for all the masculine heads in the neighborhood to come into view."[3]

Major Tom Williams recalled that on February 16, 1865, when the first regiment of the Confederate cavalry was stationed in the countryside of South Carolina and heard about the capturing of Columbia by Sherman's troops, they weren't much interested. They wanted to hear what happened to Marie Boozer. Confederate soldiers had been "struck dumb with speechless admiration" for her. In fact, Williams declared that if she had accompanied them at all when Sherman was in the state, they would have marched directly into Columbia and surrendered to the Union army. That's how charismatic she had become by the age of eighteen.[4]

Marie inherited some of her allure from her mother, Amelia. Forty-six years prior to the taking of Columbia, distinct wails were heard from a modest Philadelphia home, signifying Amelia's birth on January 30, 1819. She was the youngest of six girls. Her mother, Mary Carr Sees (1786–1871), born in Philadelphia two years after her family emigrated from Northern Ireland, spoke to her infant affectionately with words softened by a British lilt. Amelia's papa, George Sees (1781–1835), who grew up listening to the French language, was equally as loving to the baby. The couple had wed during the chilly evening of February 5, 1807.[5]

The Sees house was in a historic city so bound to the legacy of American independence that it commemorated the Fourth of July like no other municipality. In the same year Amelia was born, the artist John Lewis Krimmel sensed the merriment of the annual event and depicted Philadelphia's citizens in celebration—men in military uniforms, women in stylish Empire frocks and bonnets, and playful children shooting off toy pistols and cannons. Above the festivities an American and Pennsylvania flag fluttered in the summery sky, and pride and patriotism reigned.

Patriotism also extended to Amelia's family. Her paternal grandfather, George Sees Sr. (1754–1783), emigrated from France with the Huguenots and fought as a lieutenant in the Fifth Battalion Philadelphia Militia during the American Revolution.[6] Her father was a respected merchant and city constable (elected in 1820 by a large majority), involved in local politics and entrusted to maintain the firearms in the Philadelphia arsenal. Amelia's maternal uncle was Colonel Robert Carr (1778–1866), "one of the most remarkable men of the time." Carr knew Benjamin Franklin through his grandchildren, and apprenticed with Benjamin Franklin Bache. Carr also sent proofs to George Washington when he was in Philadelphia and published one of the first multiple-volume English language Bibles in America, which earned Carr a gold medal from the American Association of Booksellers in June 1804. But that wasn't the end of Carr's contributions to the United States. He became a lieutenant colonel in the War of 1812 and afterward was appointed Adjutant-General of Pennsylvania. After retiring from the military, Carr became a botanist and with his botanist/artist wife, Ann Bartram Carr, a daughter of John Bartram Jr., maintained the first botanical garden in North America, founded by Ann's grandfather, John Bartram. Historic Bartram's Garden, located along the Schuylkill River, can be visited today. Amelia's brother, John Randolph Sees, earned public acclaim from inventing an important engine air compressor, and the John M. Snyder School in West Virginia was named for Amelia's brother-in-law.[7]

It was clear that with her two surviving brothers and five sisters—Rebecca (born at Bartram's Garden), Margaretta (known as Margaret), Emily, Mary, and Catherine—Amelia was from intelligent, religious, and cultured stock. Like her family, she too became an American patriot, willing to suffer for her devotion to the Union.[8]

By 1828 the family had moved to Philadelphia's George (now Sansom) Street near Thirteenth Street, and soon Amelia became a teenager. Blessed with even features, luminous skin, a high forehead, and lustrous, thick dark hair, she was also a talented seamstress who could transform silks or velvets into fashionable Paris-style dresses copied from *Godey's Lady's Book*. Her talents prompted appreciative glances from men and an untold amount of envy from women.[9]

In 1837, two years after the death of Amelia's father, a severely ill Philadelphian named Thomas B. Harned fell in love with the eighteen-year-old Amelia and pleaded with her to marry him on his deathbed. She complied primarily out of sympathy for him, and sadly, as expected, shortly after the wedding he died on April 10 at 11:00 p.m.—just three months past his twenty-third birthday.[10]

A few years later Amelia met Peter Burton, an older, respected southerner who had traveled to Philadelphia on business. Their meeting likely occurred between fall 1839 and early winter 1840, for that summer and early fall Burton was occupied in Columbia, South Carolina, trying to defend his actions in killing a man. Burton and G. W. Hunt had been in a heated argument on August 8, whereupon both men drew pistols and shot each other. Burton's wounds were not severe, but Hunt's were fatal, leading to Burton's arrest for murder.[11]

The October trial in Columbia's courthouse on Main and Washington Streets created a whirlwind of press coverage and attracted a packed audience. Due to overcrowding, many spectators were ordered to leave the building. Those who were allowed to remain watched from early morning until late at night as two prominent Columbians, Colonel John Smith Preston, a wealthy attorney and plantation owner, and William Ford De Saussure, a future South Carolina senator, defended Burton. The defense presented an admirable case, and after only a few minutes of jury deliberation, Burton was acquitted.[12]

After meeting Amelia in Philadelphia, Burton became enamored with the twenty-one-year-old, and when he returned to South Carolina, Amelia traveled there with him. From February 1840 through at least April, she remained in Charleston, and on December 12, 1840, Amelia and Burton were married by the Reverend William Coombs Dana of Charleston's Third Presbyterian Church. The couple then set up housekeeping in Columbia, the state capital built at the confluence of the Broad, Saluda, and Congaree Rivers.[13]

Burton was a partner in business with merchants James McMahon and David and John Ewart in Columbia and Charleston (formerly with Winthrop Williams until 1839). Their company struggled during the marriage, forcing Amelia to deal with the strain of her husband's debt. The situation became so dire that in 1842 the businessmen filed for bankruptcy protection, and as required by law, the local press repeatedly posted the notices. The magistrate denied the partners' case, and the following year they were summoned to court to reassess their financial situation. Unfortunately, the newspaper postings concerning this remained in constant evidence from 1842–43, causing a great amount of stress and humiliation for Amelia. She was not the only South Carolina wife to experience this kind of financial difficulty. Many antebellum southern merchants became insolvent as they relied on northern financial credit that proved problematic.[14]

Peter Burton died around 1846, reportedly from a seizure, leaving Amelia a pregnant widow who gave birth to his child a few months later. A healthy baby girl with blue eyes and golden hair, the future Marie Boozer Beecher, Countess de Pourtalès-Gorgier was named Mary Amelia P. Burton. Amelia chose the name Mary after her grandmother and mother, Amelia after herself, and the initial P in memory of Peter. As soon as the baby could speak, she called her mother "Mamma."[15]

According to several genealogies including "Descendants of Archibald Carr," Marie's great-grandfather, Marie's birth occurred in December 1846. A biographical dictionary confirms that year, as does at least one period legal document by denoting she was an infant living in Columbia, South Carolina, before September 1847. An 1850 census also corresponds to the genealogic date by recording her age at three; however, it is difficult to pinpoint the exact date of birth because Marie later fibbed about her age, including to her own family members. She was obviously schooled in this kind of subterfuge by her mother as Amelia also concealed her age and had some relatives convinced she was born in 1825, not 1819. Amelia had also made herself six to eleven years younger in census forms.[16]

Regardless, Marie and her mamma formed an instant bond, and their closeness intensified as they were all each other had in South Carolina. In the spring of 1847, Amelia brought Marie to Newberry, a village some forty miles away from Columbia, yet connected to it through mutual friends and acquaintances who maintained a constant pipeline of talk. Amelia had planned to vacation at Newberry's Birdsfield Hotel; however, the hotel's manager could not allow her to lodge there as renovations were in process. David Boozer, the owner of the hotel whom Amelia had met previously in Columbia, was there inspecting the project.[17]

David Boozer, a fifty-nine-year-old widower familiarly known as "Big

Dave," was a wealthy farmer and real estate holder who owned numerous slaves. One who knew him described him as "possessed of great energy of Character" and having "generally a great flow of spirits."[18]

Boozer invited Amelia, who was thirty-one years his junior, to stay at his house, which he shared with several family members. Amelia welcomed Big Dave's invitation and moved in with him, whereupon he promptly fell in love with the twenty-eight-year-old widow and asked her to marry him. In spite of townswomen who insisted Amelia had plotted to hook Big Dave, the wedding took place on September 16, 1847, officiated by the Reverend Mr. Talley.[19]

Newberry, a small hamlet that was Newberry District's seat of government, was neither a transportation nor trading hub when Marie and Amelia resided there. As in many close-knit villages, gossip was the pastime, and Amelia, disdained as a Yankee out-of-towner, had snatched away one of the village's more eligible widowers. The new bride consequently remained a target for resentment, and lurid rumors were spread as soon as the marriage occurred.[20]

The pervasive gossip claimed that the infant Marie was not the daughter of Peter Burton. The tongues hissed that she was the child of an illicit love affair between Amelia and a Columbia physician named Hugh Huger Toland, whom Amelia supposedly often met by bribing one of Boozer's slaves to drive her to the trysts. Other back-fence talk purported that Marie was David Boozer's illegitimate daughter.[21]

While gossip in the Old South could be sufficiently malicious to cause a husband to divorce his wife, none of these rumors affected Amelia's marriage as David Boozer continued to love her and her little girl. He proved this by making Marie his daughter, for on November 21, 1848, Marie's name officially changed from Mary Amelia P. Burton to Mary Sarah Amelia Boozer. Big Dave, legally called Marie's "next friend," and Amelia Boozer signed the petition to change Marie's status, a decree that essentially denoted Boozer's adoption of the child.[22]

Marie was an active little girl and somewhat of a tomboy. She spent hours jumping rope, loved to play on grapevine swings, and ran barefoot up and down the village's paths and lanes. A former Newberry resident recalled Marie making mud pies with him. She regularly attended her parents' church, Aveleigh Presbyterian, and walked to services with Big Dave while he held her hand. Boozer would often call her "my little golden fairy."[23]

This domestic bliss changed drastically on February 10, 1850, when in less than three years after his marriage, David Boozer committed suicide by shooting himself in the head because of financial reversals. "The change in this respect, although he was still surrounded by an ample estate, unsettled his reason, and led to the rash, mad act which he committed." The death of a loving father devastated Marie, and she and Amelia mourned deeply the "great loss" of Big Dave. Nevertheless, Marie relished the love and attention of her mother, which the child clung to and strived to maintain throughout young adulthood.[24]

David Boozer's estate was worth approximately $10,000–15,000 that year. According to his will, Amelia inherited the profits of the estate to maintain and educate Marie, and when Marie was of age or married, she would inherit two of Boozer's slaves and their children. Marie would become the heiress to the entire estate after her mother's death. Big Dave had also bequeathed $1,000 for ample space for his burial place alongside his first wife's and eventually Amelia's with a structure to cover the three graves.[25]

Aside from the wrenching loss of another husband, Amelia had to endure more rumors about her perpetuated by envious females. Amelia was in church when Boozer committed suicide, but some women slandered her as his murderer, and further gossip precipitated Aveleigh Church elders to enforce charges against her. However, according to a recorded copy of the church's minutes, Amelia was accused not of actually murdering Boozer but driving him to suicide from her overextravagance; for instance, collecting payment for a large amount of cotton in Columbia and then spending the profits on herself. Further accusations included Amelia arguing with Boozer hours before he committed suicide and telling Boozer that Col. William Maybin gave her a gift, causing his jealous wife to try to poison her.[26]

These were serious character wounds upon Amelia, but instead of shrinking from them and making a hasty retreat out of town, she asked the elders to hold a church hearing to clear her name. She then traveled to Columbia and collected sworn affidavits from prominent men including those mentioned in the accusations. At the hearing she was defended by Chancellor Job Johnstone, Judge John B. O'Neall (Boozer's friend), Dr. Toland (prompting more gossip about an affair), and Amelia's stepson (Boozer's son from his first wife). Toland and Maybin attested to Amelia's virtuousness, Mrs. Maybin declared she merely gave Amelia medicine that upset her stomach, and others swore Amelia was not a spendthrift. Consequently, the church found her innocent of every charge brought against her. Later, Dr. Toland moved out of Columbia, allegedly to escape his embarrassment and his wife's irritation about the rumored affair, and eventually settled in California to become a world-renowned surgeon.[27]

Amelia remained in Newberry for around a year to settle the estate and sell Boozer's properties. An intelligent woman, she was more than capable to handle such widow's affairs with help from her attorney and Boozer's executor, Judge John B. O'Neall, but some legal minutia between them remained problematic.[28]

After Amelia sold Boozer's properties for cash, which she was permitted to do according to Big Dave's will, and partially settled the estate's legal issues, she bought some of its furniture and three of Boozer's slaves. Then she and her daughter moved back to Columbia leaving a trail of gossip behind them.[29]

Marie and her mamma were once again all each other had in South Carolina. They moved into a commodious house Amelia had purchased on Washington Street. She then employed a governess for Marie and had a mother/daughter daguerreotype made to signify their bond.[30]

Amelia was not overly wealthy and she struggled to keep her daughter in an aristocratic lifestyle. David Boozer's bequest made up the bulk of their money, but Amelia also supplemented a comfortable existence through rental property investments (using cash from Boozer's properties) and her skill with a needle and thread—earning an income as a dressmaker for elite Columbia matrons. While this was a respectable career for middle-class southern women, it permitted the upper social strata to consider Amelia beneath them.[31]

Meanwhile, the same year David Boozer committed suicide because of his financial status, Amelia's uncle, Robert Carr, and her Aunt Ann filed for bankruptcy and were obliged to sell their botanical garden and personal items at auction.[32] This challenging difficulty again taught Amelia the pain caused by the lack of money—always a detriment to one's comfort and well-being, yet rarely accompanied by any redeeming features. Amelia learned this lesson well and determined to make Marie's future as secure as possible.

Life for Marie was bound to change as the daughter of an attractive, available widow. This occurred after Amelia met a merchant named Jacob "Jake" Jefferson Norris Feaster while settling Boozer's estate. Feaster (fig. 1) was only four years older than Amelia—closer to her age than Burton and Boozer—and belonged to a prominent, cultured family from Feasterville in Fairfield District. He had a distinctive profile and kind eyes, and like Burton and Boozer, fell in love with Amelia. Consequently, she and Jacob were married at the First Presbyterian Church of Columbia on August 14, 1852, at three o'clock in the afternoon in a ceremony officiated by Reverend Benjamin Morgan Palmer.[33]

Fig. 1. Jacob Jefferson Norris Feaster, ca. 1880, Wilson-Battle-Connell-Park Papers.

Soon Marie's family grew. On June 23, 1853, at six-thirty p.m., her half sister (Mary) Julia Carrie Bell (a.k.a. Isabel or Belle) was born in Columbia, followed by a half brother, Jacob "Jakie" Andrew, born on

October 9, 1855, at seven a.m. while the family was living in Greenville after a brief stay in Alston. Another half sister (Amelia) Ethland Brooks ("Tutu") was born in Greenville on March 7, 1857.[34]

Greenville was a pretty little tree-lined town in the 1850s. Near scenic mountains and waterfalls, it served as both a trading center and health resort for those who made the yearly trek to the up-country to escape mosquito-born illnesses of the Lowcountry. Marie attended the Baptist Sunday school while the family lived in town.[35]

Jacob had established a partnership in a grocery store and the business flourished, with ample prices for provisions. He also tended a garden, which produced the most successful vegetable patch he had ever beheld. Amelia, whose Uncle Robert and Aunt Ann were expert botanists, likely gave Jacob some helpful tips on horticulture.[36]

After living in Greenville for a few years, Amelia and her family moved back to Columbia. The city's tree-shaded streets at that time were appointed with gracious brick-and-white-columned governmental buildings, stately churches, Columbia Female College, South Carolina College, a handsome library, and grand mansions—many reflecting the Greek Revival architectural style. Cottages with white-railed porches complemented the larger homes. Lush wisteria overgrew other foliage and structures, and moss-cloaked live oaks framed scenic walkways. The municipal park at Arsenal Hill bloomed seasonally with magnolias, and multicolored flowers in private gardens also adorned the state capital.[37]

Living in Columbia was quite different from small town life in Greenville. Columbia was alive with parties, balls, and other social activities when the general assembly was in session. When the legislature adjourned, the capital reverted back to a relaxed yet clique-filled community. But politically, high conflict arose between supporters of secession and those advising southerners not to be rash in their actions. Regardless of battling politicians and their competing factions, Columbia's citizens would soon be captivated by the teenaged Marie.[38]

CHAPTER TWO

Columbia's Scarlett O'Hara

*When Columbia became the great military centre, Marie Boozer
was recognized as* La Fille du Regiment, *and many a wife has
felt the stings of jealousy on her account.*

—Correspondent to the *Florida Times Union*, 1885

In the late 1850s Jacob and his brother, Trezevant DeGraffenreid Feaster
(1826–97), called "T. D." and "Trez," owned a grocery store at 194
Richardson Street near Amelia's home on Washington between Richardson
and Sumter Streets. Their neighborhood included the mayor's house and a
mansion owned by the city's Renaissance man, Dr. Robert Wilson Gibbes.
A journalist, newspaper owner, physician, scientist, educator, and former
mayor, Gibbes held an important painting and rare book collection. His
distant nephew, James Shoolbred Gibbes, also became a noted collector
and would later found Charleston's first municipal art museum.[1]

Amelia had introduced Trez Feaster to her Philadelphia family members, including her sister Margaret Sees Collins Cubbison (1809–83),
widow of Charles Collins and James Cubbison, and Amelia's nieces, Julia
Collins, Mary Carr Cubbison, and the youngest, Sarah ("Sallie") Cubbison.
In 1854 Trez married Julia and brought her family to live with him. After
Julia died in February 1858, Trez married her sister, Mary Carr Cubbison
on October 23 that year while temporarily living in Alston.[2]

Reverend Daniel Bragg Clayton recalled that on the day of the wedding, he and Trez Feaster chatted while Mary sewed and Sallie worked in
the kitchen with her mother, Margaret. After about an hour Feaster asked

21

the time, and when told that the train would soon leave, he said, "Mary, if we are going to get married, I guess we had better attend to it. Are you ready?"

"Yes," Mary replied, and they stood before Rev. Clayton, who called Sallie and Margaret to join them. Immediately after the brief ceremony, the bride returned to her sewing, Sallie resumed her work in the kitchen, and the preacher boarded the train "with a five-dollar-bill in his pocket that he had not carried there, feeling that he had officiated at about as sensible a wedding as he had ever attended."[3]

After Mary's marriage, Margaret continued to reside with the Trez Feasters in Columbia, and the extended Sees-Cubbison-Feaster family became a close, happy one. Marie particularly enjoyed being with her cousin Sallie, who was around Marie's age, and later described Sallie as a "very quiet, refined girl."[4]

Amelia had been providing a fine education for Marie from her governess, Miss Josselyn (see fig. 2), but Marie may also have been educated at the Zimmerman School run by Dr. Charles and Hannah Zimmerman, German immigrants who opened their school in 1848. It was near the house where her "cousin-in-law," Maria Louisa ("Lula") Feaster, later resided while attending the school.[5]

While Amelia had a resolved, dominating personality and could be manipulative at times, she was a loving mother to her children. She doted on them and wrote at least one metaphorical poem describing them, in which her son became an "eagle bird," the embodiment of America itself, and her daughters were symbolized by flowers in the colors of the American flag—a red rose, white lily, and blue violet. Marie was the "Lily" of the poem. She was blessed with Amelia's intelligence and a high forehead crowned with shimmering strawberry-blonde hair that appeared more auburn in dim light:

> My Lily's hair of auburn hue—
> Her eyes of darkest deepest blue,
> Displaying from her very birth
> A Heart of warmth, a mind of worth,

Fair child of promise now for Thee
I cull the Flower of Purity
Oh! May thy pathway all through life
Be sweetly calm and free from strife
Thy mind to knowledge early given
Thy Heart to Virtue and to Heaven
This Lily is my prayer for thee
The eldest of my daughters three.[6]

Fig. 2. Miss Josselyn, Ethland (around three), and Marie (around fourteen), ca. 1860,
courtesy Wilson-Battle-Connell-Park Papers.

Amelia wished her daughter Julia, to "go forth and bloom in sweetest grace/perfect in features, heart and face / May life glide sweetly on with Thee / Like sunbeams on a summer sea." For her baby, Ethland, Amelia hoped: "Oh! May thy life be one bright dream / Untouched by sorrow, free from sin / Reward thy parent's tender care / With holy love and strive to be / Fit emblem of the name you bear, / Of charming little Modesty." Amelia proclaimed her son, Jakie, "Thy boyhood pure, thy manhood bright / thus shalt Thou be Thy Mother's joy, thy sisters' pride, Thy Pater's honest boy" and wished him to "Go forth and gain a noble name / Devote thy talents, then to fame. Fear not! Be just thou then will be / Thy country's Honor / And a Noble Son of Liberty."[7] These were the hopes of a well-bred, pious, and patriotic mother, clearly belying the gossip that still clung to her.

In the fall of 1858 Amelia's famous uncle, Robert Carr, mourning the death of his wife Ann, escaped his loneliness by visiting relatives in New York and then evaded the frigid air of Philadelphia by staying at Amelia's house in Columbia for the entire winter of 1858–59. Obviously, the close rapport between Amelia and her Philadelphia family remained no matter where she resided and regardless of what the fates were planning for America.[8]

The *Columbia Bulletin* interviewed Carr and as they reported, the octogenarian could walk for thirty-one miles and did not need reading glasses. He enjoyed spending time with Amelia, Margaret, and his grandnieces, and liked the city so much he considered relocating there permanently—a sensible decision as his nieces could take care of him if necessary in the future. However, Carr's plans to live with Amelia in Columbia came to a halt in 1860 when South Carolina's leaders convened at the city's First Baptist Church to separate from the Union.[9]

Secession or not, the Feasters were relatively comfortable with Jacob's monetary worth of about $30,000. Marie fared nicely as well by captivating Columbia and its environs. By then she had left her tomboy days of carefree girlhood and entered the crinoline restraints of maidenhood (see fig. 2). She also became a nonboarding first collegiate class "day student" at Columbia Female College in 1860. While the college was located in the center of town, it was self-contained and independent of the city—conducive to keeping a watchful eye on students. During the time Marie attended, the enrollment was based on the academic ability of a student, not necessarily age.[10]

The course of study involved the arts, sciences, and "polite accomplishment," with the French language available for students of all grades. The college also included in its curriculum subjects based on the textbook *The Class Book of Nature*, originally written under the auspices of the Society for Promoting Christian Knowledge. Chapters concerned the nature of the universe, the human body with its hygiene and maintenance, and the animal and plant kingdoms. A section devoted to "Temper and Passions" discouraged ill feelings and complaining, and promoted a cheerful attitude in life. It did not approach the predicament of sexual passion—natural urges healthy young women experienced—and the word love was used primarily in respect to the Creator.[11]

Marie grew into young womanhood, and the more lovely she became, the more myth and mystery cloaked her. Still known as Mary, she sometimes arrived at school in a carriage with both a driver and footman on board, but more often on a handsome, lively horse accompanied by an African American groom on another mount. Her classmates, who described Marie as beautiful, enigmatic, and petite, were in awe of her as she was fashionably attired, wearing a "velvet riding habit with a long train," its color depending on the particular day of the week. A matching hat with a long, plush feather or silken scarf elegantly draped over one shoulder completed the outfit.[12]

Marie was an exceptional student, and this coupled with her magnetism prompted female classmates to be so enrapt with her they ignored their teacher. One young woman who sat behind Marie became entranced with caressing her thick hair curling down her back. Marie was "always friendly" with these girls "but in a cool way, never becoming intimate." While they invited her to parties she did not reciprocate with this particular group of admirers.[13]

Her reserved behavior in school, ingrained in her by her governess and her mother, reflected the approved conduct of aristocratic young ladies instructed in their era's deportment books. But however aloof

Marie appeared in classes, there was at least one female schoolmate she considered a close friend, Sally Buchanan Preston, called "Buck." Buck was a true southern belle, her enchanting likeness captured by the sculptor Hiram Powers when she and her family lived in Italy. Her father, the distinguished General John Smith Preston, who had defended Marie's biological father in his 1839 murder trial and who collected fine art, called Marie "'the most beautiful piece of flesh and blood' his eyes had ever beheld."[14]

Marie was still living a rather aristocratic life on the precipice of Civil War, her relative wealth endowed by David Boozer's estate. The young belle was the delight of those gentlemen attending South Carolina College just before the war began. David Augustus Dickert, a young collegian, gushed: "None ever saw this marvel without being entranced by her bewildering beauty. The writer of this sketch . . . must confess to having been speechless with wonder and admiration the first time he came in the presence of her matchless beauty and dazzling splendor. She was the patron saint of the South Carolina College . . . and her ball cards were filled weeks in advance by the young swains of the bluest blood and most aristocratic families of the state."[15]

Dickert added that Marie possessed a brilliant wit and perfect manners, and crowned her "without dispute the social queen of Columbia." Others who knew Marie agreed that the demure teenager was accepted into the highest societal realms. The upper echelon did not, however, welcome her mother, Amelia, into their sphere as Jacob Feaster lacked great wealth and was a mundane grocer. No matter how personable Jacob may have been or how successful at his career, he was categorized by his position and therefore not socially embraced by the ranks of elite Columbians. Additionally, Amelia had worked for wealthy matrons as a dressmaker between marriages, lowering her in their eyes. Their disdain further intensified as Amelia's antecedents were neither aristocratic nor southern by birth. The fact that her family was historically significant to Pennsylvania did not impress the local upper class. However, what

Amelia's daughter lacked in pedigree, she more than made up for in charisma. A Columbia historian, who knew many acquainted with Marie, reported the general consensus of the townspeople: "Her beautiful face and figure, and sweet and modest demeanor had secured for her, in spite of some protest from the grandes dames of society, the entrée into circles in which her mother never could have appeared." He added, "It is fair to say that her conduct in society . . . was irreproachable."[16]

Yet another admirer described Marie: "No artist could do her justice. Here was a beauty that dawned upon you like sunshine, and is seldom seen more than once in a lifetime. The young and the old, male and female, raved over this beautiful girl. Strangers called and asked to see her, as they would to see a fine race-horse."[17]

A former Columbia resident recounted the legend that one evening an elderly farmer called on Amelia and asked to see the "purtiest daughter in the world." Amelia complied, and after he gazed at Marie's radiance he agreed, declaring she was indeed "no. 1." He then audaciously asked to see Marie in the daytime, as if her natural beauty would be compromised in unkind morning light. Amelia again conceded to the senior's wish, and after inspecting Marie the next morning, he declared, "Folks can worship you, young lady, without committing idolatry, for there's nothin' like you in the heavens above, or in the earth beneath, or in the waters under the earth."[18]

After the Civil War began, Marie enrolled in the Academy of the Sacred Heart (now Manhattanville College) then located at 132nd Street and St. Nicholas Terrace in New York City. Many parents living in the South sent their daughters to this reputable academy to avoid the local perils of the Civil War. Some of Amelia's relatives, including her only surviving brother, John, and his wife, lived in New York, and Amelia's friends did as well, so the decision to send Marie there was logical. While the family was not Roman Catholic, the school was well known for providing an excellent education to students of all denominations. They encouraged French conversation and taught it for half of the day. Courses in philosophy, science, mathematics, literature, and musical performance were also part of the curriculum.[19]

When the term ended Marie returned to Columbia and remained there until school resumed in the fall. Social functions in the state capital were numerous during the first year of war, and private citizens, feeling unthreatened, set time aside for such leisure activities as parades and horseback riding—a pastime Marie enjoyed. She often rode sidesaddle on property abutting the Arsenal, turning military students' heads as she dashed by.[20]

On August 2, 1861, Marie and her mother attended a dress parade at the school accompanied by Jacob's sister, Margaret Narcissa Feaster (1839–79), visiting from her home in Feasterville in Fairfield County. Narcissa spent time with Marie and Amelia at Amelia's house, and Marie made frequent afternoon and evening calls on Narcissa as well. With her sister, Sarah ("Sallie") Feaster Butler, Narcissa delighted in coaching through Columbia with Amelia in her rounded carriage drawn by bobtailed horses, and at other times, when Narcissa and Marie were not taking tea or having dinner, they enjoyed riding through town with Trez.[21]

Marie socialized with other Feasters as well. Jacob Feaster's grand-niece, Lena Norwood Mitchell, explained that her mother, Mary Emma Feaster (Norwood) and Marie were "young ladies" in Columbia and were often together at "Uncle Jake and Aunt Amelia's" or Aunt Drucie's house (Mary Drucilla Feaster Rawls, Narcissa's sister).[22]

Aside from maintaining warm family connections, Marie soon became immersed in Columbia's female Civil War efforts. Both Northern and Southern women played significant roles in the war, primarily nursing sick and wounded soldiers. Women sewed and knitted for the cause, wrote for the cause, donated jewelry for the cause, remade chemises into shirts for the soldiers, and created social fund-raising groups in support of the war effort. For example, Narcissa Feaster supported the Confederacy by sewing and knitting for the soldiers and attending soldiers' relief meetings with her father.[23]

During the early years of war, Marie continued as a dedicated supporter of the Confederacy, spending the summers of 1862–63 in efforts to sustain the cause. She tended to the sick and injured at Wayside Hospital and spent hours at the railroad station enlivening and encouraging the soldiers coming home or en route to theaters of battle. She also danced "reels and waltzes with them" and performed in short comical plays at fund-raising events. At least one Confederate officer deemed her "a good rebel."[24]

Amelia, on the other hand, demonstrated her Unionist sympathy as soon as war drums were heard. She "steadfastly maintained her devotion to the old flag and her country's cause." Her behavior was evident despite Jacob Feaster's Confederate service in a Columbia rifle guard and a regiment commanded by General Joseph Eggleston Johnston. The couple's splintered loyalties put a great strain upon Amelia's marriage.[25]

Amelia's devotion to the North strengthened because her family was still actively engaged in making American history. Just two months before the Civil War began, president-elect Abraham Lincoln visited Philadelphia on February 22, 1861, to commemorate George Washington's birthday. Lincoln delivered a moving oration, which included the words "cherishing that fraternal feeling which has so long characterized us as a nation," and raised an American flag over Independence Hall with an additional star on it representing Kansas, the thirty-fourth state. During the ceremonies Amelia's uncle, Col. Robert Carr, read aloud George Washington's farewell address, and at the 1862 Fourth of July parade, Carr read the Declaration of Independence to the crowd, as he had done at so many other important events. Carr was an active Union supporter throughout the war as well. He collected campaign maps and communicated with generals and members of Congress, advising them from his military experience on how to proceed. Thus, Amelia had good reason to adhere to the Union, despite her southern residency and marriage to a Confederate.[26]

Apart from Southerners' allegiance to the repugnant institution of slavery, Jacob Feaster's support of the Confederacy was also understandable. Like many South Carolinians, his ancestors had been patriots and fought in the American Revolution, as Amelia's ancestors had. While southern descendants were proud and dedicated to their ancestors' memory, Confederates' patriotism was also tied to their individual state's rights guaranteed by the Constitution in 1787. When Southerners declared their independence from a neo-oppressive Union, they pledged their fidelity to a different American government symbolized by the Stars and Bars.

The hazards of war rapidly encroached upon many Southern cities, but Columbians still felt relatively safe from attack. Columbia's role in leading the state out of the Union—Charleston also had a role—would generally define it as a target, but the city had no seaport to blockade, nor did it hold a strategic fort to capture like Charleston. By 1863 some Charlestonians and Confederates from other states were refugees in Columbia because of the city's relative safety. Columbia became so festive that some deemed it unseemly. Gatherings included dinners and parties where Columbia citizens entertained high-ranking officers on leave. Dances and formal balls did not cease, and blockade-running vessels imported luxuries. Thus, while bloody battles increased throughout the South, in Columbia life remained undisturbed for Marie and Amelia.[27]

Besides riding through the city with Narcissa and others, Amelia and Marie often rode alone in their luxurious carriage Amelia had purchased from her neighbor and friend, Phineas Freeman Frazee, a prominent coach maker from New Jersey. It came equipped with silver handles and plush velvet cushions, the interior complementing Marie's flawless skin, blue eyes, and lustrous blonde hair arranged in sausage curls beneath a plumed leghorn hat. Marie caused the murmuring of both Columbia genders while riding past the citizens, and Columbians could capture the view of both mother and daughter through the carriage's folded-back glass windows, prompting the residents to call it the "Boozer glass case."[28]

Amelia, purposefully wearing somber clothing, took her place in the back seat and watched with pride while her daughter, wrapped in a sky-blue cloak trimmed with white swansdown, ruled from the front. A Columbia woman recalled seeing "Mrs. Feaster and Marie Boozer—the one rich, dark in coloring and costume, the other a girl . . . healthy, poised, delicious, pressing into the soft cushions. . . . It was an angel's seeming—and she, beautiful as Venus, the goddess of the chariot."[29]

While Marie enjoyed this adoration by the public, it was more strategic to Amelia. She may well have placed Marie on display in order to obtain a worthy husband. The attraction Marie possessed was a recognized attribute regarded by many a mother as a lure to ensnare a wealthy gentleman in marriage, thereby insuring a privileged life for her daughter and herself as well. Regardless, some Columbians, especially rebuffed suitors (of either woman) along with envious females, disparaged as vulgar Amelia's showing off her treasure.

During the early spring of 1862 while Marie was boarded at school in New York, Narcissa Feaster visited Columbia but did not have the opportunity to spend any time with Marie. Subsequently, Narcissa wrote in her diary the day she returned to Feasterville on April 13 that she had not enjoyed her Columbia stay.[30]

Marie did not remain in New York to take her final course of study at the Academy of the Sacred Heart. Instead she finished her education in Paris, most likely at a convent from 1863–64. Amelia could well afford this continental schooling due to the inheritance from David Boozer expressly bequeathed for Marie's education.[31]

Paris meandered on a path to modernity while Marie studied there. Parisians read Victor Hugo's socially conscious *Les Miserables,* published in 1862, but in 1863 the Paris Salon rejected Édouard Manet's irreverent *Le déjeuner sur l'herbe.* That year he painted the shocking nude *Olympia,* and would exhibit it in 1865 to hostile crowds who would threaten to destroy it. Concurrently, Honoré Daumier satirized the bourgeoisie, and stylish courtesans rivaled royalty for attention. Deluxe French cuisine, furniture, architecture, and fashion were adored by American visitors, especially the young student from South Carolina, and the elegance of the Second Empire ruled by Napoleon III produced a lasting effect on the impressionable teenager. She became yet another lover of Parisian cosmopolitan culture and changed her name from Mary to a more fitting Marie.

By the summer of 1864 Marie had returned to Columbia, volunteering, enjoying social activities, and claiming the center of attention at all occasions. Staying up late attending parties and waking up early to tend the sick at the hospital did not diminish Marie's attractiveness in the least. She was still "one of the most beautiful girls ever seen in the state."[32]

At seventeen to eighteen years of age, Marie rode her impressive horse through the city. She enjoyed participating in elite, British-inspired hunts and apparently inherited Peter Burton's skill with firearms, becoming known as a crack shot. Notable Confederates made up the roster of her suitors—the gallant General Martin Witherspoon Gary reportedly was one of them. Marie's hand in marriage was also sought by many of plantation owners, but she turned them all down.[33]

Despite vain attempts of many to achieve a serious relationship with Marie, she disappointed all but one when she became engaged to Willie Capers. Willie, from a religious, highly respected family, was a private in the Confederate cavalry. At least one affectionate letter written to his mother revealed his good nature, dutifulness, and faith.[34]

Marie's relationship with Capers was hardly a perfect one. His mother had never heard a negative comment about Marie; yet Mrs. Capers had opposed their marriage, primarily due to Amelia's Unionist tendencies.[35] Furthermore, Amelia would have never approved of Marie's marriage to a Columbia cavalry soldier, no matter how brave he was. Amelia guarded Marie's prospects of marrying a gentleman of wealth and society, guaranteeing avoidance of any discomfort from poverty and debt, and at this point in history, Amelia would have preferred that Marie marry a Northerner. While Amelia wanted the best for her children, she was nonetheless overmanipulative concerning her eldest beauty, especially when it came to Marie's

Fig. 3. American School, Major William "Willie" Campbell Preston, ca.1863, Bridgeman Art Library, New York.

permanent relationship with a gentleman. Amelia undeniably dominated Marie's life, grooming and encouraging her from the time she was born, and shaping her destiny into only what Amelia wished for Marie—to become the wealthy wife of a deserving husband.

Additionally, according to comments made by residents of Columbia, including members of the Gibbes family, Marie was secretly in love with Major William "Willie" Campbell Preston, Buck's handsome dark-haired brother (fig. 3). Preston, unaware of Marie's feelings for him, had been a Confederate hero, firing the cannon shot that struck the US flagpole at the April 1861 bombardment of Fort Sumter. President Jefferson Davis promoted him to major by 1863 due to his capabilities and virtuous conduct, and reportedly, Preston later achieved the ranking of lieutenant colonel.[36]

Sadly, the heroic Willie Preston did not return alive to Columbia. In late July 1864 he died from a gunshot wound to his heart during a battle in the Atlanta Campaign. In Columbia Mary Chesnut heard "a loud and bitter cry," sounding like a "broken heart: they had come to tell Mrs. Preston that Willie was killed—Willie! his mother's darling. No country ever had a braver soldier, a truer gentleman, to lay down his life in her cause. . . . Buck, now, is breaking her heart for her brother Willie."[37]

Marie's engagement to Capers remained temporarily intact, as did the townspeople's tales of her love for Willie Preston. She may have been enamored with Buck's brother at some point, missed him while he was away at battle, and mourned his death with her friend in July, but some three months later another hero named Preston would radically change Marie's hopes for long-lasting love and inspire her to rethink her national loyalties.

CHAPTER THREE

Love Conquers Confederate Nationalism

---

*I beg that you will allow me the pleasure and duty of gratitude
which I owe to Mrs. Amelia Feaster and daughter,
Miss Maria Boozier [sic] . . . to speak of their self-sacrificing
attentions to the Union officers.*

—Edward E. Kendrick Jr.
adjutant of the Tenth New Jersey Veteran Volunteers, 1865[1]

The divided loyalties of Amelia, fiercely patriotic for the Union, and Jacob, who favored the Confederacy, led to their estrangement. By December 1864, she and Feaster had separated. Without a husband to protect her, Amelia faced Columbia citizens who knew she openly supported the Union, which brought forth "undisguised aversion and annoyance" toward her. Yet she felt she had to remain amid this hostile atmosphere because her income properties in the city served as her only support by then, she still owned her house on Washington Street, and Boozer's estate sustaining Marie was not entirely settled.[2]

Mary Chesnut chronicled the Feasters' break-up in her famous diary and by mid-December seemed to resent both Amelia and Marie. Mrs. Chesnut expressed her contempt for mother and daughter and cast a shadow on the legitimacy of Marie's birth: "Mrs. Feaster (the mother of the too-famous beauty Boozer) . . . has left her husband. She has had husbands enough. She has been married three times. And yet by all showing she did not begin to marry soon enough. Witness the existence of Boozer."[3]

Amelia's devotion to the Union and her lower social status may well have prompted Mrs. Chesnut's disdain for her. However, sour feelings stemmed from not only politics and societal tiers but also from Amelia's attractiveness and the malicious gossip that had followed her from Newberry. Resentment of Marie flourished because of her supposed illegitimacy and the sharp envy Mrs. Chesnut and her friends felt as they watched scores of gentlemen fawning on the teenager.

Fig. 4. Lieutenant Samuel William Preston, USN,
Library of Congress Civil War Glass Negative Collection.

By then around twelve thousand Union officers had been prisoners of war in and around Columbia. Some were held across the street from a female academy run by Madame Rosalie Acelie Guillou Togno, a refugee from Charleston to the Columbia area to escape the beleaguered coastal city. Togno caught her students waving to the incarcerated officers, causing her to raise a tizzy.[4]

Those imprisoned officers (some in irons) and others confined west of Columbia at Camp Sorghum had been visited and assisted by Amelia and her obedient daughter, who felt sympathy for their pitiful living conditions. As Marie had lost her biological and adoptive fathers, Amelia maintained a powerful influence on her, and she relied on her mother's affection far too much not to help her in her ministrations.[5]

Disease struck Camp Sorghum and by mid-December 1864, many prisoners were relocated to the grounds of the South Carolina Lunatic Asylum within the city or to the hospital. Marie and Amelia cared for officers housed at the asylum and provided medicine, comfort, and nourishing meat for hospital inmates, who "had none supplied by the rebel authorities." [6]

Despite hardships, the prisoners tried to improve their lives. According to a former asylum inmate, they formed a club in which the detainees told stories, a glee club in which they sang, and an orchestra as well. He also recollected that when weather permitted it, dances occurred, with ladies indicating their stature by a handkerchief tied on their left arm. He remembered Marie attending a dance and sitting on the "guards' platform"; in other words, she was ostensibly on the side of the Confederacy but had permission to observe and help ease conditions of the captives.[7]

Unbeknownst to many Columbians, however, Marie had not only allowed her mother to recruit her in aiding the misfortunate but by the turn of 1865 she had wholeheartedly changed her allegiance and joined her mother in loyalty to the North. This dramatic reversal of Marie's years of volunteerism for the CSA stemmed from the loving and honorable attention of an imprisoned officer, and as a result she followed her heart, not her flag.

Fig. 5. Marie Boozer, carte de visite,
courtesy Wilson-Battle-Connell-Park Papers.

Lieutenant Samuel William Preston (fig. 4), "an American naval legend," was one of the most handsome prisoners in Columbia, easily seen through the barred window by many female admirers. Captured while leading one of Admiral John Dahlgren's divisions during the September 1863 bombardment of Fort Sumter, Preston and his good friend Benjamin Porter were incarcerated in Charleston and then shipped to Columbia; the two men were imprisoned for a total of fourteen months. A native of Metcalfe, Ontario, Canada, Preston moved to Illinois as a boy and became a Naval Academy midshipman from that state. After graduating from Annapolis at the top of his class, he served his country in many ways, including as a flag leader and aide to Admiral Samuel F. DuPont and Admiral Dahlgren, and as both admirals' go-between with President Abraham Lincoln.[8] On August 14, 1862, DuPont wrote of Preston from Port Royal Harbor, South Carolina: "He has overworked himself, and if I were to express to you the amount of his services in this fleet and the alleviation he has brought to my duties and responsibilities you could hardly credit it. He is only 21, from Illinois, and such men are born about once in a quarter of a century."[9]

A Union chaplain who met Preston while the two were in the Columbia jail described the lieutenant as "pre-eminently the courtly officer" and recounted that his "fine features" and "intelligent face . . . stamped him as a gentleman of unusual delicacy and refinement." The chaplain added that Preston was "a man of cultivated tastes and faculties, well read, and well informed." Bred to become a standout member of society, he studied foreign languages and science, could talk about any subject with ease, and was attuned to business as well. With a "high sense of honor and a sensitive conscience," he was a religious Christian, had "a poetic mind with a transcendental turn," and loved adventure and romance. All of these qualities appealed to Marie, as did his eyes as blue as hers.[10]

According to the chaplain and confirmed by a Confederate guard, Preston fell in love with Marie, who returned his affection. The affable guard, who informed the Union captives it was "their privilege to try to" escape but his "business to keep" them, recalled that he inspected letters Marie exchanged with Preston and agreed that he was an "estimable gentleman."[11]

Amelia encouraged Marie's relationship with Preston—after all, as a cultured Northerner with a head for business and a promising high-ranking career in the military, he fit perfectly into Amelia's plans for her daughter. The women bribed the guards to allow the lieutenant to temporarily leave the jail in their custody so they could take care of him at home.[12]

Marie and Preston were discreet, and their "love affair" chaste and clandestine, but imprisoned officers knew about the romance and followed it like a novel sent to them in installments. The distraction lifted their morale; it served as a respite for their meager conditions and reminded them of the hope for a sweeter part of life. The chaplain recalled that during a secret midnight meeting before Lieutenant Preston was released by prisoner exchange on October 19, he asked Marie to marry him and the two made plans for their future. As soon as the appropriate opportunity arose, she broke the engagement with Willie Capers.[13]

After Preston's release he turned down a military leave and in consequence was stationed in the North Atlantic. Marie waited faithfully for his return, but at eighteen, having grown taller and more voluptuous since her young teenage days at Columbia Female College, she had blossomed into womanhood extraordinarily enough (see fig. 5) to attract attention from other men and incite even more criticism from those of her own gender. The women's complaints were again soaked with envy and picked away at Marie's good character: "Boozer, who is always on exhibition—walking, riding, driving—wherever a woman's face can go, there is Boozer. She is a beauty—that none can deny. They say she is a good girl. Then why does she not marry some decent man, among the shoals who follow her, and be off, out of this tangle while she has a shred of reputation left?"[14] Evidently, the women had no idea of Marie's engagement to Preston.

Already ensnared in a mire of disdain and gossip claiming her clouded paternity, Marie could only escape by marrying. To remain both single and too attractive was a dangerous role to play within the circle of elite female Columbians. Marie could not stay unmarried and "good" in their eyes for long.[15]

The matrons continued discussing Marie and mentioned her breakup with Willie Capers along with pejorative statements about her supposedly stealing Capers' watch and him catching her with it, prompting the end of the relationship. Not all the women believed this accusation, however, and at least one insisted it was Marie's obvious beauty that they continually disparaged.[16]

The subject soon turned to the European prisoners of war in Columbia, who had previously fought for the Union and were recruited by the Confederates. The Secretary of War had dispatched to General Robert E. Lee, "I have given to officers supposed to be competent, in several instances, permits to raise battalions, directing them to prefer Irish and French." In December 1864, Mary Chesnut spotted members of the foreign Confederate battalion chatting with Marie during the afternoon. The sight of such brazen conviviality disgusted Mrs. Chesnut, who felt insulted that the foreigners were socializing with Marie for hours and only turned to her niece after Marie left in her carriage.[17]

By January Amelia's and Marie's humanitarian acts had expanded into the dangerous territory of furnishing officers with maps, money, "and guides to prosecute their escape." In Amelia's hometown of Philadelphia, Union officers later recalled that she was "exceedingly kind and attentive in supplying the wants and needs" of Northern prisoners and "endeared herself" to the city's officers, giving them "books, money, clothing, and necessary information to facilitate" their flights to freedom.[18]

Some Confederate officials who presumed to know the extent of Amelia's beneficence harbored hostility toward her, but wartime resentment did not deter her. However, because of her allegiance and assistance to the North, Rebels branded her with the epithet of "conspicuous Unionist." Other Unionists in Columbia were stigmatized as well; for instance, Amelia's friend, coach maker Phineas F. Frazee, assisted prisoners of war and as a consequence was whipped and imprisoned, and Rebels forcibly shaved his head.[19]

Amelia was putting her own well-being at risk; in fact she was "at constant peril." Confederates who suspected her disloyalty barraged her with insults, and according to sworn testimonies by many prisoners, local authorities arrested her twice and threatened her with execution. When Rebels eventually released her, they forbade her to enter the prisons, but in spite of the threats she continued helping Yankees by bribing guards with much of her own money. Marie, loyal to her mother and still attached to Preston, did so as well; both women's actions were accepted and condoned by the guards.[20]

Concurrently, Lieutenant Samuel W. Preston became a flag leader in North Carolina, serving along with Ben Porter. On January 15, 1865, while they awaited their ground assault on Fort Fisher, Preston felt morose and commented to their mutual longtime friend Will Cushing, "I have a prophetic feeling that I am not coming out alive." Porter tried to lighten Preston's gloom by responding, "Nonsense! You bet I am," and

Cushing advised Preston to "cheer up."[21]

During the battle, Preston, alongside Annapolis classmate Lieutenant Roswell Hawks Lamson, charged the fort against heavily armed Confederate forces. Suddenly, Lamson and Preston were confronted by a barrage of grapeshot and canister rounds, and true to his prophesy, one of the shots pierced Preston's thigh and severed his femoral artery, causing him to bleed to death. Lamson, wounded in the shoulder, began to crawl over to his friend to help him but then realized it was too late. He lamented the following day, "Poor fellow, it made my heart sick to see him stretched out on the sand, and I mourned him, not only as a dear friend lost, but as a loss to the service of the most superior young officer I have ever seen in it."[22]

Sadly, Ben Porter died as well, but his, Preston's, Lamson's, and other brave men's efforts led the US Army to capture Fort Fisher and close the Confederate seaport. As Lamson wrote to his future wife, Kate, "It has been a dreadful Sunday but we have done *something* toward ending the war."[23]

On January 18, 1865, Captain Kidder Randolph Breese wrote of Preston and Ben Porter, "Two more noble spirits the world never saw, nor had the navy more intrepid men, young, talented and handsome, the bravest of the brave, pure in their lives, surely their names deserve something more than passing mention and are worthy to be handed down to posterity with the greatest and best of naval heroes." *Harper's Weekly* illustrated the friends' pictures side by side.[24]

Marie was devastated; her hopes for a loving, long-lasting marriage with Preston died with him. She would later name her son Preston, and six US naval ships would bear the gallant hero's name as well.[25]

Just after Preston's death a charitable Columbia bazaar took place, organized by local women's aid groups to support ill and wounded Confederate soldiers, yet another example of the grand festivities held in the city during such trying times of the Civil War. It was an opulent affair, with booths appointed with elaborate drapery and silk-topped tables laden with accessories made by craftswomen and the finest gourmet foods brought through the blockade. Narcissa Feaster visited the bazaar on January 18 and 19 and described it as splendid and packed with people. She did not mention seeing Marie.[26]

Heartbroken, Marie faced her grief as stoically as possible while de-
voting her energy to the Union cause in honor of Preston's memory.
She and Amelia continued to help detained officers and receive them at
home with the authorization of certain Rebels. On January 31, 1865,
Adjutant-General W. Sidney Winder, whose name was linked with the
notorious Andersonville prison, sent a missive to a Confederate officer in
charge of prisoners of war. Winder instructed the officer to grant permission to his prisoner, Captain [M. Henry] McChesney, who had shown
gentlemanly behavior to Southerners, to pay a visit to Amelia for an evening. "You will put him on his honor not to say or do anything against
this country," Winder ordered, and added McChesney should return to
the prison at around ten o'clock p.m.[27]

Mother and daughter relentlessly yet cautiously persevered. Their
bravery was confirmed by a later report to the US Congress, wherein
more than thirty Union officers from states including Connecticut,
Massachusetts, Rhode Island, Pennsylvania, New Jersey, Iowa, and New
York signed sworn affidavits attesting to the women's courage, in support
of Amelia's claim for governmental reimbursement. Listed among the
names were Captain M. Henry McChesney; Lieutenant Roswell Hawks
Lamson, for his deceased friend Lieutenant Samuel W. Preston; and
Colonel David Vickers, a former prisoner at Sorghum and the Columbia
Asylum camp, who became a brigadier general soon after providing his
affidavit. Coincidentally, one of his daughters would be named Maria
Amelia.[28]

Edward E. Kendrick Jr., late Adjutant of the Tenth New Jersey
Veteran Volunteers testified that Amelia and Marie kept them from "suffering and starvation" and bribed guards to distribute money to the prisoners and to "gain access to us in the prison yard." His statement in part
was as follows:

> While we were deprived of animal food for five months, without
> shelter, with dilapidated clothing, shoeless and hatless, suffer-
> ing, sick and dying, they with their money, though not allowed

inside of the ground of the stockade, would place the means in the hands of the confederate . . . to buy food and clothing to be handed to us.

To the sick in the prison hospital substantial food and delicacies were received indefinitely from their hands, they not being allowed themselves to aid us under severe punishment, during the winter of 1864–65; while we were suffering from cold and wet, they sent us, in their own wagons, liberal supplies of wood to keep us warm, and (by remuneration) the guard passed it through the lines as from the confederate government, otherwise it would have been stopped and they arrested.

Their house was an asylum and retreat if we escaped, where we were concealed until the arrangements were made for guides, etc., to carry us away. The Confederate authorities were very suspicious of them; but so discreet and secretly did they manage, no positive charge of aiding us could be made against them. Their money, lavished upon the guard and officer having us in keeping, kept the secret from publicity.[29]

Emlen Newbold Carpenter, Captain of the Sixth Pennsylvania Cavalry, stated Amelia nourished him and kept him "informed of the movements of General Sherman's army" so that he knew when to make his escape. When the opportune time came as the prisoners were being transferred, he and other men eluded the guards, cut open a panel in the ceiling of an outbuilding of the asylum, and hid in the cramped space above.[30] Later Amelia sequestered Carpenter in her house prior to "the entree of General Sherman into the city," while Columbia was "filled with Rebel troops." Emlen Carpenter's 1891 obituary confirmed that a lady in Columbia concealed him in her cellar until the early morning before dawn when "a negro took him into an empty outhouse" so that he could see Sherman's troops approaching the city. Carpenter's memoriam from the Military Order of the Loyal Legion of the United States commented that he was indeed fortunate that a lady befriended him by hiding him in her cellar after the men fled from the loft of the asylum outbuilding. That lady, of course, was Amelia. It was because of Amelia that Carpenter returned home to Germantown (Philadelphia) in March 1865, beset by only a temporary case of Vitamin C deficiency and rheumatoid arthritis, and lived a fulfilling life complete with a marriage and study of art in Europe.[31]

Lieutenant Gilbert E. Sabre of the Rhode Island Cavalry hid out with Captain Emlen Carpenter and some thirty other Yankees in the outbuilding's space above the ceiling. However, Sabre was much more descriptive about the incident in his 1865 memoir. He related that after two days without food, he and several others emerged from their hiding place and cautiously left the building. Those who remained at large knew Amelia was sympathetic to the Union and hastened to her home around four in the morning in a desperate attempt to obtain food and sequester themselves from the Rebels.[32]

Amelia was startled by the knock on her door but tentatively opened it and saw the group of men standing in the dark. In a hushed tone she asked who they were and one of them replied, "Friends." She then asked if they were Union officers, and after they answered that they were, she invited them to quickly enter the house. They told her of their harrowing escape, whereupon she immediately provided them with meals as well as hiding places in her apparently roomy cellar. Indeed, by the time General William Tecumseh Sherman entered the city, these Union officers were secreted in Amelia's home. And Columbians still had no idea of the extent of the two women's support for the Northern cause.[33]

None of the printed sworn testimonies claimed or implied that Amelia or Marie had ever furnished Union officers with confidential information from Confederate forces. That the women gave information from the Union army to Union officers does not accurately define espionage; in other words, Marie and Amelia were Union sympathizers and humanitarians, not spies.

Amelia angered many of the citizens when on February 16, 1865, she displayed an American flag as Sherman's troops arrived in Columbia. South Carolinians threatened her for doing so, many perceiving the flag as loathsome and symbolic of a despotic government. Other Unionist women also waved banners from their windows, and freed slaves sang and danced in the streets. The joyous freedmen offered, as did some traders, buckets of whiskey to placate the Union soldiers. By then many supporters of the Confederacy knew it was over. The Yankees had come to destroy white Southerners' comforting traditions and ruin their lives.[34]

CHAPTER FOUR

Columbia Aflame

I trust I shall never witness such a scene again.

—David Conyngham, 1865[1]

On February 17, 1865, Columbians awoke to an uncertain future in a municipality controlled by Sherman's troops. Julia and Jakie Feaster had left Columbia the day before when General Sherman was some seven miles from the city, and had arrived safely at Feasterville to stay with their grandparents, Andrew and Mary Norris Feaster.[2]

Confederate Colonel James G. Gibbes (son of Robert Wilson Gibbes) contended that Union soldiers were already plotting to destroy the city, obtaining his information from a woman, with the coincidental name of Mrs. Boozer, who like Amelia and Marie had provided food to incarcerated Yankees. She warned Gibbes that it "was about to be burned," but he did not believe her. Mayor Thomas Goodwyn had been assured by Major General William Tecumseh Sherman himself that he would not torch the capital; however, she insisted she knew for certain the conflagration was about to transpire.[3]

If true, these soldiers would have been planning to act against the orders of their generals. Sherman wrote that he had no intentions of burning the city as the mayor had already surrendered to him before his troops entered it. He intended to only destroy the railroad depot and various other public buildings strategic to the military (as he had in Atlanta). Major General Oliver Otis Howard, who returned to battle after losing an arm and would later help found Howard

47

University, also stated that he gave no orders to burn the city. He claimed the Confederates started the fire by igniting bales of cotton in the street before the Yankees entered Columbia.[4]

Amelia recorded that earlier in the day the only buildings on fire were those at the railroad depot. It was from that burning depot due to an explosion of a magazine next to it, the torched piles of cotton in the streets, and the addition of a strong, sustained wind, that the later widespread destruction was born.[5]

However, the conflagration intensified due to mob fever. Soldiers unlocked the prison, letting loose wartime Yankee captives and hardened criminals. The gallons of available alcohol, weapons, intoxicated young soldiers, and freed convicts combined with incendiary material and long-held grudges incited the mobs to a frenzy. Rampant destruction and pillaging by inebriated soldiers and other thieves commenced throughout the city.

The Columbia fire was said to be "the most monstrous barbarity of the barbarous march."[6] First, troops would steal or destroy fine treasures within the elegant interiors and then they would ignite the once beautiful homes of the city, sparing the few mansions utilized as Yankee headquarters. Looting by some newly freed slaves occurred as well. By nighttime, the burning and ransacking of Columbia became a horrifying, chaotic, hell. Unquenchable flames devoured rooftops and leapt from one house to another. "The very heavens seemed at times alit by fire."[7] Choking smoke caused women and children in their nightclothes to rush out of their burning homes. Some children went missing, desperately sought by their panicked mothers. Gunshots and screams were heard, signifying murderous rampages; women were threatened and assaulted; yet no violent crimes of rape and murder were reported.[8]

Around ten o'clock that night, Amelia's house and the nearby outbuildings were lit by Yankees while she watched in horror. She pleaded with them to desist, but they paid no attention to her. A fire engine threw water on her house but some of "the Federal soldiers would catch hold of the pipe and hose and throw the water away from

Fig. 6. Artist unknown, portrait of Amelia Sees Feaster,
oil on canvas, ca. 1860, private collection.

the building."[9] With the assistance of Marie, Captain McChesney, and other former prisoners whom she helped escape, Amelia moved her bed onto the street a safe distance from her blazing house, along with trunks full of clothing, a few family valuables such as some silver and jewelry, and precious archives. These included the poem she had lovingly written to her children, daguerreotypes of them, and those of Amelia's Philadelphia family dressed in fine clothing. Another important yet cumbersome memento was a gold-leaf framed portrait of Amelia wearing a burgundy velvet gown, its canvas pierced by a Yankee's bayonet or sword while he was pillaging her home before setting it on fire (fig. 6). Restored over sixty years ago, the painting still shows remnants of a former puncture to the left of Amelia's face. There was no time to safely remove the rest of the oil paintings, a collection of fine furniture, a large library of valuable books, and other expensive items.[10]

After helping her mother remove the few household goods she

could, Marie held onto and protected the American flag so proudly unfurled when Sherman's troops entered the city. While she and
Amelia stood by their belongings, their friend Mr. Frazee warned
her, "You had better put your bed and trunks in my corner house."[11]

"Hell!" exclaimed one of the federal soldiers. "Do you think
them buildings won't be burnt? If you want to save your bed you had
better keep it where it is; them buildings will burn before morning
and everything else in this city." (In her recollection of this, Amelia
wrote "H—ll!")[12]

General Sherman was personally involved in the efforts to save
Amelia's house, working with the officers, including Lieutenant
Sabre, but it was too late. Amelia could do nothing but remain in the
street with her precious items next to her and watch her home and
other properties and Frazee's home and business (including several
buildings and inventory) burn to the ground. Marie stayed by her
mother, as did Lieutenant Sabre and Captain McChesney. Sherman
corroborated that the fire consumed Amelia's house entirely, reduc-
ing her "to poverty and want." Amelia later attested that all her properties were "set on fire by soldiers in the United States Army," but
she also acknowledged and offered gratitude for the Federal officers'
efforts in trying to arrest the destruction. Union soldier-diarists concurred with Amelia's declarations; one wrote that while the cotton in
the streets was burned by Confederates, the Union soldiers set fire
to the rest, "as that is the prevailing tendency of Sherman's men." He
also noted that Sherman and Howard tried to stop the devastation.[13]

Colonel James G. Gibbes, who became the acting mayor of
Columbia (Mayor Goodwyn suffered a breakdown after Sherman
left), later purported Amelia's alleged actions during the burning of
Columbia and mistakenly professed Amelia was an Englishwoman
because of her accent influenced by her mother. He stated Amelia
had the forethought of "a sharp woman who in the time of trouble
looked ahead." He went on derogatorily: "Mrs. Feaster was known as
a very smart woman, not overscrupulous. While the city was on fire
and the house she occupied was burning, General Sherman passed

by. She immediately made herself known to him as a Union woman and one who had done a great deal to assist Federal prisoners, and aided some to escape. She called his attention not only to her house . . . but showed him a large store house at the opposite corner, then burning, which she told him was her husband's, and that it had been filled with flour, bacon, and tobacco—the truth being it was a government storehouse in which her husband was employed."[14]

Gibbes's spurious account implied Amelia tried to deceive Sherman; but on the contrary, if she pointed to anything it was her home and her own storehouses. In a handwritten petition to President Abraham Lincoln, she affirmed her ownership of these properties, filled with not only tobacco but also "seventy bales of cotton" and a large amount of sugar, salt, leather, and carriages. In truth, Amelia had no faith in the future of Confederate money, foresaw its demise, and invested heavily in real estate and material goods. Moreover, the Union officers Amelia assisted actually described her heroism to their military superiors. Lieutenant Sabre added, "We saw the home of one who had been really a friend to us destroyed. It was now our turn to reciprocate the kindness tended to us." Consequently, the officers asked for Amelia and her family to have the protection of the federal troops and leave Columbia with them.[15]

To add more defamation, newspaperman Julian A. Selby and his friend and partner William Gilmore Simms purported that Amelia had been renting her destroyed Columbia house from Confederate Colonel John Bauskett instead of owning it for some fifteen years. However, the *Daily South Carolinian* on March 7, 1865, reported that Bauskett's house on Bridge Street had burned but didn't mention any destroyed house he owned on Washington Street. James Gibbes repeated the Simms/Selby allegation in his later *Who Burnt Columbia?*[16]

Gibbes's and Selby's allegations about Amelia's false statements of ownership are irrelevant, for later she was not compensated for any destroyed property. She merely took control of a chaotic, hazardous episode as best she could and once again displayed her self-reliance.

But in the light of Gibbes's claims penned years later, there were dire consequences for Amelia's and Marie's actions before Sherman arrived and of their fraternizing with the enemy after the Yankees had devastated Columbia. Amelia and Marie would forever be scorned and publicly labeled as con artists, spies, thieves, and worse.

CHAPTER FIVE

Northward with the Yankees

O, the sorrow and misery of this unhappy town!

—Emma Le Conte, February 18, 1865[1]

On February 18, 1865, the once beautiful Columbia was a city of ruins with dazed, homeless women and children filling the streets. Around one-third of the city's gracious edifices had been annihilated, including its 1790 statehouse, academies, churches, and splendid homes. Scattered historical structures remained standing; yet many were merely burned-out shells. Other parts of the city contained nothing but darkened piles of rubble.[2]

The stench of charred buildings and despair hung thickly in the air. Amelia's cultured neighbor, Dr. Robert Wilson Gibbes, lost his priceless fine art, historical artifacts, and rare book collection in the destruction. He would die less than a year later.[3]

Union officer Thomas Ward Osborn entered in his journal that "three Irish girls," referring to Amelia and her daughters, were the most prominent of the paltry number of Columbia citizens who had helped his prisoners, being the most "faithful" and had "done most everything possible for the cause." He added, "They will go north with us."[4]

The family decided that Ethland, Marie, and Amelia would leave Columbia with Sherman's army. Ethland's African American nurse, Lizzie, also readied herself for the trip north. Jakie and Julia remained in Feasterville, South Carolina, with their grandparents.[5]

On February 20, 1865, Marie, Amelia, Lizzie, and little Ethland exited the ravaged city near the front of a lengthy train of refugees led by Major General Oliver Otis Howard. A cavalry unit was in front and two brigades protected the war-weary refugees from behind.[6]

The departing citizens included many freed African Americans but "at least 800 whites," some, such as Amelia and Marie, who "feared revenges" from the Confederates. Generals Oliver Howard and Alfred Terry later endorsed Amelia's explanation that she left Columbia to "escape the fate which she well knew threatened her upon the return of rebels to that city," and Howard added in his autobiography that "those who had been especially kind to the Yankees had signs of coming retribution." Major George Ward Nichols went further in his prediction, entering in his diary that for the "generous, self-sacrificing friends," to remain in Columbia "after our visit would be certain death."[7]

Essentially all the material goods Amelia had in the world were her portrait and the items in those trunks, which were prepared to be carried north in their "beauty box" carriage. Amelia was one of the more fortunate ones; many of the journeyers had no personal goods and began the long, arduous trip on foot. And ultimately, Amelia and her daughters left in a far newer and larger carriage than their old, worn coach.

Acting Mayor James Gibbes later purported what Amelia supposedly contrived: "When the army moved out, she managed to get General Sherman to furnish her with two horses, which she hitched to her carriage, an old round-bodied affair, familiar to all the old residents, and started in company with the army. In the outskirts of the city, when passing the residence of Mrs. Elmore, she concluded a fair exchange was not robbery, so she left her old equipage and took in its place a fine carriage of Mrs. Elmore."[8]

Amelia did not exchange her coach for Mrs. Elmore's. The decision to give Amelia a better carriage came from General Howard himself. Gibbes's account was refuted by Mrs. Elmore's relative, Mrs. Thomas Taylor, who later wrote that Harriet Elmore's landau was taken along with provisions by Yankee soldiers under orders from General Howard, albeit for Amelia. According to Mrs. Taylor, Mrs. Elmore followed the Yankees on their way out of her property and confronted the soldiers:

"That is my carriage," said Mrs. Elmore, on reaching the tree. "What are you doing with it?"

"We want it for a good Union lady," said No. 1.

"Then you do not want it for any one you will find here," said Mrs. Elmore.

"Oh! Yes; we've got two loyal ladies, and we've got to have a carriage for them to go along with us," spoke No. 2.

"But that is my carriage," persisted Mrs. Elmore, "and your loyal ladies have no business with it. If you have any Union ladies, you must have brought them with you."

"No, we didn't; they've been here all the time," replied the soldier. So they had been, and hiding a spy in their home, under the shadow of the State House.

"The carriage must go," said the guard—"the fortune of war," but whether Mrs. Feaster and Marie Boozer went in it I cannot tell. But they also went, and must have enchanted those amongst whom they settled.[9]

As recompense for Harriet Elmore's loss of a carriage, her house had not been destroyed. And later the mayor gave Mrs. Elmore the Boozer coach in exchange.

Leaving with the enemy conjured up more Southern resentment, and it spread far beyond Columbia. A correspondent sent to the Augusta, Georgia, *Daily Constitutionalist* a list of the more prominent among the hundreds of "Yankee runaways" who left Columbia with Sherman's troops, forecasting that their published names would "consign them to infamy." The first couple he named was Mr. and Mrs. Kelly, and the second, "Mrs. Feaster and her daughter, Miss Boozer." The correspondent labeled all the refugees, including Marie, Amelia, and Phineas Frazee, as "a pestilential set of inhabitants, a set of croakers, harpies, spies, [and] traitors."[10]

Despite the insults, one can't blame Columbians for feeling anger toward Amelia and Marie. Much of their lives and city was destroyed. Innocent citizens lost everything they owned, including their homes, businesses, irreplaceable art objects, family photographs, and precious Bibles. Moreover, their Confederate money was already worthless, and they were forced to realize that their existence would never be what it was prior to the war. Then when soldiers and private citizens observed Marie and Amelia making their exit in a coach owned by another Columbian, and Marie fraternizing cheerfully with the enemy, it was too much to bear. A South Carolina-born woman later contended, "No crime of murder or rape or arson or theft could equal that of conviviality with the Yankees."[11] Indeed, in Confederates' minds, Amelia and Marie *were* the enemy. The gallant officers of the CSA felt that their beloved *fille du regiment* had betrayed them. It was as painful as a saber's cut.

Conversely, the Yankees felt nothing but admiration for both women. Two cavalry troopers personally escorted Amelia's group and the carriages with household items were protected by an officer and his soldiers as well. When the long trip began, officers were not only in front of Marie's carriage but also behind it, "and at each window . . . in the continual struggle to be near her, to catch the sound of her voice or even a flitting smile."[12]

Talkative townspeople remarked upon Marie's exodus from Columbia, and the gossip raged on while the train of humanity moved slowly northward. Mary Chesnut recorded that Columbians particularly singled out Marie as they spotted her leaving: "She went off with flying colors. . . . And she has married a Philadelphia officer." "No doubt. . . . And by this time she has married one from Boston—from New York—indiscriminately. Will she marry the Yankee army?"[13]

Columbians gleaned this tidbit from newspapers including one written by Columbia correspondent Se De Kay (Charles Dobyns Kirk, responsible for the "harpies, spies and traitors" comment) printed in the *Daily Constitutionalist* on the exact day of Mary Chesnut's diary entry—March

10, 1865. It was one of the first reported instances of the supposed promiscuity of teenaged Marie. It purported that the "fast and fascinating"
Marie married a Yankee prisoner of war by the name of Captain Sadlee,
who had been hidden in Amelia's home. According to the correspondent,
Sadlee stole a carriage for his new wife, whereupon they swiftly galloped
off to their honeymoon. Subsequent articles concluded that *"on dit"* (it is
said) Sadlee was already married, and that Amelia and Marie, while leaving Columbia in a phaeton, returned miserably in an oxcart, sadder but
wiser. Another newspaper added as a caveat that this was merely "common gossip."[14] It didn't matter, however. It stuck in the minds and pens
of diarists, letter writers, memoirists, and other future authors who refed
it to the scandal-hungry public. The gossip vaguely referred to Marie's
engagement to Lieutenant Samuel W. Preston, whose death precluded
their marriage, and the name "Sadlee" was likely a corruption of Gilbert
E. Sabre, one of the officers concealed in Amelia's home. In 1865 he
wrote a memoir about his experience and did not mention marrying
Marie. Furthermore, Marie was called "Miss Boozer" the entire route
northward, and she and Amelia never returned to Columbia in any type
of vehicle.[15]

James G. Gibbes added more libelous gossip concerning Amelia: "It
was said that when passing Society Hill she by mistake loaded up and
took off the family silver of the Witherspoons, a prominent family, at
whose house she stopped, and who had put their silver in her room for
safety."[16] Here Amelia, the pious daughter of a city constable, became a
scapegoat for the rampant pillaging by Yankee soldiers and escaped convicts throughout the South, but it is unlikely she stole the Witherspoons'
silver. Society Hill was not even mentioned by General Howard, Major
Osborn, or Lieutenant Sabre, who personally protected Amelia. Howard
described spending time in Cheraw, eleven miles north of Society Hill.[17]

Marie and Amelia were targets for libel and slander because they
were women with second-class status and without the protection of husbands, thereby lacking any powerful means of retaliation. Marie was fod-
der for gossip because by 1865 at the age of around eighteen she had

already become an object of men's sexual fantasies and the celebrated "social queen of Columbia" before "betraying" the Confederacy. From the morning of February 20, 1865, her fame was repaid in humiliation.

Negating her virginal status was the key to her disgrace. The widespread attitude toward women in the mid-nineteenth century, called the "cult of domesticity or true womanhood," may have been at its peak from 1850–60, but the belief was still alive as late as 1869, when an article in the *Southern Review* opined that women were inferior to men but this inferiority "exalts" women, rather than lowering them. A woman's attributes were heavenly—not merely of this earth. Notwithstanding their assumed mental incapability, feminine "moral purpose, in purity of thought . . . in sublimity of soul," resulted in ladies soaring far above men.[18] In fact, as long as women were perceived as saintly, pure, and moral, they could convince themselves that they were superior in the utmost manner—equal to that of the divine. Once they became incompatible with men's and other women's righteous expectations of them, the unfortunate females would plummet to earth and be condemned to a life of scorn and exclusion.

Thus, in the nineteenth century the most opportune way to denounce a beautiful young woman was to spread rampant rumors of her promiscuous sexual behavior. Several southern male writers accomplished this strategy with excellent skill. Marie would be eternally remembered as a teenage harlot who had sexual relations with at least one Union general.

CHAPTER SIX

The Kilpatrick Myth

*Utterly surprised and demoralized, the federals were struck down
or routed. Kilpatrick himself fled in his night clothes, abandoning
his companion, the beautiful Mary Boozer of South Carolina.*

—Manly Wade Wellman, 1962[1]

Many men who were aware of Marie's appeal subsequently told tales
concerning her sexual relations with a so-called lecherous Union general during the sojourn through North Carolina. These legends about
her and General Hugh Judson Kilpatrick were included in several memoirs, novels, encyclopedias, and many nonfiction historical narratives.
They portrayed Marie making her journey from Columbia with General
Kilpatrick's troops, bedding down with him on at least two occasions,
and being caught with him while he was surprised in his nightshirt by
Confederate troops under Lieutenant General Wade Hampton III on
March 10, 1865, at Monroe's Crossroads. The event came to be known
as "Kilpatrick's Shirttail Skedaddle."

Why would a young woman proclaimed the most beautiful of all
South Carolina females risk her reputation by engaging in sex with
General Kilpatrick, described as one of the most unattractive men in
the Union army? The answer is she didn't. Marie was absolutely not
with Kilpatrick during his embarrassing skedaddle or anywhere else
during her trip north from Columbia. Marie traveled with General
Oliver O. Howard's troops, confirmed by several sources, including Sherman in his memoir, two affidavits by Amelia, and a sworn
statement dated March 12, 1865, by Captain Emlen N. Carpenter,

averring that Marie and her mother were "under the protection of Major General Howard."[2]

Other interesting facts that support Marie not traveling with Kilpatrick's troops were revealed by the unusual duo of Sherman and a Southern woman who despised Marie. Sherman wrote: "Having utterly ruined Columbia, the right wing began its march northward, toward Winnsboro, on the 20th, which we reached on the 21st. . . . In person I reached Rocky Mount on the 22d, with the Twentieth Corps, which laid its pontoon-bridge and crossed over during the 23d. *Kilpatrick arrived the next day,* in the midst of heavy rain.[3]

The second piece of the puzzle comes from one of the South Carolina women who scorned Marie—Mary B. Poppenheim. On February 23, when Kilpatrick was nearing Rocky Mount, North Carolina, Miss Poppenheim spotted Marie in Liberty Hill, South Carolina, some 240 miles away from Kilpatrick and his troops: "While waiting for the Yankees to pass . . . the refugees from Columbia who followed Sherman's army began to pass; among them, I recognized Mary Boozer and her mother in a carriage, she in a lively conversation with a gay looking officer riding by the carriage; the scene is so sickening, I beg Mrs. Brown to let us return."[4] Major Thomas Osborn confirmed Marie's location when he recorded that he and the rest of Howard's troops were in Liberty Hill on February 23, 1865.[5]

But the most compelling evidence that Marie exited Columbia with Howard's troops and remained with him was offered by General Oliver Otis Howard himself. On March 14, 1865, he endorsed Amelia's letter to Abraham Lincoln in which the general attested that she and Marie were under his protection during the entire trek north. He also wrote to his wife ca. March 12, 1865, from Fayetteville, North Carolina, explicitly noting both Marie's and Amelia's names and relating that he and his officers had often been in the company of the sweetheart of Columbia and her mother during the some twenty-one days they had traveled from the state capital.[6]

Nevertheless, false statements by former Confederates and their sympathizers could and would not be vanquished. Edward L. Wells in an 1884 article mentioned it was an unidentified "damsel" who was caught with Kilpatrick at Monroe's Crossroads, but in his 1888 and 1899 accounts she was no longer a generic woman. On the contrary, a soldier knew she was the "exceedingly pretty girl from Columbia" who rode in a Victoria and "with her mother had left Columbia as refugees," because the soldier "tracked the wheels for hours." There was "no chance to mistake the wheel-marks of that Victoria among these heavy wagon trains. She is in his camp and we will see her in the morning." The men responded to this by whispering an enthusiastic, "By Jove!" The inconsequential evidence of a carriage track did not seem to matter—diehard Confederates deemed it as fact. It was also of no consequence that Wells inspected Kilpatrick's bonneted paramour more closely the following morning and she, to the dismay of the Rebels, was not Marie at all. On the contrary, she was a not-so-beautiful, not-so-young, and not-so-blonde "'school marm' from Vermont." Marie's detractors completely ignored this clarification as well, because they still felt the lingering bitter indignation from Marie's betrayal of them. Later this resentment became coupled with a post–Civil War unflagging devotion to the Lost Cause, and so the Kilpatrick/Boozer legend was born. It was just that—a legend, portraying Marie as a common Yankee-loving floozy caught in a humiliating situation that simultaneously ridiculed a Union general. It used Marie as a sexual scapegoat to assuage the sore feelings of former Rebels over and over again.[7]

The *Confederate Veteran* published several early-twentieth-century memoirs naming Marie as Kilpatrick's lover—memoirs frequently relied upon as facts. For example, in 1911 Confederate veteran Private Joseph A. Jones played out the Boozer/Kilpatrick myth: "Before morning, Brevet Major General Kilpatrick and Marie Boozer had returned to the main house. . . . Kilpatrick, concerned that his horses would be fed, chose this moment to step out onto the porch of the main house. Expecting to be out only a moment, he was dressed only in his shirt and drawers."[8]

The following year, a scenario of a gentlemanly Confederate risking his life to save Marie after being caught in her chemise with General Kilpatrick at Monroe's Crossroads was recalled by J. W. DuBose in the *Confederate Veteran*:

> Surrounded, Brevet Major General Kilpatrick's staff . . . were virtual prisoners in the Monroe House. Appreciating the displeasure of her fellow countrymen at the presence of Yankee cavalry and sensitive to her own compromising situation, Marie Boozer decided to leave. She appeared on the porch, gazing forlornly at her Victoria carriage. Expecting her to be shot down any second, a young Confederate officer galloped up to the porch. Dismounting quickly, he escorted her through a shower of clapboard splinters erupting from the exterior walls of the house. The couple made their way to the safety of a ditch beside Blue's Rosin Road.[9]

And then there was the 1916 account of Lawrence W. Taylor, the nephew of the beleaguered Mrs. Elmore, in *Boy Soldiers of the Confederacy*: "This was a lot of prisoners that Gen. M. C. Butler had captured the night before when he ran General Kilpatrick out in his night robe, also Miss Mary Boozer of this City (Columbia), who had left here in my aunt, Miss Harriet Elmore's carriage."[10]

The virulent sexual rumor revolved around the daughter of a Union sympathizer, and many future scholars and distinguished publishers swallowed it whole. How could they not when there was such a floodtide of southern literature purporting the legend as fact, including from those who supposedly witnessed the incident and identified Marie (or thought they saw her) as Kilpatrick's partner?

In 1956 (and reprinted in 1996) the noted professor emeritus John G. Barrett, who referred to Marie as the "indecorous Mary Boozer," wrote in a footnote to his fine book, *Sherman's March Through the Carolinas*: "The true identity of Kilpatrick's companion was never determined. In all probability it was the beautiful Mary Boozer who was still traveling with the Federal army at the time."[11]

The myth bloomed anew in a 1980 respected, well-read historical trade publication entitled *Sherman's March: The First Full-Length Narrative of General William T. Sherman's Devastating March through Georgia and the Carolinas* by Civil War expert Burke Davis, who explicitly named Marie Boozer as Kilpatrick's teenage lover.[12] And in 1986, editors noted in the informative *The Fiery Trail: A Union Officer's Account of Sherman's Last Campaign,* "In reality Kilpatrick's guest was Marie Boozer."[13]

Authors perpetuated the Kilpatrick/Boozer fantasy into the eve of the twenty-first century. In 2000, Kilpatrick biographer, Samuel J. Martin, included Marie in *Kill-Cavalry: The Life of Union General Hugh Judson Kilpatrick,* and maintained she was the general's concubine at yet another stop on their way north.[14]

That year, however, a Civil War authority acknowledged Marie's *not* being with Kilpatrick and also cited Howard's ca. March 12, 1865, letter to his wife. The scholar Mark L. Bradley maintained that Kilpatrick was never in Columbia as well and wrote (as Wells did in 1899) that a northern schoolteacher accompanied Kilpatrick at Monroe's Crossroads. However, this important material was largely buried in an endnote.[15]

In 2003 a research librarian at North Carolina State University noted that most Civil War experts were in agreement that Marie and Kilpatrick were together during at least two instances. The legend was so delectable that renowned historical novelist E. L. Doctorow scooped it up for *The March.* The best-selling author fully identified Marie, noted her fame, and expounded upon the legend in detail. The fact that the Kilpatrick/Boozer affair was untrue was probably not known to the prize-winning author or his publisher; after all, they had previously published *Sherman's March,* in which author Burke Davis professed the same fantasy as authentic.[16]

In one of twenty-five nonfiction books published in the last fifteen years that parrot the Kilpatrick/Boozer legend as truth, an author reprinted a poem located in a museum devoted to Monroe's Crossroads. The poem describes Marie's beautiful blonde curls, the disdain she received from straight-laced southern women, the destruction of Amelia's house, and Marie's sudden decision to relinquish her maidenhood and become an officer's mistress in order to succeed in life. It concludes that Marie left Columbia with Kilpatrick and had sex with no less than *four* Union generals.[17] Not only does that fantasy make Marie quite ambitious but it also brings to mind how considerate Kilpatrick was in sharing her.

CHAPTER SEVEN

The Real Road North

This time we have not been deprived of ladies' society. . . . Miss
Boozer and her mother Mrs. Feaster . . . I mention them because
we have seen so much of them in the last three weeks and I have
learned that ladies can campaign.

—Major General Oliver Otis Howard,
March 12, 1865[1]

While the seeds of a virulent legend were being sown, Marie Boozer and the other refugees under General Howard's care continued their arduous way through South Carolina. Howard commented that Mrs. Feaster although once wealthy became instantly poor because of the burning of Columbia.[2]

Tradesmen had joined the throngs of sojourners, hoping to make money selling provisions for their comfort, but Howard turned many of them away as they added too much "freightage" to the already huge number of refugees. The bumpy, harrowing trek encompassed many hardships and barriers, including floods from severe thunderstorms and a mile-wide shallow stream they had to cross. There was thievery as well—degenerate Union soldiers stole from the refugees.[3] However, it is unlikely Marie and her mother experienced this outrage, considering the attention they received from officers who extended only the most courtly, celebratory treatment to the women. For instance, Amelia and Marie were feted on at least one occasion by Howard's high-ranking Colonel James T. Conklin, quartermaster of the corps. Despite the hardships, the women enjoyed themselves during the trip and looked forward to a new life in the North.[4]

As the Civil War had not yet ended, at times deadly skirmishes between both armies took place in front of the group, and the Confederate cavalry tried to impede the formation's northern movement. Freed South Carolina slaves became Union soldiers enlisted by Howard to fight the Confederate forces ahead, and with the legions of freedmen, Howard's troops pushed back the Rebels and quenched at least one fire at a bridge they started.[5]

In the midst of these ongoing battles, General Howard made specific mention of the particular capabilities in military maneuvers possessed by Amelia and Marie: "I have learned that ladies can campaign," he wrote to his wife. What else would one expect from descendants and nieces of warrior patriots?[6]

Amelia and her party reached North Carolina on March 8, 1865, one day after celebrating little Ethland's eighth birthday. The news had spread by then that Marie, the beautiful bewitcher of Columbia, was among the travelers. It was as if "some Oriental queen or princess were driving through her realms to receive the plaudits and worship of her blinded subjects," recalled a former Confederate scout.[7]

Southern-born gossip about Marie and Amelia continued along their journey northward, but the wisecracks and disparagements were later contradicted by General William T. Sherman when he honored Amelia by mentioning her name and her daughters in his memoir. The entry concerned a steamboat by which Captain Ainsworth had arrived in Fayetteville, North Carolina, on March 12, 1865, to dispatch mail from General Alfred Terry to General Sherman. This boat would take Amelia, Marie, Ethland, and Lizzie from Fayetteville to Wilmington, a port that had been captured by the Union on February 22, 1865: "After a few minutes' conference with Captain Ainsworth about the capacity of his boat . . . I instructed him to be ready to start back at 6pm. . . . I also authorized General Howard to send back by this opportunity some of the fugitives who had traveled with his army all the way from Columbia, among whom were Mrs. Feaster and her two beautiful daughters."[8]

In the midst of a calm evening on March 12, 1865, Marie, Ethland, Amelia, and Lizzie—joined by Col. James T. Conklin—boarded Ainsworth's small tugboat, *Davidson*, bound for Wilmington. The boat parted the waters while it chugged steadfastly toward safety, carrying precious letters from the men to their loved ones—a reestablished, tenuous link that had long been absent. In one of those letters General Howard informed his wife that Amelia was returning to Philadelphia.[9]

David Conyngham, a captain in the Union army and war correspondent for the *New York Herald*, wrote in his memoir that he was in a vessel accompanying the mail boat to Wilmington. En route they saw remnants of Confederate fires on the banks, but their particular group was not fired upon. He continued: "The night was lovely, with a full moon shedding its rays over the sparkling waters as we shot along the silvery stream. All were cheerful, for it was like waking to a new life, after being so long shut from the outer world."[10]

After Amelia, Marie, Ethland, and Lizzie arrived safely in Wilmington, Amelia, General Alfred Terry and General Howard (with his endorsement written from Cade's Plantation, North Carolina while with the Army of the Tennessee) collaborated in a transcription to President Abraham Lincoln dated March 14 and March 15, 1865, that appealed for Amelia's remuneration.[11]

One of Amelia's former house guests, Lieutenant Gilbert Sabre later revealed that not only had he been among those officers who arranged for Amelia to join Sherman's army but he also protected and accompanied her and her family to Fayetteville and later the port of Wilmington. There he personally saw that they safely reunited with her Philadelphia kin, who eventually brought the tired refugees back to Amelia's hometown.[12]

On Thursday, March 23, 1865, Amelia and her party had already checked into Philadelphia's five-year-old Continental Hotel on the corner of Ninth and Chestnut Streets. Amelia signed, "Mrs. J. N. Feaster, two da. (daughters), and do (domestic servant)" in the hotel's guestbook.[13] This negates another of the many false tales by Julian Selby alleging that Amelia and Marie were about to board the ill-fated steamship General

Lyon, which sank on March 31, but because the ship was overcrowded, they boarded the General Sedgwick, a ship close to the Lyon disaster on the same date.[14]

Amelia's mother, Mary Carr Sees (fig. 7); two of Amelia's sisters, Emily Sees Snyder and Rebecca Gale Sees Moore (fig. 8); and Rebecca's daughter, Mayme, were Philadelphia residents at this time. The families established a warm environment especially for little Ethland, who was around Mayme's age. Marie liked her young cousin and stayed in touch with Mayme, who would grow into an elegant woman (fig. 9).[15]

Fig. 7. Marie's grandmother, Mary Carr Sees, ambrotype, ca. 1862, courtesy Wilson-Battle-Connell-Park Papers.

Amelia, Ethland, Marie, and Lizzie were still lodging at the Continental Hotel on April 9, 1865, when Lee surrendered to Grant and a week later when the press announced the shocking news of Abraham Lincoln's assassination. In May, amid frightening accounts in Philadelphia newspapers that Confederate sympathizers were plotting to burn down the entire city, the press lauded Marie for protecting from fire and safely bringing north the family's precious American flag unfurled in Confederate Columbia.[16]

Local papers declared that Amelia's Good Samaritan efforts saved "Union soldiers in the death-pens of the traitors in Columbia, South Carolina," and her ministrations should "forever endear her to every lover of the Union in this city." Residents of the City of Brotherly Love planned on showing Amelia a warm reception she would always remember, and journalists called on every "loyal Philadelphian" who should

Fig. 8. Marie's aunt, Rebecca Gale Sees Moore, ca. 1885, photograph by L. Husted & Co., Philadelphia, Reed family papers, courtesy J. Reed Bradford.

Fig. 9. Marie's cousin, Mayme Sees McManus, ca. 1885, photograph by L. Husted & Co., Philadelphia, Reed family papers, courtesy J. Reed Bradford.

offer their gratitude for her brave patriotism despite the threats from Rebels she encountered.[17]

Numerous Philadelphia officers—many whom Amelia and Marie saved—acted upon the local press's suggestion and respectfully called on Marie and her mother. The soldiers expressed "the greatest delight at meeting one who was their friend amidst so much peril." The *Philadelphia Inquirer* and *Bulletin* repeatedly praised the two women and predicted Amelia would be reimbursed by the federal government for the heroic hardships she incurred.[18]

While staying in the City of Brotherly Love, Amelia supported her friend Unionist Phineas F. Frazee in his attempt to be compensated for his aid to prisoners of war and for property destroyed by Sherman's troops. She signed one affidavit in Philadelphia and another in New York, for later in 1865 Amelia, Ethland, Marie, and Lizzie relocated to Manhattan. Amelia had friends and investments in New York as well as relatives there, including her brother John, who continued to obtain patents for his engineering inventions.[19]

Manhattan was the ultimate environment in which the travelers could easily slough off the conformism and provincialism of their former Confederate home. The three women and one girl had survived the war and anticipated new horizons. However, southern resentment accompanied Marie and Amelia to the big city and would not relinquish its grip.

CHAPTER EIGHT

Four Freshly New Yorkers

Mr. Sherman presented the memorial of Amelia Feaster, praying to be reimbursed for moneys expended in alleviating the condition of Union officers confined in the rebel prison at Columbia, South Carolina.

—Journal of the Senate, 1866 [1]

Soon after the four former Columbia residents arrived in New York, the steadfast Lizzie returned to South Carolina, retrieved Julia and Jakie, and brought them back to the arms of their loving mother. The war had been over for months by then and Lizzie was a free woman—able to travel to and from the South with little fear of stumbling into a battle or being kidnapped and enslaved. She eventually settled in Brooklyn but remained in contact with the family, especially Ethland.[2]

Post–Civil War Manhattan was prosperous, with aristocratic and new money pouring into its coffers. Horse-drawn trolleys, carts, and carriages of every quality ambled down the city's busy streets and circled its planted squares. Downtown was replete with brownstone buildings, some accented with red-and-white-striped awnings. Within those buildings industrialists, financiers, railroad, and shipping barons were rapidly making New York a mercantile, financial, and artistic hub of the world. The ultimate pursuits were money and power—the have-nots struggled for a bit of both and the haves strived for more.

Amid them, Amelia was still largely homeless and penniless; however, she and Marie had arrived in Manhattan as celebrated Civil War heroines with important Union generals vouching for them. The women also had verbal and written support from prominent New York citizens as well as

71

Columbian Unionist expatriates. As a result, in a gentlemen's agreement, substantial members of the Union League Club joined forces to help Amelia and her family. These men included Thomas Murphy—future New York state senator and William T. Sherman's and Ulysses S. Grant's close friend—who financed Amelia's entire stay at the Astor House, and publisher and politician Thurlow Weed, who recalled that he and others gave her a donation totaling $10,000. Like the Yankee officers, these upper-crust men were simply paying a debt to exceptional patriots. After all, to "preserve the Union" in the midst of Civil War, the Union League Club had separated from the Union Club because that aristocratic organization retained Confederate membership.[3]

Columbia's Colonel James G. Gibbes claimed in his memoir *Who Burnt Columbia* that while staying in New York, he received a note from Amelia begging him to visit her at the Astor House. He found her at the hotel "living in style, with a handsome suite of rooms and surrounded by a number of army officers."[4]

Gibbes contended that Amelia wanted him to write a statement on her behalf, certifying to the government she was a widow. While Amelia had indeed been a three-time widow, her current husband, Jacob Feaster, was still alive and well, and Gibbes noted sardonically that he had recently seen Feaster and therefore could not certify Amelia as such. In other words, Gibbes accused Amelia of trying to defraud the United States regarding her marital status to obtain more compensation. In opposition to his account, she did not formally claim she was a widow in the signed affidavits; her petition to Abraham Lincoln from Wilmington, North Carolina; or appeals she made in Philadelphia and New York. Furthermore, in the index of congressional petitions for bills of remuneration, the term "widow" was written after other women's names but not after Amelia's. However, at least one Union officer wrote in his affidavit that it "appeared" that Amelia was a widow living in Columbia at the time of its capture. Nevertheless, this had no effect when it came to her legal declaration of status in the North, where again, she did not defraud governmental authority.[5]

After Senator John Sherman, brother of General William Tecumseh Sherman, stated Amelia's case for remuneration before Congress, it was claimed she had "incurred an outlay of $60,000 in her benefactions" for Union prisoners of war. Her former traveling companion, General Oliver Otis Howard declared that the "government of the United States cannot do too much for those kind friends to our prisoners who were in that sad extremity. I . . . would be glad if some relief could be granted." This was concurred by Generals Ulysses S. Grant, Alfred H. Terry, and ironically the rascally Hugh J. Kilpatrick.[6]

The problem was that under federal law, Amelia could not receive compensation for property lost as a casualty of war. However, Secretary of War Edwin M. Stanton agreed that she should be repaid for her kindness, meritorious behavior, and expenses outlaid in helping the Union cause. As a result, in July 1866, after a unanimous vote in the Senate, the appropriation passed, which called for a reimbursement of $10,000 "to make a partial return for her work of patriotic love."[7] While the House of Representatives set aside the Senate bill in December 1866 among numerous other pleas for relief, Jacob Feaster's grandniece, Lena Norwood Mitchell, disclosed that many years later Amelia's daughters Ethland and Julia were reimbursed for Amelia's loss in the amount of thousands of dollars.[8]

South Carolinians reacted strongly to the Senate bill. Aristocratic Columbian citizen Mrs. Thomas Taylor expressed contempt for it: "We heard they got $10,000 for burnt cotton which they never owned."[9]

Another Columbian who complained about the bill's passage was the aforementioned Julian A. Selby. If ever there was a staunch Confederate, it was he. Selby, formerly with the Dr. Robert Wilson Gibbes–owned newspaper, the *South Carolinian* in 1864, published with William Gilmore Simms the *Daily Phoenix* in Columbia from 1865–78. Selby named it the *Phoenix* because the paper was born out of a portion of a printing press retrieved from ashes of the *South Carolinian*. He also published Confederate sheet music.[10]

Like many other Columbians, Selby loved his city and was horrified at its devastation. After the war he remained devoted to the memory of the South's struggle for independence and respectfully dedicated the first issue of the Phoenix to the "heroes of the tented field."[11]

In 1866 Selby reported the news of the Senate bill passage to compensate Amelia, which he deeply resented. His *Phoenix* editorial, republished in other southern newspapers as well, clearly revealed this. Interestingly, it inaccurately deemed Amelia as a pro-Confederate during the war:

Mrs. Feaster . . . was a resident of this city until the departure of General Sherman's army from its ruins which army she accompanied. We do not know that we have any right to grumble at any disposition of Uncle Sam's money the radicals may make . . . yet we would suggest that the Committee on Finance of the House give the . . . claim a thorough investigation. Mrs. F., at the beginning of war, and, indeed we believe, was throughout until her departure, an ardent female "rebel," and all our citizens will remember the grand hubbub in front of her house, when, from her own piazza, she presented a banner . . . to that gallant company, the "Butler Guards," from Greenville. There were other small evidences of her loyalty to the now "lost cause," but we will not mention them. As to her present claim we have not definite information; but if she supplied these necessaries to the Union soldiers in prison here, we do not think five citizens of Columbia were aware of the fact. We know this, that the Confederate commissary stripped this market and the surrounding farm-houses every day to feed the prisoners while they were lodged here or in the camp over the river; so that we think it but proper this claim should be properly "ventilated" by the new "retrenchment committee" of Congress.[12]

This hostility toward Amelia's proposed compensation festered in Selby. In 1878 it found full expression in his spurious *A Checkered Life: Being a Brief History of the Countess Pourtales, formerly Miss Marie Boozer, of Columbia, S.C.*, which would be most injurious to Marie and the memory of her mother. And, perpetuating Selby's myth, another less vindictive, more intellectual, and respected South Carolina gentleman, Yates Snowden, would later write the introduction of that pamphlet's reprint.

It is clear that most of the outlandish rumors about Marie and Amelia emanated from Columbia. Years later, a South Carolina author confirmed that the tawdry, wild tales of Marie's life were made public in a constant stream stemming from within the city limits, and were the fruits of chronic grudges against mother and daughter. This animosity for the women was exacerbated by the Senate enactment of reimbursement for their humanitarian actions. Some South Carolinians would continue to shred to bits both mother's and daughter's names, and it would last for over a century.[13]

CHAPTER NINE

The Beechers of West 17th Street

*At the Club House yesterday there were many celebrities of the
metropolis congregated. The ladies were particularly charming . .
. and the gentlemen were divided in their attention to their fair
companions and their pecuniary interest in the races.*

—"American Jockey Club Races,"
New York Herald, June 7, 1872

Well before the government tribute to Amelia in July 1866, the
family had moved to the residential Clarendon Hotel, using funds
from the Union League's contribution. While staying at the upscale
hotel, Amelia and Marie met prominent merchant and widower
John S. Beecher, born in Woodbridge, Connecticut, on August 14,
1826. The Clarendon was Beecher's *pied-à-terre* when not at his
"country" house on Staten Island, where he avidly participated in
the sport of fishing. His first wife, Jane, had died in 1859 at the age
of thirty-three.[1]

Similar to the legions of Marie's admirers before him, the thirty-
nine-year-old Beecher became immediately attracted to the teenager.
Amelia encouraged the pliant Marie to respond to his attention, and
following her mother's wishes, she and Beecher began a courtship.[2]

While Beecher was some twenty years Marie's senior and had a
prominent double chin, he was not unattractive. He stood five foot
nine inches tall, and his curly brown hair topped a round face that
was "full of expression, very genial, and animated," accented with

an aquiline nose and gray/blue eyes. With an affable personality, he could tell humorous stories that sent his listeners into fits of laughter, but Marie saw him as merely a pleasant old man.[3]

Nevertheless, Amelia was certain she had at last found in Beecher a suitable husband for her daughter. He was wealthy enough to establish Marie in a secure financial environment; he was mature enough to shape Marie into an appropriate matron who would satisfy Amelia's expectations; he was a recognized socialite, affording Marie a life in elite circles; and he was willing to furnish a residence for Amelia and her entire family. Amelia and Beecher consequently arranged a marriage between him and her bankable daughter as if it were a business transaction. To sweeten the deal, Beecher offered a large sum of money as a dowry—around $150,000 (which Marie retained for many years). He could well afford it. He had in 1855 formed a highly successful wine, liquor, and tea importing company with Frederick E. Ives, located by 1865 on Manhattan's Front Street. The company, whose success was primarily in the whiskey trade, advertised nationally and enjoyed a renowned repute. Beecher also owned real estate holdings and other investments that paid profitable dividends.[4]

Amelia, from her marriage to Peter Burton, knew well the stigma and stress that accompanied a bankrupt husband. Additionally, she lost her third husband by suicide due to financial troubles. Furthermore, her aunt and uncle lost their business and historic garden because of a bankruptcy. Amelia obviously wished none of that kind of fiscal suffering for her children and wanted only the best in life for them. Was this an excuse to manage Marie's life? Perhaps Amelia felt Marie would grow to love Beecher as she matured. Certainly, Amelia did not wish Marie to be in an unhappy marriage, but convincing a teenager to marry a much older man was not necessarily a prescription for happiness.

Marie did not love Beecher but she loved her mother very much and once again acquiesced to Amelia's command. Thus, Marie's future was realized when on January 22, 1866, she wedded John S.

Beecher at an exclusive, small Episcopal church—the First Church of the Intercession, located in Audubon Park in Washington Heights overlooking the Hudson River. (Today the area comprises 155th and 158th Streets between the Hudson River and Broadway.) The charming first church, built in the 1840s when the area was called Carmansville, held services until a new church was built in 1872. Beecher's partner, Frederick Ives, attended the wedding and later recalled that Reverend Smith officiated.[5]

The marriage was yet another missed opportunity for Marie to achieve a loving relationship with a man. She hinted in a letter to Ethland that after Samuel Preston's untimely death, her mother's domination ruined any hope for love: "I had no chance—you had and see how differently we have managed." Marie also revealed her morose wedding-day feelings by declaring in an interview, "My mother sacrificed me at the altar of marriage to an old man of wealth and position."[6]

To make matters worse, Marie, contrary to fictional accounts, was not sexually experienced and not aware of the complexities of an intimate relationship. She disclosed that when she married Beecher, she was "too young to understand the responsibilities, the sacred duties of wife." Marie nonetheless entered her marriage in the stoic manner she handled her prior sadness—by suppressing emotional pain and making the best out of an uncomfortable situation.[7]

There were definite perks to this sacrificial union and they included a luxurious environment. Beecher moved out of the Clarendon and purchased a grand townhouse suitable for his beautiful bride at 30 W. 17th Street, not too far west of Fifth Avenue and in the proper location for acceptance into society. It had ample room for Amelia, Ethland, Julia, Jakie, and plenty of servants.[8]

Mr. and Mrs. John S. Beecher became a part of the fashionable social sphere that lived south of 34th Street from Madison Avenue to just west of Fifth. The old-moneyed New Yorkers at that time primarily lived below 23rd St. on or near Fifth Avenue. Some of the nouveau riche lived largely on Fifth Avenue above 34th Street and were looked down upon by Manhattan aristocracy. That opinion changed radically in the late 1870s when a member of the Vanderbilt family began building his mansion on Fifth Avenue in the fifties.

Fig. 10. Jennie Jerome (Lady Randolph Churchill), photographer unknown, author's collection.

The Beechers' mixed in a circle whose society leaders were members of the Union, Manhattan, and Jockey Club set with names including August Belmont and William R. Travers. Aside from private clubs, socializing would take place at Delmonico's restaurant, where the elite often met for lunch.

Another prominent member of the New York haut monde was Leonard Jerome, a financier. The successful stockbroker and his family had moved to Manhattan from Brooklyn and lived in an opulent mansion a bit northeast of the Beechers on Madison Square at 26th Street and Madison Avenue. Jerome partnered with August Belmont to build the Jerome Race Park in the Bronx, where Marie, who loved to gamble, spent many an afternoon with her husband and other members of the privileged class. In fact, Mr. and Mrs. Beechers' names would be mentioned in the society columns just after Mr. Travers and Mr. Belmont.[9]

Leonard Jerome was a close friend of the Beechers, and the two families spent considerable time with each other. Marie was especially fond of Leonard's young daughter, Jeanette (Jennie), who later left for Europe, married Lord Randolph Churchill, and became Winston Churchill's mother. Jennie (see fig. 10) was also the subject of scandalous articles and gossip due to the swiftness of the

Randolph engagement as well as her penchants and exploits during and after the marriage. The future relationship between Marie and Jennie may have been somewhat strained or kept secret as there are no existing letters between them in the Churchill archives. Whether or not Jennie consigned them to the fireplace is unknown but she would remain friendly with Marie's son, Preston, for decades.[10]

Meanwhile, Marie was a nineteenth-century version of a trophy wife, and Beecher delighted in displaying her as such. Dressed in the latest Paris designs, she would promenade with Beecher through Madison Square or ride through Central Park in her stylish phaeton on her way to Jerome Race Park or out for an afternoon drive. Central Park was a prime place for high society to be seen; the benches along the main thoroughfares were installed so that the ordinary folk could sit while gazing at the upper classes as they rode past. It was a form of free urban entertainment offered by the city's oasis.

Marie became the center of attention during those rides, just as in Columbia. Both sexes also admired her at several social destinations, including the Jerome racecourse clubhouse, where the smart set focused their opera glasses on other spectators as well as the horses. Reporting on the glamorous clothing on women before the details of a race, New York newspapers drooled over sumptuous ensembles of a rainbow of silks, embroidered cashmeres, scalloped velvets, bonnets trimmed in multicolored lace, and exotic shawls. Marie's particular outfits, hairstyle, and jewelry were not only noticed by the public but "always the envy of every lady" who saw them. Sightings of Marie in her private opera box were often the subject of report, awe, and envy as well. While privileged New Yorkers fawned on her because of her grace, loveliness, intellectual abilities, and vivaciousness, she was too young to be a society leader. Instead she reigned as a princess of Gotham—a potential doyenne of her social realm.[11]

Mrs. John S. Beecher instantly transformed into "Mamma" when the birth of (John) Preston occurred on January 6, 1867. Ostensibly happy, wealthy, and with numerous staff to wait upon her and her baby, Marie fulfilled her role as a young mother. While she still had not grown to love Beecher, she was certainly in love with her son. She affectionately snipped a lock of his baby hair to keep close to her and inscribed on its tiny packet, "Hair taken from baby's little head when three weeks old, Monday, Jan. 28th, 1867, Mamma."[12] And one can imagine Amelia relishing her part as the baby's grandmother. Preston's birth in the beginning of 1867 was an especially welcomed blessing to Amelia as the end of 1866 proved daunting. In November, her brother John died in Philadelphia, and in December, the House of Representatives set aside her claim for remuneration.[13]

Marie's well-cushioned life continued for the next few years with John Beecher reveling in it. He still earned about $100,000 per year from his liquor and wine business alone, and spent it as fast as the money came in—but not only on Marie. He also indulged in his own pleasures, such as yachting, and outlaid generous amounts of cash pleasing his friends, including Leonard Jerome.[14]

In the interim, Ethland enrolled and boarded at the Academy of the Sacred Heart in Manhattanville, the school Marie had attended. Course of study continued to be varied and included Christian doctrine, ancient and modern history, literature, English, Latin, mathematics, the natural sciences, and the obligatory study of French. They gave "special advantages . . . for French conversation" and primarily stressed the "training of character and the cultivation of manners."[15]

Marie's half-sister Julia Carrie Feaster may also have attended the Academy of the Sacred Heart as a "Julia Feaster" appears in their records. Preston Beecher later recalled Julia from the time they were both living on W. 17th Street. He wrote she was "quite pretty" and "used to wear curls hanging down at each side of her face, which was the fashion."[16]

In 1870, Amelia, who had done everything in her tumultuous past she felt was beneficial for her family, and who had been suffering for a lengthy amount of time from an ovarian tumor, died from its swelling on the second of March. Mourners were welcomed at the Beechers' home on West 17th Street, and on the following day, like so many other members of the Sees family, Amelia was buried in Philadelphia. This refutes yet another false statement by Julian Selby—that Amelia was buried in a pauper's grave in New York in which John Beecher was a stockholder. Marie's maternal grandmother, Mary Carr Sees, outlived Amelia, died at age eighty-four the following year in December, and was buried in Philadelphia as well.[17]

Amelia's burial record noted she was forty-one, around ten years younger than her actual age—the same as Amelia recorded in the 1860 census. Marie perhaps filled in the discrepant age on the death certificate as a final favor to her mother. Marie then had to contend with the pain of losing the parent on whom she depended for most of her life—the woman she loved to such an extent that she let mold her from the time she was a little girl. Marie may have felt, aside from the deep sadness of permanent separation, an unfamiliar sense of freedom, for suddenly, despite the control of her husband, she could dare to make some decisions of her own.

After the Civil War, several of Amelia's relatives had offered her estranged husband, Jacob, attractive business opportunities in Philadelphia or New York—perhaps as a way to reconcile the two—but Feaster opted to remain in the South. As a result, Jacob Feaster and his parents (Ethland's, Julia's, and Jakie's grandparents), Andrew and Mary Norris Feaster with their family in tow, had in December 1867 moved south from Fairfield County, South Carolina, to LaGrange in what was then Volusia County, Florida—a stunning contrast to the Beechers' stylish urban lives. The Feasters were courageous Florida pioneers, trekking through sand roads, lakes, and streams by mule pack and carrying household necessities, oil paintings of ancestors, and "a big, heavy, square grand piano," often played by their daughter, Julia Feaster Coleman (1835–1919).[18] They chose LaGrange for a fresh start because one of the Feaster brothers had previously purchased "considerable acreage" of wilderness in the area and the settlement could easily be reached via the St. Johns River. It was also around two miles from a trading post called Sand Point, now known as Titusville, located on the banks of the wide, sparkling Indian River, a salt-water sound fed by fresh water streams. Titusville and LaGrange would become part of Brevard County by 1879.[19]

Fig. 11. Portrait of Julia "Belle" Carrie Feaster Field at sixteen, pastel heightened with gouache, courtesy J. Reed Bradford.

The Feasters, headed by Andrew who was a Universalist, founded a nondenominational church in LaGrange in 1869. Two more Feasters joined the church after Amelia died, as Julia C. Feaster (fig. 11) and Jakie (fig. 12) moved to Florida to be with their father. By then, Julia had grown into a beautiful, gracious young woman. Julia's well educated aunts—Julia Feaster Coleman and Margaret Narcissa Feaster (who had enjoyed spending time with Marie in Columbia)—resided near Jacob Feaster's house in LaGrange. The refined Feaster women added culture to the frontier community. Narcissa taught children in a log cabin, one of the first public schools "between St. Augustine and the Keys," and Julia Feaster Coleman taught Sunday school and brought music to the settlers through her piano, the only one in the area.[20]

Ethland stayed in New York and at age thirteen was under Marie's care, residing with her or boarded at the Academy. Marie was a loving half-sister to the much younger Ethland. The two were as close as any two sisters might be, and Marie mothered her with considerable affection. She was in charge of Ethland's well-being, guidance, and education, which helped shape Ethland into the lovely

Fig. 12. Jacob Andrew "Jakie" Feaster, ca. 1870, tintype, Reed family papers, courtesy J. Reed Bradford. According to Marie's niece, Ethel Battle, Jakie died at a young age.

young woman she eventually became.

In May 1870 John S. Beecher encountered a vexing problem with the law. A conspirator judge accused him of contempt of court when, as an assignee, he allegedly appeared at a bankrupt gentleman's place of business and tried to collect property without having a summons. Consequently, two men questioned him at his store, and two other individuals claiming to be deputy sheriffs confronted him in lower Manhattan on his way to Brown Brothers. They took him to court, and after the judge heard Beecher's side of the story and had a conversation with one of the men who manhandled him, he asked Beecher to rise and then told him he was allowed to leave.[21]

Beecher worried that if he left he might be re-arrested. He asked the judge, "Where shall I go, if you please?"

The judge offered the following options: "You can go to Ludlow street jail, or to the bosom of your family, just as you like."

Beecher replied respectfully, "I shall do whichever you direct."

The judge responded, "Well, I should advise you to go home," whereupon Beecher returned to Marie and little Preston.[22]

Beecher's arrest was declared illegal. And the unscrupulous judge behind it, who prevented Beecher from acting as a rightful assignee in a bankruptcy case, was John McCunn, a Tammany Hall politician and the target of charges by the New York State Legislature.

With the assistance of Beecher and others as witnesses, the legislature consequently removed McCunn from the courts.

John S. Beecher remained an upright citizen and businessman as well as an attentive husband and father during the early 1870s. But he was also a member of the set in which dalliances with women were acceptable as long as one was discreet. He, according to Marie, lived up to that role and became unfaithful to her.[23]

CHAPTER TEN

Passion Sails In

---

*If a gentleman approaches you with words of flattery and profuse
attentions, especially after a short acquaintance, extend no
encouraging smile or word; for a flatterer can never be otherwise
than an unprofitable companion.*

—Emily Thornwell,
The Lady's Guide to Perfect Gentility, 1856[1]

Situated between Leonard Jerome's mansion and the Beecher townhome
was the grand residence of John Beecher's friend, Lloyd Phoenix, at 22
W. 23rd Street, perched in prime New York social territory, just off Fifth
Avenue and Madison Square Park. The attractive Lloyd Phoenix, born in
1841, was a scion of New York society. His mother was Mary Whitney,
daughter of Stephen Whitney, and his father was Jonas Phillips Phoenix,
a distinguished congressman. This background afforded the young
Phoenix the means to live his life as a gentleman of leisure as well as to
gain entry into the best of New York's circles and private organizations,
such as the Union, Knickerbocker, Metropolitan, and Manhattan Clubs
that catered to urban socialites.[2]

A former Union officer who entered Annapolis in 1857, Phoenix as a
midshipman was accused of minor delinquencies, some entailing socializing during study hours and after taps, having his hands in his pockets
during a drill, no gloves during an inspection, smoking, and "lounging
on the bed during the day."[3] After graduating from Annapolis, he became
a Civil War naval lieutenant, enlisting in 1861. In the subsequent three

years Phoenix endured the challenge of naval combat. He was involved in the famous battle of Hampton Roads, in which the *Monitor* went against the former USS *Merrimack* (CSS *Virginia*), and also spent much time sailing on the US steam frigate *Wabash*. In fact, as long as Phoenix was wrapped up in the excitement of fighting Confederates, he was largely contented and an admired sailor.[4]

Although he resigned from the navy after the war, Phoenix maintained a love for the sea that no woman could supplant. He continued his maritime romance as an enthusiastic yachtsman and prominent member of the New York Yacht Club, becoming Rear Commodore from 1867–68. Club Commodore DeCoursey Fales remembered Phoenix fondly in relating his generosity to the club by funding it whenever it was necessary. In fact, Phoenix became "one of the leading spirits in American yachting," and so important to the yachting world that a regatta and trophy are named for him today.[5]

Second to Phoenix's nautical passion was his attachment to freedom. He refused to be anchored to any one woman and changed them as frequently as he changed his yachts. His yacht in 1871 was called *Restless*, reflecting Phoenix's fickle personality, and by 1872 he had been cruising on his recently purchased *Josephine*, a Stonington, Connecticut–built ninety-five-plus-foot schooner. When he wasn't sailing, he was at the raceway "driving fast horses," and when he tired of that, he frequented museums, galleries, shops, or auctions, collecting fine art, rare books, and antique objects.[6]

John S. Beecher and Lloyd Phoenix were members of the Union and Manhattan Clubs, but Phoenix, being a bachelor, was a bit more adventurous. He was similar to his friend, fellow playboy James Gordon Bennett Jr., the heir to the *New York Herald* known for his party hopping. Bennett took time out from cocktailing to send one of his correspondents, Henry Stanley, to Africa to seek out Dr. David Livingstone, which resulted in their famous meeting reportedly beginning with "Dr. Livingstone, I presume?"[7]

Phoenix and Bennett were the leaders of New York's golden youth, the champagne-guzzling "fast set." Their hedonistic escapades were celebrated within their circle but usually kept muffled by the press with handsome payoffs to newspapers and generous tips to the restaurants in which some of these carousals occurred. These young men were exceedingly popular, likeable fellows who held substantial positions in the social strata and wielded power the likes of which nineteenth-century women could never possess.[8]

Marie and Phoenix were often at the same social functions in New York—for instance, a charity ball at the Academy of Music benefiting the Nursing and Child's Hospital. Phoenix was the manager of that event along with other notables, and Marie likely attended as Beecher often bought her "a place among the patrons at the ball."[9] They also had

Fig. 13. Rear-Admiral Samuel Francis DuPont and staff on the USS *Wabash* in the harbor of Port Royal, South Carolina, in 1862. From left to right: Captain Christopher R. P. Rodgers, commander of the *Wabash*; Admiral S. F. DuPont, commander of the South Atlantic Blockading Squadron; *Lieutenant Samuel W. Preston, admiral's aid* (third from left); Secretary Alexander McKinley; Lieutenant Thomas H. Corbin; Lieutenant Alexander S. Mackenzie; Surgeon George Clymer; Assistant Surgeon Philip R. Voorhees, of the *Wabash; Lieutenant Lloyd Phoenix of the Wabash* (third from right); Commander William Reynolds, of the *Vermont*; and Lieutenant John S. Barnes. Samuel Francis DuPont photographs, ID: 2010_269_W9_18842 (Accession 2010.269), Audiovisual Collections and Digital Initiatives Department, Hagley Museum and Library, Wilmington, Delaware.

someone quite significant in common—Marie's former fiancé, Lieutenant Samuel W. Preston, who had died in battle some six years before she met Phoenix by 1871. Not only were Preston and Phoenix at Annapolis with each other but they also served together aboard the *Wabash* (see fig. 13).

John S. Beecher introduced Marie to Phoenix at the Union Club during an evening ladies' reception, one of the only occasions in which women—with an escort, of course—were allowed inside. At that time Phoenix was in between the young graduate of about nineteen as seen in fig. 14 and the mature clubman at around sixty as seen in fig. 15. He had thick dark hair, full sensual lips, and gazed at women with penetrating, soulful eyes. His frequent runs aboard his schooner kept his skin bronze and rugged, which intensified the contrast of his eyes, and he retained his good looks even as he aged.[10]

Marie was as lovely as ever that evening at the Union Club. One can easily imagine her animated blue eyes in the candlelight, her hair styled in a half upsweep with a torrent of curls down her back, and her off-the-shoulder silk Paris gown with plunging neckline, narrow waist, and voluminous folds cascading onto the floor behind her. Indeed, the initial encounter between the two was no doubt spellbinding with an undercurrent of sensual energy smoldering amid pleasant conversation.

Phoenix, who had an inexhaustible sexual appetite, was a muscular dish of trouble. Prior to meeting Marie, he had been involved with a courtesan/prostitute named Harriet "Hattie" Blackford, a.k.a. Fanny Lear (1848–1886) (see fig. 16). She was born Harriet Clarissima Ely in Philadelphia, the daughter of a Presbyterian reverend, Ezra Stiles Ely.[11]

The witty Mrs. Blackford said she was forced into a life of prostitution by "bad men and inconsiderate women."[12] She married a so-called jealous alcoholic whom she met in West Virginia and had a daughter with him in 1865 named Caroline. Hattie's husband later died in a largely unknown way after allegedly stabbing her, and thereafter she preferred being photographed in high-collared clothing. While Caroline lived with Hattie's mother, Hattie applied her profession, trading sexual encounters for money from primarily wealthy men and obtaining cash from them in other creative ways. For instance, early in her career she was said to have

Left, Fig. 14. *Lloyd Phoenix*, USNA 1861, Special Collections and Archives Department, *Nimitz* Library, US Naval Academy.

Right, Fig. 15. *Lloyd Phoenix*, reproduced from Lewis Randolph Hamersly, *Men of Affairs in New York* (New York: L. R. Hamersly, 1906), 279.

threatened to sue a respectable Philadelphia artist for breach of promise until she received a settlement of thousands of dollars.[13]

Blackford then moved on to loftier conquests in New York City. She first met Lloyd Phoenix around 1869 at a New York brothel in which she was working. He took her to London where they lived together, during which time Phoenix introduced Hattie to British royalty. The relationship between the yachtsman and prostitute flourished until Phoenix betrayed her. Phoenix allegedly promised to marry her but unbeknownst to Hattie he was already betrothed to a New York woman. Hattie, however, did not shrink away quietly or suffer demurely in silence. She instead returned to New York, declared she had indeed married Phoenix in London, and threatened to sue him for breach of promise, just as she had done to the Philadelphia artist. Phoenix quieted her and obtained his release by paying her an amount of money reported to be over $100,000.[14]

From then on, Hattie was well known by the press as "Phoenix," "the Phoenix," "La Phoenix," "Mrs. Phoenix," and "Miss Phoenix." She

Fig. 16. Hattie Blackford, ca. 1875,
image courtesy Eva and Daniel McDonald.

called herself the same, declaring, "My name is Blackford after the man who married me and Phoenix after the man who wronged me." She named her lap dog "Lloydy" as a further ironic tribute to Phoenix.[15]

Hattie did not let the failed affair slow her down. She became the courtesan of a Scottish earl and had a liaison with the Prince of Wales, the future King of England—Edward VII.[16] In 1874 she was at the center of a scandalous international affair involving a grand duke in tsarist Russia and would also become Marie's friend.

Phoenix did not marry his New York intended, and after he terminated his relationship with both Hattie and his former fiancé, he cast his net in Marie's direction. He was the definite hunter in this sport of seduction. Very reliable sources—Phoenix's own attorneys, who included Clarence Armstrong Seward (raised from age seven by his uncle, William Henry Seward, Secretary of State under President Abraham Lincoln) and Samuel Blatchford (later an associate Supreme Court justice)—averred that Phoenix tried to seduce Marie, not the other way around. However, the flirtatious Marie, attracted to his sexual energy and his compelling connection with her former fiancé, welcomed and responded to the yachtsman's attention.[17]

Aside from her aborted relationships as a teenager, Marie was relatively inexperienced with men other than her husband, and she had never met up with Phoenix's kind of aggressive, all-consuming male force. The desire brewing between them at subsequent encounters was overwhelming, despite her eroding loyalty to John Beecher, whom she knew had been unfaithful to her as early as April 1871. As a result, she had little guilt in contemplating an affair with Phoenix, and by May of the same year she had fallen in love again.[18]

Meanwhile, John S. Beecher was more than suspicious of his wife's supposed infidelity or potential affair with his "friend." Therefore Beecher sent Marie and four-year-old Preston to Europe on the Cunard line by the summer of 1871 mainly to separate her from Phoenix. It was as if Beecher were the father in a novel, sending his daughter on an extended tour in hopes of her forgetting an unacceptable suitor.[19]

Marie arranged for female companionship during her stay in Europe. She brought her younger half sister, Ethland ("Tutu"), who was around fourteen years old at this time (fig. 17) to finish her education in Paris, just as Marie had. Tutu was boarded at a convent school by the beginning of 1872.[20]

While Marie was in Europe, Beecher discovered a hidden letter from Phoenix to his wife containing promises of Phoenix's eternal adoration, as well as vowing to sacrifice anything for Marie's affection. Even more unfortunate for Beecher, Phoenix was not stifled by a mere

Fig. 17. Ethland "Tutu" Brooks Feaster, tintype, ca. 1871, courtesy Wilson-Battle-Connell-Park Papers.

ocean separating him from his object of passion and followed Marie to Europe. He surprised her while she was in London.[21]

Upon seeing the yachtsman, Marie knew she was still in love with him. Her feelings intensified as Phoenix, in such close proximity, proved his love for her by more devoted actions and speeches. Despite all of Phoenix's efforts and the scorching attraction between the two, Marie did her best to remain faithful to her husband, sending him a letter promising to try to achieve that improbable feat.[22]

Nevertheless, when she and little Preston finally returned to New York by June 1872, Phoenix followed her home and continued his pursuit of her throughout Manhattan. By the fall of 1872, Marie and Phoenix were seen together at Delmonico's and other haut monde watering holes; he perceived by those who recognized them as constantly expressing his devotion for her. This often occurred in close public view as they were not simply alone having a tête-à-tête in a dark cozy corner. On the contrary, during these occasions they were in the company of others, such as Adelaide Neilson, the acclaimed British actress, who was in New York in November 1872 playing Shakespeare's Juliet to rave reviews. Members of New York society who spent time with Phoenix and Marie included brothers Leonard and Lawrence Jerome, as well as at least one of Lloyd's female relatives from the Whitney family. John Beecher permitted his wife in the company of Phoenix with these people as many were good friends, and he was occupied with his own economic, social, and perhaps carnal pursuits as well.[23]

Phoenix continued courting Marie, promising to marry her if she divorced Beecher. The yachtsman's ardor and vows were exceedingly seductive, and Marie finally responded in earnest and completely gave herself to him, risking everything based on his promises. Their relationship became intensely sexual, with many intimate encounters. Presently, Beecher became suspicious of what was transpiring and hired a detective. The first evidence of Marie's affair with Phoenix occurred on February 17, 1873, when the detective observed them entering a residential building at 106 East

15th Street. This was followed by another meeting on February 18. Subsequently, in March there were multiple rendezvous detected by Beecher's sleuth—on the "fourth, tenth and thirteenth days of March" at the same place, and the "fourteenth, fifteenth, sixteenth, nineteenth, twenty-first, twenty-third, twenty-fourth, twenty fifth, and twenty-sixth days of March 1873 at 228 West 40th Street."[24]

The frequent encounters continued into April 1873 until the cuckolded husband felt it was time for a confrontation, hoping to catch the couple in *flagrante delicto*—irrefutable proof of Marie engaging in sexual relations with Phoenix.

On the evening of April 8, 1873, Beecher, along with his friend Charles Fleurry, hired a carriage and rode to 228 W. 40th Street (near today's *New York Times* building). The small apartment house had a two-room parlor (second) floor comprising squeaky sliding-glass doors separating the front and back rooms. Two men accompanied Beecher and Fleurry—the detective for protection and a tenant who lived on the third floor of the same building, providing both an easy entrance and hiding place.[25]

Beecher then returned to his home on West 17th Street while Fleurry, the detective, and the tenant settled down for the night and waited to hear any evidence of people below them. Around 10 p.m. they heard what they were waiting for—a loud screeching sound signifying the opening and closing of the second-floor sliding doors separating the front room from the bedroom.

The men waited until around five thirty in the morning, whereupon Fleurry returned downtown to Beecher's home and asked him to accompany him back to the 40th Street building. Beecher and Fleurry then met the tenant and detective upstairs, and the sleuth checked the hallways to see if it was safe to proceed. It was. All four men went downstairs to the parlor floor, and the detective opened the door of the back room—the bedroom of the flat—with a small pair of pliers. John Beecher entered first, followed closely by Fleurry.

There they saw a startled Lloyd Phoenix and Marie in bed together, he wearing a nightshirt and she attired in nothing but a chemise. Phoenix leapt out of bed and took a firm hold of Beecher, whereupon Fleurry seized Phoenix to keep him from assaulting the poor betrayed husband.[26]

There was nothing left for either Phoenix or the humiliated Marie to do. The subterfuge of their love affair had ended. And from that moment forward, Marie's life would never be the same.

CHAPTER ELEVEN

Irreparable Damage

*From the moment we can no longer serve the vanity
or the pleasure of our lovers, they leave us,
and long nights follow long days.*

—Alexandre Dumas, fils,
La Dame Aux Caméllias, 1848[1]

The same day Marie and Phoenix were discovered in bed by Beecher, he filed for divorce, retaining William J. Osborne as an attorney. The complaint charged Marie with adultery performed with the correspondent, Lloyd Phoenix. Marie answered it by hiring William Fullerton of the leading New York law firm Fullerton, Knox, and Crosby. Fullerton later represented Theodore Tilton in the scandalous trial about another case of adultery concerning a Beecher—Henry Ward Beecher—lasting from January 4, 1875, until July 1, 1875.[2]

Marie, after being caught with Phoenix, denied "each and every allegation" of adultery through her lawyers at a hearing on May 8, 1873. Marie furthermore claimed that between April 12, 1871, and April 12, 1872, and whenever she was in Europe, Beecher committed adultery with "one or more women whose names are unknown to" her as well as with a woman named Mrs. Phinney. Marie asked for custody of Preston plus alimony and child support. Beecher denied his infidelity and Marie, who unfortunately had not hired a detective, held no irrefutable proof. The lawyers then planned a further hearing to begin in the following year on June 29, 1874.[3]

Directly following the first divorce hearing, Marie, Phoenix, and John Beecher became the talk of the Jockey Club set. One dyed-blonde socialite, after gossiping about the cost of a gown's $3,000 lace trim; a fashionable new landau; and how Leonard Jerome, William Travers, and Jay Gould would ride in an upcoming steeple chase; fanned herself while prattling breathlessly about "how Mrs. Beecher had been flirting with Lloyd Phoenix and Mr. Beecher was getting a divorce."[4]

With John Beecher no longer living in their home, Marie reportedly continued to reside there in a carefree fashion, despite Beecher clearing out some of the furniture while she was at Jerome Race Park. However, Marie was not living in a lighthearted manner. She spent the rest of the spring and summer contemplating the consequences of her affair with Phoenix, as the once ardent lover was not quite as anxious to be near his former object of desire. By the beginning of August he had dashed off to Newport where he sailed his schooner *Josephine* in publicized races. Marie may have followed Phoenix to Newport, but at some point returned to Paris to be with Ethland, as she was still studying there, and Marie felt somewhat comforted by Ethland's company. John Beecher, however, remained in town, being elected to a wine and spirits council. Phoenix, meanwhile, did everything he could to publicly alleviate his guilt and distance himself from the entire humiliating situation. He twisted the facts of the affair, declaring to his friends that the sultry *Marie* pursued *him*, and try as he might, he could not escape her seduction.[5]

By October 1873, Phoenix and Marie were back in New York. Faced with the stress of impending divorce and possible loss of her son, she sought out her lover in order to find some kind of reassurance. She reminded him of all those gallant words he had said and written, promising to protect her and marry her as soon as she became free. But instead of supporting Marie, Phoenix coldly informed her that their relationship was over and he planned to sail to Europe alone. Phoenix reportedly "sneered" at Marie, adding to the injury of the scenario.[6]

His flight to Europe would avoid the further embarrassment from being correspondent of the divorce as well as afford an escape route from his obligation of having to marry a soon-to-be single woman. In his devotion to freedom, Phoenix had renounced his promises and betrayed Marie as he had abandoned Hattie Blackford. Indeed, according to a later statement by Marie, Phoenix's supposed intention of marrying her after her impending divorce was a complete sham.[7]

Marie was understandably shocked and heartbroken. Before the Phoenix affair she was unknowledgeable in the habits of duplicitous bachelors. By the time she was twenty, she had gone directly from the manipulation by her mother to the equally firm control of a much older husband and was unaccustomed to the experience and self-reliance of an unmarried woman. Adding to Marie's vulnerability, her mother was no longer there to advise her. Amelia would have discouraged Marie from discarding her comfortable life with Beecher in exchange for empty endearments from a known playboy. There were also few lessons about loving the wrong man in literature, considering the popular books of the day. Some women's novels of the early nineteenth century, especially when concerning a young lady moving to the big, bad city, used the theme of a villainous seducer ruining her for mere sport. But later in the century many ruination-by-seduction storylines were omitted by female authors not only because of moral convention but also a desire to show a man and woman in a more positive relationship.[8]

Finally, this period still maintained antiquated theories about sex, love, and marriage, and women in general had not yet felt an identifiable surge of united power. Marie, for all the stated reasons, had no notion or warning of Phoenix's motivations and became the proverbial lamb on its way to the hatchet—deceived as so many women before her and so many women since. Her betrayal by a philanderer breaking up her marriage and leaving her a fallen woman could be used in a tale portraying the punishment of immoral womanhood à la *Anna Karenina* or *Madame Bovary*.

But we know what actually happened to Marie was not clothed in fiction. It was stark reality with the full force of cruelty, causing irreparable wounds to her psyche. And this woman had never experienced such callousness. She had been up until then worshiped by gentlemen and treated with the utmost politeness and tenderness. No man had ever provided such ecstasy and then viciously inflicted such pain. The realization that the man she adored had shattered her marriage without caring for her and then coldly denied his former words of love hit her severely. Too devastated to remain in a mentally stable condition, she was infuriated and frantic and had wild thoughts of retribution. She told Phoenix that if he wouldn't marry her as he had promised, she would kill him and herself.[9]

Phoenix laughed at her, disbelieving she would do anything of the kind, but Marie had reeled out of control. He had severely wounded her, and she wanted in turn to hurt him. The only way she knew was to shoot him with a pistol, which, according to Phoenix's attorneys, is precisely what she did on Madison Avenue in the early evening of October 31, 1873.[10]

Marie, as mentioned, was an excellent shot and could have easily terminated the womanizer's life. She couldn't bring herself to actually kill him though, and the yachtsman merely incurred a slight flesh wound. Reportedly, Marie nicked his earlobe. Had Phoenix not wrenched the pistol out of her hand directly after firing at him, she would have turned the gun on herself. Concurrently, a gentleman waiting at a Madison Avenue coach station witnessed the dramatic scene.[11]

Apparently, the police were not made aware of the shooting. Marie was not arrested and Phoenix pressed no charges—an obvious admission of his guilt in ill-treating her and causing her emotional breakdown. His failure to press charges also indicated his wish to avoid further notoriety by such behavior being exposed in a public trial.[12]

Directly after the incident, Phoenix's attorneys Blatchford, Seward, Griswold, and Da Costa outlaid "thousands of dollars" to stifle it. They did so not only on behalf of Phoenix but also because it was one of the most mortifying cases a client ever brought upon them. In their legal memoir they discreetly omitted his name, as well as John Beecher's or Marie's (referring to her as Mrs. B____), but made reference to Phoenix in a newspaper article they reprinted as a "prominent yachtsman." In addition, the lawyers mentioned other individuals' names, which were published and linked with "Marie Beecher," definitively connecting them and focusing a spotlight on precisely who were involved.[13]

Phoenix's lawyers accomplished the suppression of the Madison Avenue incident to some extent. Only one paper that year published it— New York's *Sunday Mercury*—on November 9, 1873 (under the radar of Phoenix's attorneys), but it did not mention Phoenix, John Beecher, or Marie's name. Entitled "Female Revenge: A Lady Shoots Her Betrayer on Madison Avenue," it deemed John Beecher as "weak" but loving and generous, Marie as the "victim," and Phoenix as a "lothario," and was published while Phoenix was en route to Europe. Filed away in his attorneys' records as an accurate account, they later reprinted most of it in their memoir.[14]

The lawyers felt that their client was culpable in the matter, calling him the "villainous lover."[15] This is an interesting dichotomy; here were his advocates, yet they were well aware of the irreparable damage Phoenix had brought upon Marie. They understood the social ramifications as well—as she would likely be forever ruined. The fact that the attorneys made their feelings clear about Phoenix shows the weight and seriousness of the strict Victorian-era boundaries gentlemen must never cross. It was simply their courtly reaction to Marie's victimization, as many women in the nineteenth century were driven to exclusion and some even prostitution after being deceived by a scoundrel.

After the shooting, Marie reportedly discovered which steamship Phoenix would take to Europe and waited for him at a New York pier where he was supposed to board. But when his carriage pulled up to the wharf, he saw her there and duped her by driving off and taking another ship already scheduled. On the way to Europe, Phoenix confined himself to his cabin bed, a doctor attending to his gunshot wound. Phoenix's lawyer Clarence A. Seward wrote to the yachtsman after he sailed, informing him that Marie intended to embark on a steamship in the following week and was determined to meet up with him. According to Seward, Marie planned to make certain that if she couldn't be with her former lover, no one else could as well. This was a frightening threat, and he advised Phoenix to do whatever he could to avoid contact with Marie. Seward added that her extreme feelings of anger and hurt would mellow throughout the length of time it took for her to find Phoenix, and pointed out that the expense she paid in looking for him would after a period be a hindrance in the irrational attempt to confront him. Therefore, Phoenix should try not to associate with his circle of friends in Europe, making it more difficult for Marie to locate him. Seward promised to correspond with Phoenix as long as he made him aware of his whereabouts.[16]

Marie left New York for Europe the following week on Wednesday, November 4, 1873, aboard the ship *Russia*. That day John Beecher (or his attorneys) placed a classified personal advertisement on the front page of the *New York Herald*, asking for the witness who saw the shooting to contact him: "Personal: Will the Gentleman who witnessed from a Madison Avenue stage the discharge of a pistol between Thirty-first and Thirty-second Streets on Madison Avenue, at about 5:45 P. M., October 31, please send his address to box 217 Post Office, New York, New York. If an interview is granted it will be treated as confidential."[17] Beecher and his lawyers obviously wanted to gain more evidence for his divorce proceeding as well as suppress any further public embarrassment. If the gentleman did respond to the advertisement, a substantial payoff may well have been offered.

One wonders if Marie spent time in Paris waiting for Phoenix outside of the Washington Club, an organization where the yachtsman and other wealthy American males lodged and gambled. Regardless, despite the attorney's advice to his client, she and Phoenix made contact on the continent. But instead of killing him, Marie participated in some heavy gambling with Phoenix in Nice. It is unknown if they reprised any sexual involvement but their relationship was not to be revived by Phoenix, at least not with any more promises of eternal togetherness. It was over and Marie had to deal with the pain of separation from him as if she were being weaned from an addictive drug.[18]

In Nice, Marie stayed at only the most luxurious resorts, such as the Grand Hotel Chauvain, and held court in the casino's ballroom when not involved with games of chance. She kept company with one of the most famous social leaders of New York, Annette Wilhelmina Hicks, a widow who later became Mrs. Thomas Hicks-Lord after she married a multimillionaire almost twice her age. Marie and Mrs. Hicks were noticeable and discussed by the press, as both were poised, spectacularly dressed and coiffed, and beautiful. Marie especially dazzled a New York correspondent, who called her "a perfect siren among men, who was young, of perfect manner, faultless of form and features," and with an enchantingly sweet speaking voice. But as always, although she and Mrs. Hicks were constantly surrounded by interested gentlemen, Marie was particular to whom she spoke. The two women led a clique of American travelers who frequented the Côte d'Azur gathering place.[19]

While in Nice, Marie called herself a married woman, but soon those in social circles whispered that she was already divorced. In 1873 divorce still stigmatized the woman involved. If an American man committed adultery, it was somewhat excusable and accepted, but when the woman was declared the adulteress, she could be ostracized from polite society. The situation in Nice was exacerbated when a few of Marie's New York detractors let loose a flurry of unkind gossip concerning her romance with Phoenix, her shooting him, and her fleeing New York to follow him to Europe.[20]

The once idolized and celebrated beauty realized her reputation was destroyed. Condemned first in the South and again in New York, she had become a fallen woman who could no longer live among the foremost American social sphere in which she was accustomed. She quickly returned to Paris where Ethland had been studying.[21]

When Ethland was not boarded at the convent, she lived with Marie in a magnificent mansion built during the Second Empire at 85 Rue de Pompe, near the Eiffel Tower (now the eleven-room Hotel de Glamour). Ethland, already a gifted young lady, had written in a French composition, "Gratitude is one of the noblest sentiments and most learned of human nature. It is a perfection of love inside, it indicates a pure morality." By 1873 she had formed a literary society, and on neatly written, floral-embellished paper she invited "poets, painters, enigma and conundrum-makers and all who wish to shine" to become members at no charge.[22]

Clearly, Marie had shown the clever Ethland the best French education and the glories of *joie de vivre*—staying at only the finest addresses. Ethland's generous older sister also brought her to such vibrant attractions as the *Jardin Mabille,* an open-air dance floor frequented by many American tourists (and courtesans), and to other opulent fêtes in Paris and the South of France. Apparently, Marie was not only a guardian and big sister to Ethland but also her veritable Auntie Mame, exposing Ethland to the culture of foreign countries and treating her to fabulous parties.

By the time Marie had returned to Paris in late November 1873, she had moderated her outrage against Phoenix but was still in love with him and still pursuing him. Her life, while greatly altered, had to somehow endure despite her grief, and as long as Phoenix was out there Marie held onto an obsessive hope of reconciliation.

When Ethland was free from school, the sisters planned a vacation, ostensibly for some relaxation and merriment. They sailed for England at the end of the month. Marie's sixteen-year-old sister was about to be schooled in a part of life she could have never imagined.

CHAPTER TWELVE

Scandal in London

The Lady Abroad: Gentlemen's Attendance—After twilight . . . it will be well to request your husband, or some one of your relatives, to . . . wait upon you; you will, in this way, be entirely free from that harsh criticism . . . concerning even the most innocent acts.

—Emily Thornwell,
The Lady's Guide to Perfect Gentility, 1856[1]

One of the sisters' first stops in England was the seaside resort of Brighton, where years before, King George IV as Prince Regent built the Royal Pavilion, sparking a burgeoning popularity among the stylish. His exotic, Orientalist palace became the focal point among many hotels, and Marie chose one of the most sumptuous of these along the ocean— the Grand Hotel.

Marie, who had been through life's devastating learning experience with Phoenix from New York to Europe, was a changed woman. Any naïveté she possessed in the Columbia years had been long since squashed, replaced with the agony of Phoenix's betrayal and subsequent gossip. She knew that within a year she would have to face the Court of Common Pleas decision of her impending divorce and a custody battle for her son, and she still felt abandoned by the yachtsman. She tried to suppress her grief by donning more layers of aristocratic pretense and an increased desire for the luxurious, hedonistic pleasures of life. By day and evening Marie played the part of the still-married society woman, riding horses through the countryside and attending social functions. She was also the attentive older sister and guardian of Ethland—continuing to help shape her into a polished young woman. But late at night, Marie enjoyed a lively private party with champagne and/or other intoxicants to ease her emotional pain. When Marie and Ethland were in Paris during Third Republic, partying until the wee hours was decidedly more acceptable than in the staid circles of Victorian England.

While Ethland and Marie were staying at the Grand Hotel, Marie was introduced to William Foster and his brother, Arthur, a thirty-year-old governmental clerk. She and Ethland got along well with the brothers and a friendship was formed. Both brothers also shared an attraction for Marie.

At the end of December, the two sisters arrived in London where William and Arthur lived. However, there was an underlying reason for Marie's visit to that city. Lloyd Phoenix was in town, and according to his attorneys Marie had followed "the villain" there.[2]

On December 29, Marie took lodgings at the small, private hotel on Dover Street near Berkeley Square owned by Mr. and Mrs. Frederick William Denyer. Also a wine merchant, Frederick Denyer may well have known John S. Beecher as they were in the same type of business.[3]

Accustomed to her French nighttime merrymaking—again remarkably unlike the behavior of the Victorians—Marie had forewarned the landlady of the hotel that she kept late hours. Marie also ensured that Ethland's sleeping quarters were further separated from hers and expanded their suite of rooms on two floors. Unfortunately, about three days into their stay, Marie, who had a habit of letting candles burn all night, damaged a cabinet with hot wax and was charged £2, which she paid immediately.[4]

While Marie may have intended to have an interlude with Phoenix, it did not occur, at least not at her place. And it wasn't long before Marie's penchant of soothing her hurt feelings with "gaiety and pleasure" came to a humiliating conclusion prompting a court trial in which she was exposed to public disgrace.[5]

The case concerned William Foster's brother, Arthur, who was arrested and held on the count of an assault upon Mr. Denyer, the Dover Street hotel proprietor. Foster had beaten Denyer's bald head around four times with the heavy knob of a walking stick until it broke into pieces. The victim spurted a stream of blood and was rushed to the hospital.[6]

What would cause Arthur Foster, an otherwise reasonable gentleman, to behave in this manner? The answer began with a small late-night private party. According to a hotel waiter, William Foster had remained in Marie's suite into the early hours of the morning. The waiter, who had been listening at the door of her suite, informed landlady Harriet Denyer of this Victorian-era impropriety, and the following day Mrs. Denyer, as she later testified, gave notice to Marie to leave the premises. Marie countered that it was outrageous to be asked to leave for something that was no one's business but her own, and felt that her socializing with either of the Fosters was entirely proper. She and Ethland consequently stayed on at the hotel.[7]

Arthur and William visited Marie the following evening and remained until past 12 a.m. Mrs. Denyer later recollected that her bedroom was under Marie's suite, and between 11 p.m. and 12 a.m. she heard a loud noise emanating from upstairs. She climbed the stairs to the suite, and when Marie came to the door, which was slightly ajar, Mrs. Denyer asked her to "lull the noise and allow her visitors to go away, as there was a lady ill" who couldn't bear it.[8] According to Marie, it was presumptuous and impertinent of Mrs. Denyer to ask the Fosters to leave as they weren't creating a disturbance of any kind. So, displaying the aristocratic insolence culled from her years in Columbia and as Mrs. Beecher of West 17th Street, Marie demanded the brothers stay.[9]

At about one o'clock in the morning, Mrs. Denyer returned to the room and again "requested the gentlemen to retire" as they "were making a noise and disturbing others." She then added that "if they were gentlemen they would kindly retire." Mrs. Denyer was angry and insisted that the "house was quiet and respectable, and that they never had such late hours." The Foster brothers again refused to leave.[10]

Following this, Frederick Denyer visited the suite and asked the Fosters to leave the premises. Arthur, after politely offering Mr. Denyer his card, remained adamant that they would not go. Denyer returned with a constable and asked the officer to arrest Arthur, but the policeman felt there was no cause and subsequently did nothing but exit, as did the brothers about one hour later.[11]

The next day Mrs. Denyer went upstairs and saw Ethland standing in the living room and William Foster lounging on the sofa. The landlady reported, "I spoke to him of the previous night, and said I was sorry to see him there." She returned at eight o'clock in the evening and William was still in the suite. She implored him, "For God's sake, and in the name of peace, leave," but he still refused. As a result, Mrs. Denyer "gave instructions that . . . Arthur or William should no longer be admitted to the hotel." Arthur did return to the hotel, however, to see Marie and ask how she was getting along after such shoddy treatment by the Denyers. When he requested to see Marie, Mrs. Denyer informed him that Marie and Ethland were not in, although Ethland was in fact in the suite. Arthur responded by asking if he could "go up and write a note for Marie," to which the landlady replied, "Certainly not," and later explained to the court that "he may be a gentleman and he may not," and she "could not admit him as the ladies had valuables lying about."[12]

Mrs. Denyer admitted there were "no other improprieties" perpetrated by Marie or the brothers but when Arthur lingered at the hotel, Mrs. Denyer's servants "seized" him "and put him out." The landlord then insulted his brother, William, while he joined Arthur outside. In the meantime, Ethland had spoken in French to Arthur from the hotel's balcony and explained that Marie had been denied food by the Denyers.[13]

Marie returned to the hotel around ten o'clock in the evening and went upstairs to her suite. Whether or not she had been involved in a disappointing meeting with Phoenix is unknown. Subsequently, according to Arthur, "two bullies, like bricklayers' laborers" (a plasterer and builder employed by the hotel) entered the house. The laborers sought Marie out, making references to her as being an immoral, common, and loose woman—a "Polly Skittles." ("Skittles" a.k.a. Catherine Walters was London's famed prostitute in the 1860s, who rode through the streets in the finest carriages and set fashion trends such as the pork pie hat.) The workmen also made snide remarks concerning William, but Marie's aspersions were more precise, shocking, and detrimental to her reputation as the court testimony was reported throughout England and reprinted in the United States—including in the *New York Times*. This unfortunately fed her gossip-crazed detractors with fresh, satisfying material.[14]

Prior to this first hearing on January 17, Marie's attorney, Mr. Alsop, cautioned her not to testify and risk being cross-examined, but Arthur and his lawyers pleaded with him that their case depended on her story, so Alsop allowed Marie to tell her version of what occurred. She explained that the day after the incident in which Arthur and William were asked to leave, she planned on visiting Lady Victoria Yarborough but was concerned about Ethland alone at the hotel and did not make the trip. She corroborated Arthur's testimony, that after she returned to the hotel in the evening, the laborers walking back and forth insulted her. They also entered her suite and verbally tormented her, and that after hearing such disgusting phrases from the workmen, Ethland became frightened and tried to leave the room. One of the men grabbed her by the shoulders and shook her violently, prompting her to scream and run onto the balcony where Marie joined her, threatening to jump off if the laborers made any more lewd statements.[15]

Marie added that the Foster brothers were never in the bedroom of her suite and insisted she never received a notice to leave the hotel because of her late hours, but the owners subsequently refused necessities because they wanted her to leave. She also avowed that "she had been frequently subjected to unpleasant remarks" and "annoyance from the landlord and landlady."[16]

Attorneys then put sixteen-year-old Ethland on the witness stand, who confirmed what Marie and Arthur Foster had said about the harassment by the hotel owners and the workmen's insults. Ethland could not bring herself to repeat the words but said, "They were to the effect that her sister was a loose, good-for-nothing woman." Ethland also recalled the landlord saying to Marie "that she was no better than she should be." The first hearing then concluded with a lawyer affirming that after Arthur Foster assaulted Denyer on the morning of January 6, 1874, the sisters packed up and left the hotel.[17]

The trial continued on the twenty-third of January, in which the presiding judge denied the considered bail amount of £2,000 as Mr. Denyer could not attend due to his severity of injuries, although his condition had improved. Arthur Foster, who had by then realized the seriousness of his assault, wrote a letter of apology, asserting that he had no intention of harming Denyer, but Marie's telling of the way she had been insulted by the workmen and treated so abominably by the Denyers provoked Arthur's emotions to overcome his discretion.[18]

During the second hearing, the hotel's waiter testified, insisting "the ladies' ways were not ladylike," and explained why—"They kept late hours and wanted coals brought up in the middle of the night!" which prompted laughter in the courtroom. He also declared the shocking revelation that he heard a gentleman there on New Year's Eve at 2:40 in the morning! Attorneys then called the builder to the witness stand, where he denied entering Marie's suite and said his plasterer did not as well. The workman further insisted neither he nor his associate touched Marie or Ethland, yet she screamed. When the builder saw Arthur, he asked him to go away if he was a gentleman and Arthur replied that he wouldn't speak to such "low blackguards."[19]

Then the builder added: "About twelve o'clock Mrs. Beecher came to the door with a candle, and said 'You, what do you want here? Let's have a look at you.'" He alleged that "she was not conducting herself as a lady; but it was excusable as she had been drinking." She then supposedly remarked, "You won't give me anything to drink." He said he produced a bottle of brandy and gave it to her.

"She drank some and spat it out, and said it was not strong enough; she had something stronger upstairs which she would give him. She kept bellowing upstairs to her sister, 'make a note of that too.'" He also denied ever calling Mrs. Beecher "Polly Skittles," a blatant lie contradicted by Marie, Ethland, and Arthur, who swore the builder used that term. He was twisting the event and embellishing the truth, stating Marie was acting as an immoral woman, yet denying he ever denoted her as such. He ignored the fact that her impressionable younger sister was within earshot as well. Marie adored Ethland and as her guardian would not have become that drunk in front of her and acted out so demonstratively when Ethland could hear what she was saying. Furthermore, no matter how intoxicated Marie may have been, if able to speak, she would certainly not have spoken to either of these members of the lower working class. She was known for her snobbishness, only associating with those in high societal standing. Even at school she was said to be, while somewhat friendly, rather reserved. A Confederate major who knew her in South Carolina also remarked about her slight haughtiness, and in Paris it was observed that she only was seen with persons of high rank. After all, at least one deportment book advised, "It is almost needless to say that taste leads us to avoid low or vulgar associations. It is of great importance, in the formation of good manners, that a young lady should be accustomed to mingle in good society." Still, the builder's words were damaging, especially after his working-class associate concurred with his statement that Marie called the builder a "jolly fellow," yet another British expression.[20]

Despite the contradictions in various testimonies, the allegations became more severe, and witnesses further battered Marie's character. A chambermaid testified that she saw William Foster walking from the dressing room to Marie's bedroom and then to the living room. The maid also said that two baths had been ordered for the dressing room and later Mrs. Beecher rang for them to be taken away—both having been used. Foster's lawyer then countered that the baths were used for washing a long-haired collie. The chambermaid would not relent, however. She insisted upon relating a story that Marie asked her to copy a letter from Marie's lover "Charley" who wanted Marie dressed only in white muslin, but the maid could not produce the copy of the letter, leaving no evidence to corroborate her story.

Regardless, Marie's reputation had been dumped in the mud puddles of London and splashed before countless eyes of transatlantic newspaper readers. Her attorney advised her not to take the stand again as he was afraid she would be further denigrated, but she re-entered the witness box after the judge argued it was necessary to answer the derogatory charges against her character. She denied ever making noise in her apartment and didn't understand why she and Ethland were even called as witnesses or why they were made to appear "notorious." She stated Mrs. Denyer came into her rooms in a "violent passion" and requested the brothers to leave, and Marie "requested

Fig. 18. Mabel Grey,
photographer unknown, author's collection.

them to stay." Marie deemed Mrs. Denyer "extremely rude" and related that William, whom she called "Willy," asked Marie "why she submitted to such impertinence."[21]

Marie admitted that one of the Foster brothers dined with her every night but she confirmed it was indeed a dog that William Foster was washing in Marie's dressing room. Then, when her attorney asked her about some of the workmen's specific vulgar remarks, she wrote them down for the judge rather than experience the humiliation of saying them aloud. They were "Come, come, can't you do without your Willy tonight? Now Willy, go away and get some other woman"; "Willy said he didn't care to sleep with her"; and "She ought to be put out of the house. She was a common, low woman, but could not impose on them. They had seen her before and her face was familiar to them."[22]

Interestingly, one of the most photographed women in London was the beautiful courtesan/prostitute Mabel Grey (see fig. 18), whose features resembled Marie's and who shared Marie's coloring, both having strawberry-blonde hair and blue eyes. Mabel Grey often promenaded down the busiest streets in London, and images of the famous Miss Grey were consistently displayed in London shop windows. The workmen may well have confused the two women—a mix-up which would also occur in the future.

In her continuing testimony, Marie claimed she never said the words that the builder accused her of saying and did not "ask him for anything to drink or accept brandy from him." When she was questioned about the chambermaid asking her to copy the "letter" from the supposed lover named Charley who wanted to see Marie only in a muslin chemise, she said the story was absurd. She also denied that William Foster was still in her suite at 2:40 a.m. on New Year's Eve, and said that he had never been in her bedroom, nor had there ever been any impropriety between Arthur, William, and herself.[23]

Marie's statements seemed largely truthful to the judge; however, there was one glaring inconsistency provoking another denouncement of her character—not brought forth from a lowly laborer or

Cockney chambermaid but from the pen of British nobility. As mentioned, the previous week Marie had testified she was planning to visit Lady Yarborough but had stayed at the hotel from her concern about Ethland. But at the January 23 hearing in which Marie was retestifying, she was confronted with a letter signed by Victoria Yarborough herself: "Sir—In reply to your letter of the 21st inst., the statement that Mrs. Beecher was about to visit me is false, and I have no acquaintance with her. If an opportunity occurs, I should like this to be stated in the police court. –I am yours truly, Victoria Yarborough."[24]

Severely humiliated when hearing the letter read aloud to the court, Marie responded by gathering her composure and stating, "After that letter there would be no further acquaintance with Lady Yarborough." Marie insisted she had an "acquaintance with Lady Yarborough before that letter" and she "was going on a visit with some friends to Lady Yarborough." But Marie knew she had been defeated.[25]

While Marie may have been acquainted with Lady Yarborough through her friendship with Jennie Jerome, who was then engaged to Lord Randolph Churchill, we don't actually know who told the truth in respect to the supposed visit. The point must be made, however, that Lady Yarborough was already aware of the tawdry details printed throughout British papers, and if Marie was in fact honest with her testimony, Lady Yarborough as a member of the nobility realized that any relationship with Marie by connection would stain her own reputation. Therefore, she found it necessary to do what women of the upper echelons of society have always done in this sort of situation—remove any evidence of their acquaintance and exclude Marie from polite English social circles. If Marie was not telling the truth in this case, she was blatantly caught in the act of lying. Either way, this letter might have affected her other testimony concerning the allegations made against her moral character. Fortunately, however, Ethland and Arthur had corroborated most of Marie's statements.

After the mortifying letter was read, Marie, her attorney, and the judge felt that it was quite enough questioning about the Yarborough matter. Marie then answered a few questions concerning John Beecher and their marital status, stepped down from the witness box, and was free to leave, never reappearing at subsequent hearings.

On February 14, Denyer had improved a bit and while he was still "in somewhat delicate health," the marks of violence visible at the first examination had nearly disappeared. Bail was finally set at £2,000 and met by Arthur Foster's friends (paying £1,000 each), releasing him from jail. The judge declared that the case should be moved to Central Criminal Court—Old Bailey—where Foster should be tried for the more serious crime of intending to do grievous bodily harm.[26]

Of course, if judge and jury believed Marie and Ethland, Arthur Foster would be essentially vindicated as to the criminal intent of his act. The notion that Foster did not plan to assault to the victim but was carried away by his emotions in reaction to a wronged young woman would certainly help his case. The judge admitted that gross insults and maltreatment had been perpetrated against Marie; thus the testimony during the trial also harmed the Denyers' reputation, disclosing "a grave outrage . . . and was calculated to bring great discredit on the prosecutor." They might be declared guilty participants capable of harassing their guests, and if that occurred, potential tourists would think twice about planning to stay at the Denyers' hotel.[27]

Marie's, Ethland's, and Arthur's testimonies were ultimately believed, for the verdict on April 7, 1874, stated that Arthur was guilty of merely unlawfully wounding Denyer—a misdemeanor and precisely what Foster had pled before any testimonies. Accordingly, Arthur Foster received a fine of £500 and was released on his own recognizance.[28]

However, a fact that wasn't recorded in the annals of Old Bailey and unbeknownst to newspaper court reporters, Lloyd Phoenix's attorneys had been deeply involved in the case. This was a result of both Phoenix and John Beecher's embarrassment about Marie's London misadventure. Phoenix's lawyers, who used Arthur Foster's and Denyer's name in their memoir, recollected that the favorable verdict for Foster whom they deemed "gallant," stemmed from their negotiations with the British law officials, concluding amicably for all those involved. The lawyers made certain no aspersions were cast upon the reputation of the Denyers' hotel and that the proprietors had not been guilty of any wrong. The attorneys also arranged for Foster's discharge.[29]

The legal situation may have been resolved and the Denyers' names protected, but after Manhattan newspapers publicized the case using Marie's full name, her reputation was further damaged in the minds of New York society members. She was not only a known adulteress and perceived by some as a would-be murderess, but because of the London scandal she was seen as a liar and a prostitute. While Arthur Foster would remain a loyal friend to Marie, she had to accept the cold lesson of having to deal with the permanent brand of notoriety.

Chapter Thirteen

To Russia and Back

*The Lady Abroad . . . should not turn her head on one side and
on the other, especially in . . . cities, where this bad habit seems to
be an invitation to the impertinent.*

—Emily Thornwell,
The Lady's Guide to Perfect Gentility, 1856 [1]

Sometime in their travels Marie took Ethland to tsarist Russia where
they hobnobbed with Russian and other foreign aristocracy. It was
later recorded that Marie would have lived in Russia, she enjoyed it so
much. [2]

In Saint Petersburg, Ethland and Marie had their photographs taken
at the studio of renowned Charles Bergamasco, photographer of celebrities and British, Italian, and Russian royalty. The photograph of Ethland
(fig. 20) can be dated to after May 1873 as the reverse lists an award
won by Bergamasco at the Vienna Exposition held during that time.
Therefore, it is reasonable to assume that Marie and Ethland were in
Saint Petersburg either from the late summer to early fall of 1873 or
shortly after Marie's appearance as a witness at the London trial in late
January 1874, a more likely presumption.

Marie, as she had in London, caused a gentleman to lose his temper
and violently act out. The gentleman, named Vladimir and perhaps of
royal birth, cut into Marie's Russian photograph, causing a deep gash
across her forehead. The image of Marie (fig. 19) has since been digi-
tally restored.

Marie noted on the back of the carte de visite albumen print the reason for the scratched condition of it. However, a part of Marie's inscription was cut off, leaving it a mystery. In the nineteenth century it was the custom to frame photographs and portraits as ovals, so Ethland unfortunately trimmed the image into an oval shape to fit it into a frame, thereby deleting the rest of Marie's cryptic message, which read in part, "Russian . . . [of] course you unders[tand] . . . Vladimir scratched i[t] . . . brought them to Johnstone." The inscription was no longer important to Ethland but very important to us. We want to know more about this Vladimir who marred Marie's image perhaps in a jealous rage. The name is an oft-used Russian one, but as Marie was known to only have associated with those of high rank, it invites speculation whether or not it could be Grand Duke Vladimir Alexandrovich, son of Tsar Alexander II. His Romanov relative Grand Duke Nicholas Constantinovich was the lover of Marie's friend Hattie Blackford, and historically, Grand Duke Vladimir was capable of dramatic outbursts. But what makes this message even more interesting is, by the beginning of 1872 Grand Duke Vladimir was allegedly the lover of that infamous English courtesan, Mabel Grey, who resembled Marie, and Marie Beecher's and Mabel Grey's names would soon be linked by the press. The other name mentioned on the back of the albumen print, "Johnstone," also gives cause to ponder. An English baronet by the name of Sir Frederick Johnstone was both a racehorse owner and member of the British parliament, and in 1874 he belonged to the Newmarket Jockey Club along with Grand Duke Vladimir. And we know how much Marie enjoyed horse racing. Regardless, we can only surmise what, if anything, transpired either in Russia or England between Johnstone and Marie to cause Vladimir to deface Marie's picture, and we can only guess Marie and Grand Duke Vladimir were involved before he became engaged to his wife in April 1874. The royal couple's long, happy, and fruitful marriage began in August that year.[3]

The Paris police later recorded talk concerning Marie knowing Hattie Blackford in Saint Petersburg, and they were likely seen together in 1874 as both Hattie and Marie frequented the same aristocratic crowd. Thousands, including the Prince of Wales, were in Saint Petersburg for

Left, fig. 19. Marie. Right, fig. 20. Ethland. Bergamasco Studios, Saint Petersburg, Russia, carte de visite albumen prints, ca. 1873–74, courtesy Wilson-Battle-Connell-Park Papers.

festivities and social whirl beginning in late January 1874, revolving around the wedding of Grand Duchess Marie of Russia to Prince Alfred of Edinburgh, Queen Victoria's son. One might speculate that Lloyd Phoenix had introduced Hattie to Marie as early as 1871 in Paris when they were all there or perhaps in the fall of 1873—when Marie followed Phoenix back to Europe. Ethland knew Hattie as well, and she and Marie would become much better friends in Paris by the end of 1874.[4]

The two sisters were back in England by mid-May 1874. Knowing she had to meet with her attorneys before appearing in court in June, Marie left from Liverpool and arrived in the United States on May 25, 1874, traveling as Mary Beecher, an American spinster, age twenty-eight. Seventeen-year-old Ethland, a "finished" young lady, waited nearly two weeks to sail from Southampton on the *Donau*, as that ship's final destination was Baltimore, Maryland, where she could then take the Baltimore and Charleston Railroad and Steamship's line through the Deep South to Jacksonville or Palatka, Florida. From there she could board a steamboat on the Saint Johns River and eventually arrive at LaGrange to reunite with the transplanted Feasters.[5]

The divorce trial of John S. Beecher and Marie A. Beecher began on June 29, 1874. Beecher's longtime partner, Frederick E. Ives, gave his testimony first and confirmed the date of the Beecher's marriage at First Church of the Intercession, the acknowledgment of the Beechers' seven-year-old son, Preston, and the fact that the Beechers were no longer living together within the past year. Charles Fleurry, the second witness, revealed much more to the court, including Marie's adulterous guilt in what had transpired between her and Phoenix on that fateful morning in April 1873 in the back bedroom of the parlor floor of 228 W. 40th Street. After Fleurry's damning testimony, the trial adjourned until July 11, whereupon John S. Beecher approved the appointment of a referee to continue the proceedings.[6]

The judgment of Marie's divorce was presented July 21, 1874, at the Court of Common Pleas in Manhattan with Marie declared "guilty of adultery" and Beecher awarded custody of Preston. Two attorneys had confirmed in writing that "all the issues in the action" had been "referred to a referee to hear and determine" the case. But while William J. Osborne Esq. represented Beecher that day, Marie had no lawyer there to oppose him. Evidently, she thought she no longer needed Fullerton or his associates or could not obtain them. Not being represented by an attorney was a considerable error on her part, for while the first section of the document mandated, "It is judged that the marriage between the said Plaintiff, John S. Beecher, and the Defendant, Marie A. Beecher, be dissolved, and the same is hereby dissolved accordingly, and the said parties are and each of them is freed from the obligations thereof"; the second section was appalling and unjust. It read: "And it is further adjudged that it shall be lawful for the said John S. Beecher, the Plaintiff, to marry again in the same manner as if the said Marie A. Beecher, the Defendant, was actually dead, but it shall not be lawful for the said Marie A. Beecher, to marry again until the said John S. Beecher, the Plaintiff shall be actually dead."[7]

According to the law, Marie was still beholden to Beecher and unable to marry unless he predeceased her. This law was applicable—if the plaintiff deemed it so—to the guilty party in an adulterous marriage whether it was a man or a woman, and not challenged until 1880. According to that landmark divorce case, the male adulterer was unable to remarry until the ex-wife's death but he remarried in another state, and the appellant court declared that marriage legal. (This did not preclude the "no remarrying" clause to appear in subsequent divorce cases.) However, in Marie's 1874 divorce judgment only Beecher held the freedom to remarry, and because Marie declined to contest it, she not only held the potential of permanent ruination but also the reality that she would have to remain alone for the rest of her life.[8]

Marie later briefly described the details of the property settlement and custody of Preston: "I was cheated out of my home and prosperity by J. S. B. who made me sign a paper—on condition of having P. with me but afterwards he kept Preston and the property too. . . . Oh how I shudder to think I might always have been under his control."[9] She was about to learn what it was like to be under no one's control—her mother's, her husband's, or her former lover's.

Marie returned to Paris. Still young, beautiful, and vivacious, her failed affair with a self-indulgent lover had left a bitter legacy with few options in a puritanical world. Subject to sexual longings but unable to remarry until John Beecher died, Marie needed an emotional release. As a result, she felt she had no other route but to take on a lover as well as socialize with a group of sophisticated Europeans who embraced her despite her damaged reputation and permanent label as the "notorious Mrs. Beecher." By the end of 1874, Marie, a survivor with social skills well beyond the norm, had accomplished this. She had become a denizen among continental circles where she could conceal her past as best she could. She was living permanently in Europe, associated with the French beau monde, and had secretly accepted the offer of becoming the mistress to a wealthy, married American who maintained her in grand style, along with Beecher's dowry and alimony. While neither contented nor fulfilled, this was temporarily an advantageous situation for Marie. Her wealthy lover could not control her as his situation was far more dangerous than hers. After all, she was already a fallen woman; what could she lose? But he, being married, faced the possibility of relinquishing his wife and children plus a considerable amount of money if Marie made their relationship public.[10]

He needn't have worried, however. Marie knew well how to keep a secret and wasn't about to threaten to sue him as Hattie Blackford had done to a former lover. Although the two women had become friends by 1874, that was one of the differences between them. Marie would not as a rule invite publicity by suing a lover—it simply was not her style of cautious living with an appearance of the highest-tiered socialite. And Marie had only been betrayed by one man. Hattie, however, had been mistreated, robbed, ruined, and otherwise wronged by more than one lover. She had adopted a different attitude toward men and seemed to thrive on her scandalous reputation.

Another difference between Hattie and Marie was Marie's penchant for discreet behavior, compared to Hattie, who publicized her past for the right fee. Marie continued keeping her past and present sequestered as best she could, despite the gossip that swirled about her. The silent dominance and sexual power Marie held over her lover by becoming his mistress, plus the freedom of being a single woman with a newly adopted way of life and making her own decisions, would give her a taste for hedonism and luxury, Parisian style.

CHAPTER FOURTEEN

Among Les Grandes Horizontales

Those who love . . . unfortunately . . . are not apt to suffer from
dearth of sensation. . . . I think one is especially thrilled to have her
nature stirred to its depths. 'Tis a great privilege . . . to feel the entire
life in intense motion. Every pore agape with life, every pulse panting
with it, every drop of blood hot with it.

—Ada Clare, 1861[1]

By the end of 1874 Marie, at some twenty-eight years old, had been
freed from a domineering, philandering husband and was relatively
well-off living in Paris. Supported in style by Beecher and her married lover, she encountered a heady feeling that may well have been
overwhelming. Paris, with its ravishing atmosphere, was her tonic.
Indeed, possibilities were endless in Paris, one of the most beautiful
cities in the world. The City of Light teetered on the brink of the *Belle*
Époque. By 1875 Patrice de MacMahon led France as president of the
Third Republic, but the aristocracy and nouveau riche still worshiped
luxury and pleasure as they had in the Second Empire. In fact, the
two greatest aspirations of that time, much as in post–Civil War New
York, were money and power. Fashion remained luxuriant with silks
and satins embellished with embroidered and bejeweled artistry. A
good portion of the town floated on a cloud of art, beauty, and gaiety.
A new opera house opened with a grand gala, and Georges Bizet pre-
miered his avant-garde *Carmen* there in 1875. Concurrently, Émile
Zola was writing naturalistically and Frédéric-Auguste Bartholdi was

in the midst of constructing the Statue of Liberty. A powerful liquor called absinthe rivaled champagne in popularity—think of Degas's *The Absinthe Drinkers* (1876) with the artist Marcellin Gilbert Desboutin sitting in a café next to a forlorn woman portrayed by actress Ellen Andrée with a vacant look in her glazed eyes. Other painters, including Renoir, Monet, and Pissarro joined Degas in transforming reality into luscious, light-filled, impressionist canvasses and were ridiculed by the unappreciative, academically inclined press. Paris celebrated the demimonde as much as the haut monde, and members of these worlds interacted in public venues as well as clandestinely. For example, celebrated actress, artist, and courtesan, Sarah Bernhardt mingled in both spheres.[2]

Without Ethland to look after and with John Beecher retaining custody of Preston, Marie's only responsibility was to herself. She could devote herself entirely to her favorite pastime—hedonism—entailing gambling, extravagance, parties, drinking, dancing, and sumptuous dining. She embraced these rituals, hoping they would numb her misery, and longed for the one elusive morsel of fulfillment she could not obtain through such actions—love. Indeed, her freedom had its price—that of loneliness. Marie had not yet recovered from her failed romance with Lloyd Phoenix, she didn't have her son, she couldn't enjoy the companionship and adoration of her younger sister or have her mother's affection to comfort her, and she could not remarry.

Nevertheless, amid the stimulating French *joie de vivre* atmosphere, Marie had taken her public place in the upper echelon of Parisian society, associating with the haut monde who didn't know or simply didn't care about her past. As soon as she began attending events such as grand operas and horse races, she became a fashion icon and quickly earned the reputation as a gracious hostess who gave lavish dinner parties. She simultaneously inhabited the demimonde as a high-styled courtesan with that rich, older American who maintained her and a young French army officer who excited her. In other words, Marie was a bona fide demimondaine—a pleasure-seeking woman who took on a wealthy lover to support her lifestyle. She had also found a small circle of female compatriots who like Marie had been removed from "polite" American society—courtesan Nina War (a.k.a. Wilton), who had lived with Marie until maintained at another residence by her distinguished lover, and of course, Hattie Ely Blackford.[3]

There was a clear demarcation between a courtesan and a prostitute in France during the latter half of the nineteenth century: "The question first arises 'what is a prostitute?' To this the law answers, that it is one, who openly and with little or no distinction of persons, sells her favors for money: and who with this object endeavors to make herself publicly known as a prostitute. On the contrary, the woman, who does not court notoriety, but admits few lovers and in secret, although she receives money, cannot, and dare not, under penalty of damages for libel, be called a prostitute."[4]

Men of the arts were creatively inspired by these women. Zola would later have his book *Nana* published about a character based on the high-styled, sensual Parisian courtesans and prostitutes. Édouard Manet, Henri de Toulouse-Lautrec, and other great masters would portray them on canvas.

According to Parisian authorities, Marie was by no means a prostitute who met strange men in *"établissements publics"*— public whorehouses permitted in only certain sections of the city. Marie also did not attend *"maisons de rendez-vous"*—private receiving houses. In other words, she did not frequent any kind of brothel and refused to be completely ruined like women who became prostitutes after the abandonment of men who victimized them; nor did she join the multitude of lower- and working-class enterprising females who simply turned to the oldest profession as a way of earning a profitable living. Marie was also a minor player amid the demimonde with only two lovers, remaining reasonably faithful "in her fashion" to the wealthy American, called in the language of the demimonde, her "protector."[5]

Many of the protectors who supported courtesans were married to other women, yet these upper-crust men were necessary to the courtesans for providing them with cachet, a fine address, and cash. Indeed, the women could earn upward of 10,000 francs per month from their protectors, not to mention gifts of jewelry, furs, and other fineries. The expression first written in the seventeenth century, "Living well is the best revenge," became their credo. As fast as they earned money in bed or elsewhere, it was spent, flowing through their well-manicured fingers for the finest designer *haute couture* as well as carriages, furniture, more jewelry, art objects, and horses. While ultraluxurious extravagance acted as a salve for any past or present unhappiness, it was primarily a strategic means to secure an elevated status so that a courtesan herself became a luxury item and therefore could command more money for sexual favors. More cash and notoriety meant more power, independence, and freedom at a time when most conventional women held little advantage over circumstances.[6]

In Paris, courtesans who were maintained by their lovers or protectors of titled rank could be called *les grandes horizontales*. One of the grandest was Englishwoman Emma Crouch, better known as Cora Pearl (1835–86) (see fig. 21), some ten years older than Marie. When Cora was a young girl, a man victimized her by getting her drunk and raping her. From that episode she detested men so excessively she vowed never to marry as she could never obey one. In her prime she selected protectors from the highest echelons—Napoleon III had been among her numerous titled lovers.[7]

Cora Pearl was recognized as a wit and known for her beautiful figure, dressing in fabulous clothing to accentuate it and her worth. She, like other courtesans, set stylistic trends and rivaled nobility with their presence at exclusive social affairs, just as they had in the Second Empire. With the frequent sharing of her body, Cora became both courtesan to royalty and prostitute to the everyman. The morals squad of the prèfecture de police called her "le plat du jour," a title given to those designated women offered daily to clientele in a brothel. That moniker is ironic as Cora supposedly was once carried by four strong men into a dinner party while lounging on an oversized silver serving platter and wearing nothing but a side of garnish. Cora created a scandal with Alexandre Duval, the son of a wealthy family, whom she had bankrupted and who shot at her and then himself at her doorstep. As a consequence, she was temporarily expelled from France and relocated to Monaco.[8]

Hattie Blackford (a.k.a. Fanny Lear) was another leading member of the demimonde. While she too worked at brothels in Paris, her most lofty titled conquest occurred in Russia during the early 1870s when Hattie met and became the lover of Grand Duke Nicholas Constantinovich, grandson of Tsar Nicholas I. The grand duke was

Fig. 21. A.A.E. Disdéri, Cora Pearl, courtesy private collection.

exceedingly in love with Hattie, calling her his wife, his soul, and his greatest passion. He also gave her some of his family's precious jewels he pilfered because of debts. Consequently, in the spring of 1874 Hattie was arrested and expelled from Russia.[9]

The fact that Marie and Hattie were companions in Paris is interesting in that they had both been in love with the same womanizer who betrayed them—Lloyd Phoenix. But instead of regarding each other as competition, they may have realized that a relationship with Phoenix would never again occur, and at least he was a subject the women had in common.

The two women were often confused with each other as well, despite the fact that Hattie had chestnut-brown hair and Marie was a strawberry blonde. For instance, an aristocrat met Hattie in Monte Carlo and later wrote, "I am not sure whether originally she came from Philadelphia or from one of those charming cities in the Southern states." Additionally, several later detractors would pin Hattie's adventures on Marie. Furthermore, at least one French photographer called Hattie "La Belle," which a southern novelist would later utilize for Marie.[10]

After Hattie's expulsion from Russia because of the scandalous jewel affair, in which Marie and Ethland had absolutely no part, Hattie returned to Paris and became the toast of the city. She had *"Prends tout"* ("Take all") printed on her note and calling cards and it was clear she had taken all of Paris. Her home was an extravagant salon adorned by abundant damask silk, *doré* (gilded) bronze, fabulous *torcheres*, and fine oil paintings—some copies of old masters depicting bacchanals and sexual liaisons. Royalty, artists, and writers frequented her grand apartment and crowded it with offerings of devotion—baskets of flowers, jewelry, and other expensive gifts.[11]

Similar to Marie, Hattie possessed a fine mind and owned over 550 volumes of French and English literature. Her clothes, like Marie's and Cora Pearl's, were conceived by leading Paris designers and stitched on the most sumptuous of fabrics. During a grand evening reception, a baroness spotted Hattie wearing a gown made of "opal-coloured royal satin, profoundly trimmed with Burano lace, a corsage covered with real opals, and strings of black pearls." In love with Russian culture, some of Hattie's attire reflected this. She liked to dress on chilly Parisian evenings in a cloak of Russian sable "entirely trimmed with rose miroir velvet."[12]

Hattie owned a stable of horses (Marie deemed them more like ponies), and drove through the *Bois de Boulogne* in a luxurious calèche (open carriage resembling a chalice) pulled by two Russian horses. She frequently rode with Marie where they were often stared at by the park's pedestrians—many of them Americans—and were also seen at the *Jardin Mabille*. In fact, the two flamboyant women created a sensation. By riding in Hattie's carriage, Marie ironically garnered attention similar to when she was back in Columbia as its reigning queen in the Boozer coach and later in New York's Central Park, recognized in her phaeton as a gem of Manhattan society. However, in Paris she sat next to a celebrated harlot.[13]

One day in December 1874, Hattie and no doubt Marie, described by the préfecture de police in their secret files as a *"grande blonde,"* were about to leave Hattie's home in her calèche. Her pimp stopped them, apprising her that a customer wanted a rendezvous after seeing her portrait, and he was offering twenty-five Louis (gold coins each worth approximately four francs at the time) or less. Hattie responded, "For twenty-five Louis, I can delay my promenade for a moment because it is done so quickly." She then changed into a glamorous outfit consisting of pantaloons, blouse, and boots—everything, including underclothes, made of pink silk, accessorized by garters with precious stones spelling out the day of the week. She and Marie drove to the brothel and while Marie waited outside in the *calèche*, Hattie entered the client's room. Twenty minutes later, she emerged, having performed her swift assignment, whereupon the two women went on their merry way.[14]

The morals agents of the Paris prèfecture de police were concerned with many more women than just Hattie Blackford and Cora Pearl; in fact, the number of agents burgeoned in the 1870s. They relished their control over the legions of females of the demimonde with little concern of their civil rights. As there was no effective cure for syphilis, the vice squad regulated health visits to private prostitutes as well as houses that catered to the oldest profession. However, their attention to the women went beyond health reasons as the agents also kept watch and entered data into their hidden dossiers for authoritarian and political purposes.[15]

The Parisian morals squad obtained their information in several ways—similar to American police methods—by surveillance, evidence, interrogation, and through informants. At times they had to spend quite a bit of money in their pursuit of courtesans, following them to balls, theaters, and expensive cafes. Agents were generally thorough in reporting about the women but were not always accurate when it came to spelling of names, biographical information, and reported behavior. Some accounts were based on mere gossip. According to historian Gabrielle Houbre, who made an in-depth study of the moral police's secret files in the excellent *Le Livre Des*

Courtisanes: Archives Secrètes De La Police Des Moeurs, the agents often relied on complaints, ranging from sources such as a pimp who was unhappy with private "competition" from an alleged independent prostitute, an envious female acquaintance, a disenchanted lover, a worried parent, or an outraged neighbor. Many of these individuals could hardly be proven as legitimate sources.[16]

Private women's personal lives particularly interested the police, a subject that would not usually hold the attention of a vice squad in the twenty-first century. During the Third Republic, however, these women were uncontrolled, defied police authority, and posed a certain threat. If a suspected woman was secretive and would not cooperate, i.e., divulge the names of their lovers, they would be filed in the registry and ranked among the highest of the fashionable courtesans and actresses as well as the lowest of streetwalkers.[17]

By 1875 Marie, divorced, secretive, extravagant, and dressing far beyond the norm, was added to those investigated by the préfecture de police on suspicion of being a clandestine prostitute. They noted her conduct was not at all scandalous, but her ultraluxurious public lifestyle prompted their scrutiny. Such behavior included Marie frequently riding in a grand horse-drawn carriage [with Hattie] and being on view at the Longchamp racecourse on the day of the grand prize. There she would show dazzling wealth in her attire, hairstyle, and jewelry, including earrings—one blue and the other red.[18]

The police were first aware of Marie by name in May 1875 and reported that she had leased a furnished apartment paying 900 francs per month. The opulent building, with French doors leading out to wrought-iron, filigreed balconies, was located at No. 2 Avenue de Friedland, just off the corner of Rue du Faubourg Saint-Honoré and near the Arc de Triomphe and Champs de Élysées.[19] Marie's spacious apartment was filled with personal items—leather-bound, oversized volumes of topographical, literary, and scientific studies; along with watercolors, engravings, and Japanese prints. It was tasteful, aesthetic, but also comfortable, reflecting Marie's warm personality and eclecticism.

The agents noted that Marie still enjoyed alimony from her husband but was further maintained a grand lifestyle by her "longtime" lover, the wealthy American known as Mr. "Meurice" or "Maurice." A couple of men with that last name resided at fine addresses in New York at that time—one on Fifth Avenue—but the agents sometimes recorded a name phonetically if they did not know the spelling, so he could have been Mr. Morris. Although "Mr. Maurice" visited Marie often, he did not stay over in her home, and in that regard the police accurately suspected him of being a married man. They also transcribed that Marie saw a young army officer but they did not know who he was.[20]

The morals squad confused John Beecher with Lloyd Phoenix, stating some of the Beechers' fights in New York were so violent Marie would have shot her husband with a pistol—wounding him so that he would have to spend months in bed. It was obvious by this allegation that some data in their files about Marie was, again, inaccurate and based solely on gossip and/or hearsay. They also described Marie appreciatively as blonde, pretty, with an excellent figure, and even a little too stout.[21]

Being a mistress of a rich married man and lover of a young man hardly constituted illegal prostitution in the truest sense. Marie absolutely did not meet strange men in her home, perform sex for a flat fee, and then twenty minutes later perhaps engage in a sexual encounter with another stranger. But in the agents' eyes she was an immoral woman and evasive in that she was not telling them any information about her two lovers. Of course, the prefecture had no way of knowing that Marie was already quite rehearsed in ultradiscretion from as far back as her life in Confederate Columbia when she and her mother helped Yankee prisoners. Nevertheless, Marie's fulfilling her sexual need and trying to replace the lack of affection with pure sensuality was on a personal level and not really police business, considering she posed no health or political risk to the city of Paris. However, they pursued with interrogating her and other investigations into her private life.

In Paris, Marie seemingly behaved as if she were trying to recapture her former life in New York as Mrs. John S. Beecher while experiencing her first all-encompassing love affair with Phoenix. Her wealthy older lover, who allowed her to live in the high style she had enjoyed, took the place of Beecher. Yet she also had the frivolity and sexual excitement of her young lover, the French army officer recreating the Lloyd Phoenix role, and potentially transporting her to realms of sensual pleasure not necessarily offered by the elder protector.

Marie told the agents she was twenty-six, an age of which she was particularly fond. They placed her picture, like so many others, in the margin of the prefecture's oversized portfolio of dossiers (see figs. 22 and 23). In the image Marie, appearing to be wearing no makeup, essentially challenges the photographer and exhibits neither coyness nor shyness. Instead of casting her eyes down or off to the side, a method used by many other women posing during that period, she gazes directly into the lens with a slightly amused expression, one eyebrow arched a bit higher than the other, as if to convey that she was not afraid of anyone, no matter what level of power they possessed. It was clear that her former roles of obedient daughter and slavish lover had morphed into that of a rebel. She behaved as what the French called an *insoumise*—a young *rebelle* who was unsubmissive to men, living at a fine address, secret about her sexual behavior, and defying police authority.[22]

While Marie still longed for Phoenix, she had evidently ceased chasing him. During the warm months of 1875 when she provoked public attention and police scrutiny in Paris, Lloyd Phoenix sailed to Scandinavia and Russia on the *Enchantress*, a yacht owned by his friend, the American expatriate Joseph Florimond Loubat, and Marie did not follow them. Instead, she remained immersed in the French social pool; Parisians and Americans saw her beautifully yet eccentrically attired while socializing at fashionable gathering places. The morals police remained attentive to her, yet the agents recorded in mid-October (concerning the previous few months) that Marie's lovers were the same as with whom she had been linked in the June

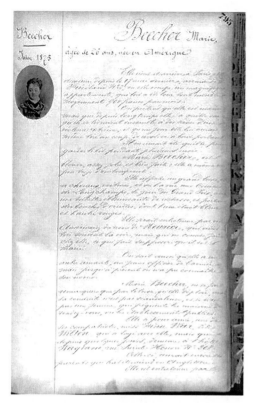

Fig. 23. Detail of Marie's photograph.
© *Archives de la Préfecture de Police.*
Tous droits réservés.

Fig. 22. Marie's dossier, BB2, the *Registre de la Police des Moeurs*, Préfecture
de police Paris, fiche 795, courtesy *Cabinet du Préfet*, Paris, France,
© *Archives de la Préfecture de Police. Tous droits réservés.*

report. The agents still lacked any evidence of her attending private or public brothels. Her behavior in the outside world remained perfect, and in private was still in keeping with the terms demimondaine and/or insoumise. The report also disclosed that by the end of September, Hattie Blackford and Marie had an argument and they no longer saw each other.[23]

Hattie's memoir about the Russian jewel scandal, *Le Roman d'une Americaine en Russie (The Romance of an American Girl in Russia)*, was published in Brussels in October 1875, which included impassioned letters from the grand duke and intimate descriptions of their love affair. It also contained her liberally burnished swipes against the Russian imperial family. For example, she contended, when describing Grand Duchess Marie, *"Qu'elle avait de quoi charmer . . . si on ne la regardait pas trop longtemps."* ("She managed to charm . . . if we did not have to look at her for too long.") As a consequence of writing such an incendiary book, Hattie was expelled from France due to pressure from Russian authorities.[24]

In the meantime, this new life of Marie's as a Paris *rebelle* comforted her as much as possible. She somewhat cushioned any longings for Phoenix by indulging in private reveling and public ostentation, actualized by her rules and on her terms. But as Marie later implied, she was experiencing emotional pain and a nagging emptiness, and she became strikingly more indulgent. Aside from gambling, overeating, and dancing, she partook in more "gaiety and pleasure," which carried with it the potential for self-destruction. The morals police recorded this alleged private yet risky behavior from the report of an informant, that in the early hours of the morning in Marie's home she frequently became distastefully intoxicated and participated in what they called *"orgies ignobles."*[25]

The 1888 *New English Dictionary* defined an orgy as merely "feasting or revelry especially such that is marked by excessive indulgence." A nineteenth-century courtesan in France wrote that an orgy was simply a dance at a public establishment wherein women were freely drinking and smoking. In fact, it would not be unusual for a courtesan to engage in an orgy—many were known to do so.[26]

However, the Marquis de Sade used the term *orgy* with the group-sex connotation, and today we also assume that orgies include sexual relations by more than three people.[27] Was Marie taking part in the sort of innocuous "orgy" where merely indulgent drinking, smoking, reveling, and feasting were occurring rather than actual group sex? Or was sex with multiple partners transpiring in Marie's private apartment? No matter what one's imagination might offer, we don't know what actually happened in her home or how many were involved. But we do know Marie was quite particular with whom she associated and spoke, let alone with whom she made love, and in that regard, it is difficult to accept the scenario of a sexual orgy taking place.

The information offered to the police was unsubstantiated hearsay and may well have been from a disgruntled neighbor who heard the noisy sounds of a raucous get-together, deemed as an "orgy" in 1875. The informant could also have been a rebuffed male who added more degradation to Marie's inebriation at a wild party, or perhaps a female rival who attended a soiree at Marie's home. Interestingly enough, the passage regarding Marie's alleged outrageous private life directly followed the sentence about the falling out between Marie and Hattie Blackford, leading one to suspect that Hattie may have been the police's informant. There is no definite evidence pointing to Hattie as betraying Marie to the police, however. Regardless, if we believe any of the report, it indeed appeared that Marie's innermost beauty was drowning in overabuse of alcohol, which could have compromised her health.

The suppression of Marie's sadness over the betrayal by the yachtsman, her divorce, the loneliness from missing her sister, and the loss of her son had enveloped her in a treacherous whirlpool of hazardous merrymaking. As mightily as she partied, she was equally as miserable, and in the unlikely event that sex with indiscriminate partners occurred, this reckless behavior could not last forever. The role of a demimondaine/insoumise was primarily a young woman's game and Marie was not getting any younger. While some courtesans eventually married their titled protectors, many died unhappily, young, and poor. The sensational Hattie Blackford succumbed to a stroke, alone and in poverty at only thirty-eight. Cora Pearl lived longer but died from gastrointestinal cancer at fifty-one, in sadness and poverty as well. During her decline, she reportedly remarked, "Look, my cheeks are furrowed with tears."[28]

By the end of summer Marie was well aware of the morals police's continued attention to her lifestyle. She knew her behavior was considered shameful and tried to hide her true identity as best she could. Protecting her family members as well as any good reputation left by reinventing herself, she informed the police that she was a twenty-eight-year-old British woman. When asked her maiden name, she reported it to be "Bourteline"—an ironic play on words, as she was on a metaphoric borderline between life and a perilous shaft plummeting one way down.[29]

Marie may well have realized the danger of this precarious line she was treading and yearned to redeem herself. By October she had sailed to England to see old friends and perhaps meet new ones as well. There Marie would make a dramatic and brilliant life choice that would not only change her future but also nurture her heart, mind, and soul.

Chapter Fifteen

Enter Count Charming

He is a charming man, my dearest and most intimate friend. . . .
He is a very handsome and distinguished man and is of course a
tie that links me with the past.

—Preston Beecher, 1921[1]

The turn of Marie's fate occurred when she began to spend time with Comte Arthur de Pourtalès-Gorgier (see fig. 24) in London. Elizabeth Boatwright Coker claimed in an essay that one of Marie's relatives thought the count had originally met Marie at a social function in Baltimore, introduced by her friend Jennie Jerome. However, that is unlikely as it would have been before the fourteen-year-old left for Europe with her mother in 1868, and Arthur was not stationed in America at that time. Jennie (Lady Randolph Churchill) did not return to the United States for a visit until 1876, so if she did introduce the two it was likely in England or

Fig. 24. Count Arthur de Pourtalès-Gorgier, ca. 1864, Geneva, signed "Arthur de Pourtalès-Gorgier" and inscribed *"Envers et contre tout, en souvenir de 1859, a mon cher ami, Alfred Dufour"* [Against all odds, in memory of 1859, to my dear friend, Arthur Dufour], author's collection.

Paris. Arthur de Pourtalès-Gorgier reported in an interview that he had first met Marie aboard a steamship en route to New York at the end of November 1875; however, that was not true as well. Nevertheless, the important point is that they were together in London by October of that year.[2]

Arthur de Pourtalès-Gorgier was born on August 31, 1844, in the canton of Neuchâtel, Switzerland. Handsome, decorous, and distinguished, he held a legal degree and had been an attaché employed in the diplomatic services with the French legation since 1866. A "gentleman of the old school in every respect," his ideals were as fine as his diplomatic uniform (fig. 25). Marie later called him "high-souled." He was near Marie's age and coincidentally may have been acquainted with the American expatriate Joseph Florimond Loubat, a friend of Lloyd Phoenix.[3]

Fig. 25. Gustave Le Gray & Cie, Count Arthur de Pourtalès-Gorgier in diplomatic uniform, inscribed in Arthur's handwriting, "Dear Old Chutter (or Chatter), Yours sincerely, 'F. Loubat,' *n'est-ce pas?* Paris, June 21, 1879" [or 1871, photo was trimmed], courtesy Wilson-Battle-Connell-Park Papers.

Pourtalès descended from a family with a remarkable heritage. His mother, Anne d'Escherny, Comtesse de Pourtalès-Gorgier (1820–1901), was a countess in her own right before she married his father, Count Henri de Pourtalès-Gorgier, the last lord of Gorgier, once a fief in Neuchâtel. An accomplished sophisticate with perfect manners and taste, Anne spent years in the aristocratic world of Paris, Rome, Berlin, and Naples where royals received her at court. Arthur's grandfather, Frenchman James-Alexandre de Pourtalès-Gorgier (1776–1855), a renowned banker, the King of Prussia's chamberlain, and made a count in 1814, was one of the most exemplary art and antiquities collectors in the world. Much of his former collection is currently owned by major museums, and his

Fig. 26. Jenny Holladay in Paris, ca. 1867, photograph by Augustin Aimé Joseph Le Jeune (successor to Levitsky), inscribed "Countess Arthur de Pourtalès-Gorgier," author's collection.

portrait by Paul Delaroche hangs in the Louvre.[4]

Arthur's first wife was an American named Jenny (sometimes spelled Jennie) Lind Maria Holladay (1851–73) (see fig. 26), whom Marie knew during her schooldays at the Academy of the Sacred Heart in Manhattanville. Jenny was the daughter of a formidable West Coast magnate, Ben Holladay, called the "stagecoach king of the Pacific" and the "railroad king." Early in his career in San Francisco, Holladay founded the stagecoach company that was eventually sold to Wells Fargo. He owned other substantial holdings in western railroads and real estate, and also tried to finance his way into the United States Senate. The family moved to Oregon but also resided in a grand residence in Westchester County, New York, due to Holladay's wife's penchant for the New York social world. After he took a financial bath in the 1873 economic panic, Holladay sold his expansive estate, complete with a castle tended by sixty servants, but he still lived an extravagant lifestyle in Oregon.[5]

Years previously, Jenny, her sister, and her mother had traveled to Europe where Jenny met Arthur. Their marriage in December 1869 was at the crest of the tidal wave of wealthy American females who married European titled men. Some of these noblemen were rich in lineage but monetarily poor. Marriages to daughters of substantial Americans secured the grooms in wealth and gave their brides ostensible storybook lifestyles as well as entrance into the highest tier of European society for which the nouveau-riche young women would have otherwise been denied.

Arthur and Jenny's marriage certainly had a storybook beginning. At that time both the groom's and the bride's family had ample cash to throw a grand wedding. Arthur's father, Henri, was blessed with an inheritance that included art treasures from Henri's father, Alexandre-James de Pourtalès-Gorgier. He had written in his will that none of his important paintings, including Frans Hals's *Laughing Cavalier* and other masterpieces by artists such as Rembrandt, Velasquez, and Leonardo da Vinci, as well as sculpture, antique jewelry, ivories, and ancient medals and pottery could be sold until ten years after his death. And prices for these works had risen considerably within that decade. Consequently, in 1865 when Henri de Pourtalès-Gorgier sold so many fabulous pieces, featured in a thick catalogue of around five hundred pages during a series of auctions lasting over a month, it drove the art-buying public wild. The salesrooms were jammed full of ravenous museum curators, private collectors, and dealers anxious to be the successful bidder for at least one work from this celebrated collection. This strategy worked well; the sale fetched record prices and netted a generous sum in the hands of the groom's father.[6]

Nevertheless, the wedding was not an ostentatious event and took place at the family home—the romantic Château de Gorgier, built ca. 1620 (see fig. 27). The bride dressed in satin detailed with orange blossoms and the groom was described as "handsome, honorable, and genuine."[7]

Fig. 27. Château de Gorgier, Phototype Co., Neuchâtel, author's collection.

As was the European custom, Arthur bestowed upon Jenny a corbeille, a gift basket packed with diamonds worth "$50,000 in gold," as well as intricately designed fans, the finest cashmere shawls, parasols, lace, and other expensive jewelry. After the ceremony, the newlyweds greeted their guests—a large company of titled individuals accompanied by the peasants of the canton who gave a profusion of flowers to the bride. The happy couple followed the grand fête by honeymooning in the South of France and Paris, and in 1871 their daughter, Maria-Pauline-Louise, was born.[8]

Jenny's sister, Polly, whom Marie also knew from the Academy of the Sacred Heart, married Henri de Bussiere, a baron, but their marriage was unsuccessful. Unfortunately, Jenny's marriage to Arthur de Pourtalès-Gorgier also ended, but far more tragically. In May 1873, en route by railway from Oregon to Chicago on the first leg of her return trip to Switzerland, Jenny died from complications of bilious fever—its symptoms similar to typhoid. Her mother was inconsolable, and as a consequence of Jenny's death and Polly's failed marriage, Mrs. Holladay immediately changed her will, stating no female descendant of hers could ever marry a man of two-generational French descent, lest she be cut out of the Holladay fortune. In fact, Mrs. Holladay was so grieved from Jenny's death that she too died shortly thereafter. Ben Holladay's bereavement, however, caused him to file suit against Arthur for custody of Maria in June 1874.[9]

Subsequently, Arthur's father lost much of his inheritance through unfruitful investments, and when he died on July 31, 1876, Arthur inherited only around 40,000 francs along with some incurred debt. Pourtalès in consequence was not soon to be rich by the time he and Marie met; in fact, the count primarily lived on his income as a diplomat, and Marie was wealthier than he was, with her dowry from Beecher still largely intact.[10]

During the winter through the summer of 1875, when Marie was a rebellious Paris demimondaine, Pourtalès had spent the season in England where he was stationed from January 15–July 27. There nobility and royalty, including the Prince and Princess of Wales, invited him to the country's most fashionable events. By August he had been made secretary of the third class at Washington, DC, a service he had performed just before his transfer to London, but remained in Europe on leave.[11]

When Arthur met up with Marie, he, like legions of men before him, became strongly attracted to the demimondaine, and she enjoyed the company of the count. Their time together quickly kindled into the count's deep love for the beautiful *rebelle*, and Marie's fondness for Arthur with his princely manner and kindness burgeoned as well. But while Marie held warm feelings for Pourtalès, they were calm and steady— quite opposed to the frantic whirlwind of emotions she had held for Phoenix. She felt a connection with the count and yearned for a meaningful relationship but did not at first comprehend that something deeper was developing between them. Arthur, however, knew exactly how he felt. Before long, the count envisioned Marie as Maria's new mother. He recognized Marie's brilliance, wit, attractive speaking voice, and graciousness, and wanted these attributes to be shared with his daughter to guide and shape the child. Within a matter of weeks the attachment between Marie and Pourtalès became serious. He was not letting her go, not even for a moment. He had found his new intended and the presumptive mother of his child and would not gamble on another man interfering while Marie was on her own. As a result of their mutual attraction and desire for permanence, they were married on November 4, 1875, at All Saints Church in the Knightsbridge section of London, officiated by the Reverend John Bloomfield. Marie's British friend Arthur Foster served as a witness to the event, as did Vicomte de Castello-Alvo, an attaché of the Brazil legation. The bride gave her name as Marie Adèle Beecher, reported she was a twenty-six-year-old spinster living at Grosvenor Terrace, and denoted her father's name as John Preston.[12]

Within a week or so the newlyweds arrived at Château de Gorgier in Switzerland to meet with the count's parents and pick up his daughter, Maria, who had been living in the castle. When Pourtalès introduced Maria to Marie, he couldn't help but notice her kind attention to his little girl, and she encouraged Marie to bring to the surface her deep affection for children.[13]

The brand-new family of three then traveled to Paris where Marie's personal items were sent to Château de Gorgier, and then boarded the *Klopstock* at Le Havre en route to New York to begin their future. As the steamship left the harbor on Saturday, November 27, 1875, Marie hoped she finally had a chance for happiness. Wise enough to take the risk of marrying the count, the Countess de Pourtalès-Gorgier abandoned her former life as a Paris demimondaine as if she were flinging it into the ocean behind her.[14]

Pourtalès was required to check in at Washington for his appointed diplomatic service and Marie looked forward to seeing her eight-year-old son, Preston, but another important reason prompted the trip to New York. Marie knew, as did Arthur, an attorney, that they had to convince John S. Beecher to add a waiver to Marie's divorce judgment in which she could not remarry within Beecher's lifetime, because without it the London marriage could well be declared illegal. Fortunately, Marie's divorce judgment did not include a "no waiver" clause.[15]

Arthur also planned to have Maria visit the child's grandfather, Ben Holladay, in New York as had been agreed upon through prior correspondence between the two gentlemen. However, unbeknownst to Pourtalès, Holladay determined not only to see his granddaughter but to also obtain immediate custody of her.[16]

Marie and Arthur decided that after the stay in Manhattan the family would travel to Washington, DC, where Pourtalès would extend his leave of absence and receive his future diplomatic orders. From there they would go to Baltimore for a week or so and consider heading south to Saint Augustine, Florida, to spend the rest of the winter. Little Maria would accompany them wherever they traveled, but not Preston as he had to eventually return to school, and Beecher would not allow him to spend that much time with Marie.[17]

During the transatlantic voyage the count and countess's relationship blossomed, and Marie formed a motherly attachment to Maria, which delighted Arthur. And by the time the *Klopstock* entered New York harbor on Monday, December 6, 1875, Marie and Arthur had become an established couple. Listed cabin passengers included a male de Pourtalès, age thirty-one and a twenty-six-year-old female de Pourtalès written directly underneath his name. Her occupation was recorded as "his lady" and that lady was Marie, once again denoting her favorite perennial age.[18]

CHAPTER SIXTEEN

How to Be a Countess

I called on the Countess de Pourtales yesterday afternoon at the Metropolitan Hotel. The countess kept me waiting about three-quarters of an hour.

—New York correspondent for the *San Francisco Chronicle*, 1876

On the day they arrived in New York, Comte and Comtesse Arthur de Pourtalès-Gorgier with Maria and servants moved into an expansive suite of rooms at the Metropolitan Hotel, a large, imposing brownstone on Broadway and Prince Street in lower Manhattan. Arthur entered "Count de Pourtalès and family" in the hotel's guest book.[1]

Five days later New York's *Daily Graphic* reported that Count and Countess Pourtalès, *"née Halliday,"* [sic] had recently arrived in New York and were later going to Washington for Christmas followed by a visit to Saint Augustine, Florida, where they would spend the winter. Ben Holladay was outraged at this reference to his deceased daughter, reading it while planning to meet with his granddaughter at the Brunswick Hotel on Madison Square. He retaliated by summoning his staunchest ally—attorney George Kingman Otis—Holladay's former agent who maintained close ties with the entire family as an advisor. Otis investigated and informed Holladay that the count's new wife was the notorious divorcée, Mrs. John S. Beecher, and Holladay became irate that a woman with such a scandalous past could be his granddaughter's new mother. After all, Marie's divorce and London incident were subjects of gossip, major nationwide newspaper stories, and minor ones such as in the *Graphic*, reporting inaccurately that Marie had been arrested in London "for assault and battery." Holladay also reasoned that because of Marie, Pourtalès might not give up the child. Consequently, he took immediate action. Although he had been living in Oregon, he still had plenty of associates, friends, property, and influence in San Francisco. He or his associates apparently notified the respected *San Francisco Chronicle* to investigate and publish a major story about this change of his son-in-law's events—in Ben Holladay's favor, of course.[2]

One cannot blame Holladay for attempting anything within the law in order to adopt his only granddaughter. He was still not over the loss of his daughter, Jenny, and his first wife died as a result of grief over Jenny's death. Holladay's adoption of Maria was foremost in his heart and mind, and it was necessary to convince the public that Pourtalès was a selfish father and to discredit Marie as the child's stepmother. The railroad magnate dispatched George Otis to accomplish this in an interview-cum-interrogation with the count, later included in the *Chronicle's* report.[3]

Otis shrewdly plotted out how to handle the confrontation, and in the beginning of the interview he and Pourtalès played one another. But Otis was no match for the scion of generations of nobility who possessed the talent for negotiating touchy situations in a diplomatic manner. Otis chided the count for not making Holladay aware of Arthur's marriage, and in deference to John S. Beecher and the legal ramifications concerning the divorce waiver, Pourtalès countered by fibbing that he was not married at all. On the contrary, he explained, the woman traveling with him was merely a beautiful lady whom he met en route from Le Havre to New York. He added that he highly regarded her and was impressed that she was so kind to his child. Otis then pried the count for the name of this mystery woman, all the while knowing exactly who it was. Again out of respect to John Beecher, Arthur hedged, but then the count hesitatingly admitted Marie's last name. Otis pounced on that revelation and emitted a long whistle. He declared Pourtalès was associated with Mrs. John S. Beecher, tainted with a well-known, scandalous reputation. He cited the British articles about the Arthur Foster trial reprinted in New York, and mentioned Marie's notoriety in Nice. But no matter what Otis said, he could not elicit a satisfactory reaction from Pourtalès. Finally, in a dramatic gesture, Otis exclaimed, "Why man, if I was in your shoes I would take a pistol and blow my brains out."[4]

Insulted and seething inside, the count maintained his savoir faire and still did not put forth the emotional or verbal response Otis was expecting. Arthur was much too resolved in his convictions to let anyone manipulate him, especially another attorney. Shortly after the uncomfortable session, Arthur returned to Marie at the hotel and told her what had happened. She may have warned him that this kind of personal attack might occur. She was accustomed to the gossip that swirled around her since her youth in South Carolina and she knew about the New York newspaper coverage of the London affair. Nevertheless, Otis likely convinced Holladay that after the interview, the count would be deterred from his relationship with Marie and give up his child to the railroad king.[5]

Eventually Arthur and little Maria arrived at the Brunswick Hotel to meet with Holladay, who was waiting there with his new wife, Esther. Still not disclosing the London marriage, Arthur pleaded with Esther "to call and see a lovely lady—a friend of his—who was down at the Metropolitan Hotel, and who had been so kind to the baby on the voyage." Esther Holladay did not, however, make the social visit.[6]

Ben Holladay reportedly claimed that he had been supporting Maria through $500–$600 per month paid to Arthur, and had extended another $1,000 to the count covering his expenses to New York so that the adoption could take place. According to the railroad king's associates, Holladay had also informed Arthur in advance that the meeting of the little girl in New York confirmed Holladay was taking custody of the child and bringing her back to Oregon. However, that was not the case, for when Holladay's attorneys offered a hefty sum for Maria and read the adoption papers to Arthur, "he refused to sign them" and terminated any of the child's financial support. Little Maria and a servant then returned to the Metropolitan Hotel. [7]

Subsequently, Pourtalès made a brief trip to Washington, DC, involved in diplomatic affairs, while Marie stayed in the Metropolitan

Hotel suite with Arthur's daughter and eight-year-old Preston. Her new title compelled the *San Francisco Chronicle's* New York correspondent to call on her for an interview on a blustery December day.

Marie projected contentment in both her life and new relationship. Her love for the count remained serene, diametrically opposed to the overwhelming and obsessive way she had felt about Phoenix. The intense infatuation she held for Phoenix may have been unequaled in her life but it was also emotionally unrequited and destructive. Marie realized that the residual pangs from their failed relationship had diminished in the face of a nurturing love that could very well endure with Arthur. While she relied on that hope, Phoenix continued to remain in Marie's thoughts.[8]

On the day of the interview Marie, the Countess de Pourtalès-Gorgier, grasped her newly received power through European title and marriage to a diplomatic attaché. Her primary motivation in agreeing to the interview was to publicize her side of the rumors that already pervaded the American printed media.

She chose to appear quite conservative for this second New York debut and selected understated and British attire—a gray, white, and brown shepherd's check suit with a "jaunty cutaway jacket" and pleated flounced skirt under a long draped tunic. She accessorized the suit with a Malines [French Victorian] lace scarf tied around her neck and a fashionable "little gray felt hat trimmed with brown velvet" topped by a "bird with plumage." Her hair was styled in intricate curls which fell in numerous *"creve-coeur"* [heartbreak] rings on her . . . forehead and temples." In contrast to her subdued clothing, Marie expressed her penchant for flamboyance by displaying a ring on every finger.[9]

Marie had an appointment at her attorney's office scheduled after the interview, so she picked up a pair of gloves before entering the drawing room of her suite. As she approached the New York correspondent from the *Chronicle,* she became nervous but graciously apologized for keeping him waiting for forty-five minutes.[10]

One could see from his questions and what was eventually printed that the correspondent bore no grudge against Marie. He was surprised she was so young—definitely under thirty, he surmised correctly. Charmed by her good looks, he described her in detail: "a beauty of the blonde type, a stunner . . . teeth perfect and white as pearls, her nose . . . slightly aquiline, her chin pointed, . . . her eyes blue with drooping lids and long lashes." If, he pointed out, she wasn't quite as tall, she would be considered "stout," but her height, gracefulness, and energetic gestures well made up for any excess poundage. He also thought Marie had a rather domineering, English horsewoman's quality about her. Her classic clothing reminded him "of the snobbish check suits affected by English tourists in America and by young Americans just returned from Europe, who aspire to be taken for English." He also described her as holding onto the pair of gloves while constantly toying with the rings on every finger and occasionally fiddling with her scarf. [11]

Marie made certain any discourse between reporter and interviewee would be under her control, not the correspondent's or his newspaper. She therefore began the session in a "very pleasant" voice, "Print whatever you please, but remember that if you print anything relating to my private affairs of a scandalous nature I will sue your paper for libel. Judge Fullerton is my legal adviser, and I give you fair warning."[12]

The correspondent assured her he would not report any injurious statements about her and stated that the paper "will print nothing except what you say—nothing, probably, but what has already been printed." Marie then touched on her past by explaining, "A certain scurrilous little sheet that is published in this city has already printed a fact which I do not deny . . . that one man was knocked down in London on account of some impudence offered to me."[13]

"Madame," the journalist responded, "I have no intention to report anything that would injure you; I name my business and errand at once, so that you may decline the interview if you desire." This prompted Marie to ask why his paper would even be interested in her. He responded that as she had married Count Pourtalès, the *Chronicle's* editor had been made aware of rumors concerning her past. Unlike Arthur, she did not disagree with the reporter about her marriage to the count—what was left of her reputation depended upon it. She then served up the main course of the interview but simultaneously began to tell half truths: "Everybody knows that I was married to John S. Beecher of this city, that I divorced him— he did not divorce me. I divorced him because I loved Lloyd Phoenix!"[14]

The journalist, noting Marie's "lovely blue eyes" as she revealed her feelings, thought her expression "would have reduced that Phoenix to ashes at once if he had seen it, or if he had already been consumed, he would have arisen from his own ashes."

Marie then went on about Lloyd Phoenix as if she were confessing to a close friend and sharing her emotional pain of the brutally ended affair, while the reporter continued to be mesmerized by Marie's beautiful eyes: "Yes, I loved him, and he professed to love me, and promised to marry me, but he was deceiving me." She then philosophically stated while "shrugging her shoulders like a Parisian . . . , 'I am not the first woman who was deceived by a villain. I followed him to Europe, to Nice; there he lost 35,000 francs gambling and I paid his gambling debts. A man is very low when he will let a woman pay his gambling debts or take her money at all.'" Truthfully, this was likely a way for Marie to have a little revenge upon the duplicitous ex-lover via the press because Phoenix was quite generous and could well afford to pay his own gambling debts. When he died at the age of eighty-five in 1926, he left an ample estate, including leaving over four million dollars to his nephews and around a half million to New York's Columbia University.[15]

Marie could not seem to let go of the Phoenix matter, speaking again without guile as if the journalist was her friend. After relating that her mother had sacrificed her in marriage to the much older Beecher, Marie explained, "Fortunately for me he was a generous man, and when he discovered that I loved another—Lloyd Phoenix . . . he released me, and then I learned how treacherous and fake a man can be. Yes, I l-o-v-e-d Lloyd Phoenix! But I hope I do love him no more! I respect Mr. Beecher: I do not love him. I hope I love Arthur de Pourtalès." This statement revealed exactly how Marie was feeling—in the midst of discovering the difference between her blossoming yet peaceful love for the count and the addictive, desperate love she had felt for Phoenix.

Marie then conceded that the description of her as a "fast woman" in one respect was somewhat correct, but "not in the worst sense I hope." A rare occurrence for the dawn of 1876, Marie essentially admitted that she had been for a time involved in hedonistic behavior—yet not as an actual prostitute—which would be considered the "worst sense."

Explaining that she loved to hunt on horseback, Marie then assured the correspondent of her solid standing in American and British high society—which in reality, apart from Arthur's diplomatic contacts, had largely crumbled. She also stated she was devoted to "gaiety and pleasure" and an avid fan of gambling. "Yes," she declared, "I gamble recklessly—that is no one's business but my own." While numerous feminine members of nineteenth-century European aristocracy gambled and imbibed while doing so, including Marie's friend Jennie, Lady Randolph Churchill, it was certainly in many puritanical minds more acceptable in males. Yet Marie let the world know that she was young, spontaneous, with a *joie de vivre*, and didn't apologize for her indulgent behavior no matter how high the eyebrows of a prudish reader might rise. Confident enough to admit her guilty pleasures, the once-jilted woman who left New York in tears and rage had returned as a resounding success—and she was proud of it.[16]

The tyro countess then challenged the press with an all-too prophetic pronouncement: "Now that I have married the Count de Pourtalès . . . I defy the newspapers to attack me." She also explained her monetary status, again showing the correspondent she was a substantial, independent woman—not to be trifled with and deserving of the utmost respect: "I am a wealthy woman. I have $150,000 in my own right [retaining Beecher's dowry], not very rich you may say, but enough for my purposes. I can bring a suit for libel and recover damages from any paper that dares to attack me." Unfortunately, newspapers would take on that challenge and attack her for the rest of her life.[17]

Subsequently, servants brought Preston and Maria to meet the reporter. The devotion between Marie and Maria impressed him as did Maria's fluency in English, French, and German, having been exposed to those languages while living with the count's parents at Château de Gorgier in Switzerland. After the children left, Marie revealed that Holladay had offered Arthur money in exchange for custody of Maria. She said Arthur would never give up his daughter to Holladay—not for any amount of money—and added, "I would think very little of the count if he was willing to sell his child. A man that would sell his child would sell his wife."[18]

Marie wanted to extend the interview as she felt comfortable with this gentleman. She explained that she was quite fond of reading and writing literature and had "volumes" of her own writings on a variety of subjects. This was later corroborated by several letters to Ethland, one in which Marie commented she was quite a "scribbler."

The correspondent asked her how was it possible to find time to read and write voraciously considering her exciting life. Marie replied: "Sometimes I seclude myself for weeks and cram, you know. I take out my encyclopedias, my histories, and scientific works . . . and cram. Yes I am devoted to literature." A true statement, as Marie had a fine collection of rare illustrated reference volumes and enjoyed reading them. Sotheby's in London recently auctioned one of her three-volume sets on geography that fetched the equivalent of around $1,500.[19]

The correspondent felt he could dig further and mentioned he had heard Marie was southern. Marie confirmed she was from the South but once again embroidered on the tablecloth of her past. She did not want a connection to South Carolina or the name Boozer, most likely because of the rumors that had plagued her and her mother, and did not want her notoriety to stain any family members. In answering the question pertaining to her relation to "the late Colonel A. G. Sumner [sic] of Columbia, South Carolina" [Adam Geiselhardt Summer (1818–66), born in Newberry but moved to Columbia where he became editor of the *South Carolinian*], Marie told the reporter, "No, no; that is a mistake." She said that although her mother was born in Philadelphia she married a gentleman named Boozier who lived in New Orleans where Marie was born. However, as a child Marie took her guardian's name, Burton. She went on to say she had lived "only a small part of my time in South Carolina" and had been whisked to Paris by the time she was three. She claimed that since then she had spent her entire life between Europe and the United States, and concluded, "My life is the old, old story."[20]

The interview ended after Marie dismissed the reporter, mentioning she was almost an hour late for her appointment with Judge Fullerton, perhaps to discuss the waiver of the divorce judgment. She may have felt vindicated and relieved that her new status and changed maiden name would be launched so prominently in the press. After all, Marie was a survivor. This manipulation of her past is what she thought necessary not only to avoid aspersions on Arthur or her half sisters but also to prevail as a wife of a titled diplomat. And prevail she did. Years later, as far as the European and American governments and genealogical publications were concerned, the so-labeled promiscuous traitor and Yankee-loving Mary or Marie Boozer, also known as the scandalous, clubman-shooting adulteress, London debauchee, and Parisian demimondaine Marie Beecher, had ceased to exist. Within six months Marie became officially known as Marie Adèle de Beauvoir Boozier, Comtesse de Pourtalès-Gorgier, born in New Orleans.[21] This has been her genealogical data in respected tomes of nobility, Pourtalès family documents, and likely inscribed on the headstone of the crypt in which she rests. However, many members of the sensationalist media, former Confederates, and those frequenting the exalted halls of higher education would keep Marie Boozer and/or Marie Beecher's name in the forefront for the rest of her life and far beyond.

No matter what name accompanied Marie, she was still flesh and blood, beating heart, fine mind, and affectionate soul. She had not ceased loving her son. She no doubt feared that the moment she left New York, her child would be back under John Beecher's control and influence and she might not see Preston again for a long, long time. Marie felt that she needed a token to take with her—something she could see, touch, and smell in order to feel close to her child. She removed a small pair of scissors and clipped a lock of his hair, which was later nestled in a packet with the tiny envelope containing the snippet of Preston's baby hair. The two precious bundles stayed together for well over a hundred years and remain so today.[22]

On Tuesday, January 11, 1876, Marie, Arthur, and Maria arrived in Baltimore and checked into a sumptuous suite at Barnum's Hotel. A few days later another *San Francisco Chronicle* correspondent sought out the count for an interview. Still perturbed at the way Otis had interrogated him and insulted his wife during their confrontation, Arthur kept the reporter waiting for a couple of hours and then declined the meeting. Marie was again available, however, and the journalist wasted no time in objectifying her, reporting that she could make a man into a "hero or a devil." Describing her as very beautiful with blue eyes and "lips to cleave to," and with a "full and charmingly rounded figure," he added she was of "ripe and eager health" and moved in a "smooth, wavy, sensuous motion" that "makes men forget their duty." He also noted her pleasing voice, "enticing" hands, and that her confidence and "worldly wisdom" belied her approximate thirty years of age.[23]

For this interview Marie dressed in a close-fitting, flounced blue outfit trimmed with silver lace and accented with a black bow around her neck. As for jewelry, she wore a gold chain wrapped twice around her arm and only three rings—most prominently "a large diamond on her wedding finger." She began, "The Count Pourtales does not wish to make a statement, and had he consulted his own feelings he would have said so to-day, but I am willing to see you as I am not afraid to meet anybody." She also made the reporter aware of her sharp intelligence and added that she was not frightened of anyone who might try to outwit her.[24]

Lacking the rapport she had with the first interviewer, Marie did not share her innermost feelings and instead began to embroider immediately: "The fact is, I am something of a diplomat myself. I inherit it. My father was a diplomatist, one of my uncles was a foreign Minister, and I have seen a great deal of the Legations abroad. On my father's side I am descended from one of the most aristocratic of Virginia families [this could have been true], and my mother was one of the Bartram's of Philadelphia." [Marie's great-aunt Ann was a Bartram.] Marie added that Charles O'Connor, head of the New York Bar Association, was her godfather. [Before her divorce from Beecher, Marie reportedly associated with Mrs. Charles O'Connor.][25]

When questioned about the Phoenix shooting, Marie replied hotly, "It is an infamous slander! . . . I never had a pistol in my hand in my life. I don't know how to shoot one, and would be afraid to handle such a weapon." Not surprisingly, she also denied her relationship with Hattie Blackford, calling her an attractive and well-bred "very wicked . . . woman of the town," but insisted that while she had seen Hattie in her coach many times, she didn't know her and never even spoke to her. Marie then admitted that she had visited the *Jardin Mabille* like other American women but Hattie did not accompany her there. Marie also stated that many people had often mistaken her for Hattie and another scandalous American courtesan in Paris named Baker [although no such courtesan by that name existed in the 1870s prefecture files].[26]

The correspondent then questioned Marie why the count had denied their marriage to Otis and Holladay. Angry at Otis for his previous comments to Arthur about her and annoyed with Holladay for sending Otis to pry, Marie retorted, "In the first place, it was none of his business. When Mr. Holladay wants information, he had better send a keener spy than Otis—I could twist him round my finger like a wisp of straw. The miserable old prowling vagabond!"[27]

Discreetly avoiding the divorce waiver issue, Marie blamed the count's reticence in discussing their marriage on a lawsuit concerning property she owned in the South. She also denied that Holladay supported Arthur, calling it a "vile falsehood," exaggerated her wealth at $300,000, and explained that the count would never give his daughter to a man with such "low tastes and low company" who only wanted to adopt Maria to spite his other children. She cited two other reasons for the count's insistence on keeping Maria—unlike Arthur, Holladay was not Catholic; and furthermore, Marie and Arthur could give Maria more advantages than Holladay. While impressing the reporter with her knowledge of libel laws, she assured the *Chronicle* that she was ready and able to sue anyone who disparaged Pourtalès or herself and stated that Arthur's friends and business associates would likely laugh at Holladay's trying to discredit the count. Then she challenged Holladay: "I wish somebody would put something in the papers about me. I would like to make $50,000," and warned, "the Holladay family had better set their own house in order before they undertake to pull down those of others."[28]

While Marie showed bravery in protecting herself and her husband, taking on Holladay as an opponent was not her wisest decision. Some two weeks later, on January 30, 1876, the *San Francisco Chronicle* ran the widely reprinted article reporting on Count Pourtalès and his custody battle with Holladay. Clearly biased toward Holladay and against the count, it portrayed him as the selfish, "ungrateful son-in-law." It also stated that Arthur de Pourtalès had given Holladay's grandchild a stepmother who was none other than the "celebrated fast beauty and divorcée, Mrs. John S. Beecher, whose career in New York and in London, Paris, Nice, and other cities of Europe is well known," and included the Otis interview that disparaged Marie. Holladay may well have wielded his power influencing the *Chronicle*, but even a Chicago newspaper clipping pasted in Holladay's scrapbook insulted Marie and Arthur.[29]

Regardless, by the time the *Chronicle* published the slanted article, Holladay had to accept his stinging defeat in Maria's adoption. An unhappy and bitter man, he condemned Marie for her perceived unacceptability and Pourtalès for his supposed duplicity about promising to let Holladay take Maria permanently, which in truth he never intended or promised. It was clear that Marie had caused the distress and ire of a very powerful man, and one who was capable of further staining her reputation.[30]

CHAPTER SEVENTEEN

New Husbands and Renewed Lives

I have watched the growth of the [Indian] river year by year with the greatest of pleasure.

—Samuel Joseph Field, September 1, 1895[1]

With no direct route, travel from Baltimore to Saint Augustine and south for a hundred miles to LaGrange in 1876 could be difficult with a little girl in tow, but if Marie managed to make the trip with Arthur and the four-year-old, she would have reunited with Ethland where she was living with her father, Jacob Feaster. He had in 1874 married a woman named Jeanette (née Twitchell) whose descendants later founded a church in Miami.[2]

When Ethland arrived in Florida, the Feasters received her as an "accomplished and lovely young lady."[3] The fact that she was so well respected and polished (see fig. 28) reflects upon Marie and Amelia and the nuns who taught and molded her. In LaGrange, Ethland met Benjamin Rush Wilson (1838–1913), a former Confederate army surgeon who came to Florida from Alabama in 1870 for health reasons. A recent widower in 1876, Wilson fell in love with the pretty, youthful Ethland who at nineteen was twenty years his junior. She returned his affection and the two were married on July 10, 1876. Ethland had the good taste to choose a worthy husband. Dr. Wilson would become renowned as "the first physician in North Brevard," the mayor of Titusville, a Brevard County judge, a Florida legislator, and father of the Titusville Waterworks.[4]

If Marie visited Ethland, she would have seen her half sister Julia as well, who lived only some twenty miles south of LaGrange. Julia had fallen in love with a former Confederate named Samuel Joseph Field who served in Macon, Georgia, as well as Pensacola during the bombardment of Fort Pickens. Three years after the Civil War ended, Field along with his family had sailed across the Indian River to frontier Indianola on Merritt Island. Although wildly beautiful, the only shelter from the elements was a tiny hut, and the pioneers arrived during wintertime amid cold weather coupled with pouring rain. "It was not encouraging," Samuel Field later wrote in a succinct understatement. Nevertheless, they built a house and stockade from pine trees and formed a historic settlement, despite facing extreme hardships, little provisions, poverty, and no professional medical services. On Julia's wedding day, September 24, 1872, the couple, after taking vows at Sand Point, celebrated in their Indianola camp with a few guests before a meager dinner of potatoes seasoned with salt made from the waters of the Indian River.[5]

Amelia had no opportunity to arrange Julia's and Ethland's marriages. As a result they, unlike Marie, had the chance to make their own choices of husbands and entered their marriages with their own hopes for the future. Regardless of Amelia's domineering parenting, she had produced three cultivated, strong women who all loved and revered their mother. Julia and Ethland each named one of their daughters Amelia.[6]

A stalwart, busy frontier wife, whose later nieces and nephews called her "Aunt Belle," Julia C. Feaster Field would have six children (see fig. 29) and live until the age of almost ninety-one, passing away on March 7, 1944. Distant from Marie when her half sister lived in Paris, Julia was not nearly as close to Marie as Tutu. In fact, Marie had no knowledge of Julia's number of children or other future events concerning her. However, Julia's daughter, Ethland Amelia "Ethel" Field Reed, who called Amelia "Grandma Amelia" even though they had never met, stayed in touch with Marie's son, Preston, long after Marie had died.[7]

Fig. 28. Ethland Feaster Wilson after arriving in Florida, photograph by Owen and Woodward, Ocala, Florida, courtesy Wilson-Battle-Connell-Park Papers.

In the meantime, on February 9, 1876, the *San Francisco Chronicle* published Marie's second interview in which she boldly challenged Holladay to further discredit her and the count. Holladay, known to be ruthless, took on Marie's dare, and on February 20, 1876, the *Chronicle* published another article about her—the beginning of numerous nationally printed calumnies. Obviously, the *Chronicle* was again expressing its sympathy "too profusely bestowed upon Mr. Holladay" and this seemed like yet another attempt to paint her as an unfit mother to Maria. The issue date—exactly eleven years from the day Marie left Columbia with the Yankees—and accurate details about Marie's early life in South Carolina also pointed to a local Columbia source of information. In fact, Nell Graydon claimed in her nonfiction portion of an epilogue that Julian A. Selby wrote the *Chronicle's* article, and because it covered so much of Marie's youth, it is highly likely the *Chronicle* contacted Selby or another Columbian. At least two major South Carolina newspapers partially reprinted it as did Selby at the end of *A Checkered Life.*[8]

The piece contained an accurate account of Marie's escape from South Carolina, and interviews with prominent New Yorkers revealed details of her stay in that city before marrying Beecher. But then the insults began when it called her a "notorious" and "reckless" woman.[9]

Aside from rehashing the Lloyd Phoenix shooting, one of the most intrusive parts included intimate details of Marie's adultery in the Beecher's divorce case that had been recorded in the Court

Fig. 29. Samuel Joseph and Julia Feaster Field family, image courtesy J. Reed Bradford. Front row, left to right: Ethland Amelia (Ethel Field Reed), Bart Field, John Field, Ida Moore Field. Back row: John E. Reed (standing with hand on post), Samuel Joseph Field (seated), Charles E. Reed (child), Emmett Field (behind child), Julia Carrie (Belle) Feaster Field, Jacob Moss Field.

of Common Pleas. That portion was not reprinted in New York or the South; perhaps it too explicitly used prominent New Yorkers' names and was too salacious for the general conservative southern readership.[10]

Any of the decree's missing melodramatic dialogue was filled in with relish by the author stating it had been reported by Beecher's detective. For example, when Beecher and company caught Phoenix and Marie in their love nest, Beecher "walked to the bed and tore off the bedclothes from his wife's head." Instead of leaping up and seizing Beecher as described in the divorce report, Phoenix also hid under the bedcovers: "Mrs. Beecher pulled off the sheets and put her arm around his neck, saying, 'Come here, Lloyd.' She then said 'Gentlemen, make no mistake; this is Lloyd Phoenix.'" Phoenix then simply "ran for his pantaloons" while the other men held onto him, afraid that he would draw a revolver and shoot them. This story would have thoroughly shamed Lloyd Phoenix if he had heard of it; no wonder it wasn't reprinted in New York.[11]

The article was also the first of the stories that had Marie frolicking in Russia with Hattie Blackford and Mabel Grey amid numerous men "late in the winter of 1874." While no known evidence existed of Marie cavorting with the golden-haired Mabel Grey, and Marie might have been mistaken again for her due to the similarity in appearance, this was an obvious twist of the facts. In truth, a madam named Marie Paucher had arranged for Mabel Grey to go to Russia from London and a high-ranking boyar (Eastern European nobleman) escorted Grey to Saint Petersburg. According to Hattie, "Mabel G____" had entreated her to be a companion in Russia since they both spoke English, and invited her to a troika party. At one of these wild bashes, Hattie threw a diamond bracelet at a group of singing and dancing gypsies to show her appreciation. At another, Hattie was tossed into the air by some of the men, hindering her digestion, she quipped. But she did not mention Marie being with them—in fact, the name Marie Beecher, Marie B___, or any phrase alluding to Marie does not appear in Hattie's memoir. Furthermore, Mabel Grey was working as a prostitute in Saint Petersburg in 1871, not 1874, and left Russia by the end of 1872. Hattie's unrestrained parties occurred around December 1871, before she met the grand duke. At that time, Marie, by no means a courtesan, was traveling with her son and Ethland in Europe, still married to Beecher and being pursued by Phoenix. The *Chronicle* had simply taken Hattie's memoir and replaced Mabel Grey's name with Marie's or added Marie to the pair of prostitutes.[12]

Baldly accusing Marie of being an active harlot, the *Chronicle* mentioned that "kissing" was a rule at the overnight Saint Petersburg celebrations. Two or three loose women among numerous lusty men at all-night, bawdy parties engendered in readers' minds numerous forbidden debaucheries.

The article also purported that Lloyd Phoenix was waiting for Marie and Hattie in Paris after Hattie was expelled from Russia. In reality, when Hattie Blackford left Russia for Paris in May, Marie was in New York (or en route) and Lloyd Phoenix had previously arrived there by April 15, 1874, having helped rescue passengers from another ship, which was sinking.[13]

Marie's published explanation concerning the confusion between her and Hattie Blackford had apparently given her detractors the idea of switching her name with the notorious courtesan, as the article purported that Marie, not Hattie, took the name of "the Phoenix." Then the *Chronicle* claimed that the journalist Donn Piatt photographed Marie, "the Phoenix," smoking a cigarette on a Paris train. In 1876 it was in poor taste for a young woman to smoke in public and those who did were considered vulgar and possibly prostitutes. Quoting from an actual 1875 article by Donn Piatt entitled "Miss Blackford," the *Chronicle* omitted the title and twisted Piatt's entire piece so that the woman became Marie.[14]

By replacing Hattie with Marie, the *Chronicle* and its southern cohort played a large part in a concerted effort to stigmatize Marie as an immoral woman. The story concluded with "We would as soon think of making love to" the murderous wife in Shakespeare's Scottish play or Vinnie Ream's marble statue of Abraham Lincoln, than "to this female American eagle." Julian Selby later added in his *Checkered Life,* "who hails from the Sunny South," confirming his manipulation of the malicious identity switch.[15]

Marie may have been unaware of the exaggerated coverage of her former "fast" behavior at the time of the article's first publication. Regardless, if Holladay had employed the *Chronicle* and Selby to destroy the relationship between Marie and the count and leave Maria without a new mother, he failed. The couple stayed together and on May 2, 1876, they took part in a second wedding ceremony—this time in Baltimore—to ensure the legality of their marriage, for by then Beecher had waived the no-remarrying portion of the divorce judgment. They chose the city for three reasons: the count enjoyed Baltimore and considered living there as he often had diplomatic business in town; it was in close proximity to Washington, DC, where Pourtalès was employed; and most importantly, it was out of New York State in deference to Beecher. His kind gesture in having his attorney add the waiver was a wonderful blessing to Marie; it gave her the opportunity to drastically change her life. It's no wonder she later wrote to Ethland about her ex-husband, "I have no grudge against him" and "I have only great joy, great thankfulness toward him."[16]

Count and countess enjoyed a second honeymoon in New York, with little Maria along as well, and checked into the Grand Hotel around May 9. There was an air of excitement in the Northeast during this time because of a phenomenal event underway in Philadelphia. The Centennial Exhibition, celebrating the one-hundred-year anniversary of the Declaration of Independence, began on May 10. It would change history and pervading taste, and raise the consciousness of fair-goers. President Ulysses S. Grant was one of the dignitaries who attended on opening day, and amid the crowd were Marie, Countess de Pourtalès-Gorgier, and her elegant husband, Arthur.[17]

Some 200,000 people attended by day's end, with throngs delighting in marching bands, eminent orators, and at one moment over a hundred bells, including the most famous of them all—the Liberty Bell—chiming in unison. Marie's friend, Lady Randolph Churchill, with her uncle, Lawrence Jerome, attended the grand fair at some point as well.[18]

The Centennial was a milestone of extraordinary progress for women. Thanks to Benjamin Franklin's descendant Elizabeth Duane Gillespie, who chaired the committee in charge of building an exhibition hall, they raised $30,000 to erect the first Women's Pavilion at an international exposition.[19]

While Marie and other American women were creating positive new lives, little had changed for Lloyd Phoenix. He repeated the sport of marriage dissolving by beginning an affair with another beautiful woman, Laura M. Thorp, someone else's bride for only seven months.

After the Northeast visit, Arthur, Marie, and little Maria railroaded west to San Francisco where they vacationed and then boarded a ship headed for Asia. Arthur's next diplomatic assignment was in Peking, China, and Marie's life was to become far more exotic than she had ever imagined.

CHAPTER EIGHTEEN

A Well-Traveled Lady

First there is Shanghai—a perfect European city, beautiful houses, horses, carriages and good society. Then Hong Kong—a perfectly lovely spot, where we remained four days—dining and being feted by the governor, who, by the by is Pope Hennessey.

—Marie, Countess de Pourtalès-Gorgier,
January 18, 1878 [1]

Marie continued her life with Arthur in a whirl-wind of exotic destinations. Following his service in Peking, he took a leave of absence on August 29, 1877, which afforded them the luxury of traveling throughout Asia, but they did not journey as far east as Japan. In contrast, Ethland was in Florida, pregnant and ill yet stalwartly overcoming the challenges of a pioneer wife. In December 1877 she gave birth to her first child—a boy—and in January she vicariously experienced international sojourns through her half sister's correspondence. [2]

Arthur's daughter accompanied the couple no matter where they went, and Marie continued to dote on the child and cherish her close relation-ship with the count. There was not a hint of un-certainty in her feelings by then. She knew she loved Arthur completely and would devote the rest of her life to him. He and his daughter served

Fig. 30. One of the emblems on Marie's stationery, courtesy Wilson-Battle-Connell-Park Papers. The letterhead was the Pourtalès family crest with the slogan "Quid Non Dilectis."

as Marie's anchors while she experienced her new roles as countess and diplomat's wife, loving stepmother, and citizen of the world. She considered herself up to the challenge as after all, she was already accustomed to travel and living in unfamiliar places; in her teenage years she had boarded away from home in New York and then in Paris where she had fallen in love with French culture. She had traveled frequently in her twenties and thought of her new exotic adventures as further cultural growth. An intelligent, gregarious, and positive-thinking woman, she had morphed herself into several different personas in order to cope, and this new part of her existence—even with the rigors of diplomacy—was a complete pleasure, especially compared to her unfulfilled and painful past.

Marie wrote to Ethland, "I cannot begin to describe to you how interesting the voyage has been. We have stopped at some beautiful port every four to seven days, that breaking the monotony immensely. Really it is a superb voyage! And well worth the time and money it costs." After visiting Shanghai the family went to Hong Kong, which Marie thought was "one of the prettiest little places imaginable." She described it as a city built onto a high mountainside with terraced streets, magnolia and orange trees, coconut palms, and the natural splendor complemented by beautiful houses. There they dined with Hong Kong's governor (from 1877–83), Sir John Pope Hennessey, at his "perfect palace of a home . . . in a large public garden."[3]

Marie also related a visit to Point Galle, the "pearl of the Indian Ocean," once in Ceylon, now called Sri Lanka. It certainly seemed heavenly, and her description resembled a lushly written travelogue with the writer captivated with the country's splendor:

Then again after two weeks having stopped twice en route before we arrived at the Paradise on Earth. . . . This place . . . is a dense forest of every tree & rare beautiful flower that grows, just fancy miles . . . of dense bushes of camellias with the clearest little rivers running through them; so clear & bright that one can see the bottom glistening with white crystallized sand, then every flower we guard so tenderly in our European hot houses growing wild and beautiful every where; then the forests of Coconuts with their long slender silvery white bodies and their long graceful branches . . . ladened with the coconuts. Then great mountains . . . the eye being enchanted every moment with the scene around and below, then . . . the Ocean beating in upon the shore in great mad blue waves. It fairly startles you, for all is so quiet a moment before, so beautifully peaceful; that the roar and the waves fairly paralize [sic] you with astonishment. And then the Natives are such a picturesque race. They look like polished Ebony, their eyes are wonderfully beautiful long and with curling lashes an inch long. They all wear their hair long—it is difficult to tell the women from the men, save by the gold ornaments that the women deck themselves out with.[4]

She went on: "They wore on their bodies a close fitting silk, or cotton undershirt, knitted and fitting like a glove, sleeveless & low neck, then wrapped around them a crimson scarf—their legs being exposed to the knees and their arms bare. They are the prettiest faced race in the world, pure Grecian faces—with such sad beautiful eloquent eyes. I wish I could better describe all, but as I said before it is beyond description even a cleverer pen than mine would fail to do justice to the scene!"[5]

By January 13, 1878, Marie and Arthur arrived in Naples, Italy. The king of Italy had recently died, so attractions were closed and they were left to "see nothing save the gay monde driving in their fine equipages." They remained for another day visiting the museum that stored Pompeian relics, which Marie called "intensely interesting," and later traveled to Rome and Florence before spending a brief time in Marseille, France.[6]

Marie closed her letter to Ethland from Marseille: "I must say goodbye and hoping with all my heart that you are well & happy and that you have got through your illness safe & have now a little one, I remain as always affectionately & devotedly yours, Marie, Countess de Pourtalès."[7]

On January 19, 1878, the family began their stay with Arthur's mother at Château de Gorgier in Switzerland with plans to remain until

May. It was wonderful for Marie to live with her husband and stepdaughter in an historic castle among personal treasured books and objects d'art sent from Paris. After their time in Switzerland, they planned to travel back to the City of Light.[8]

As Marie was building a life with Arthur and Maria, and Ethland began to raise a family in Florida, Lloyd Phoenix continued his career in dramatic confrontations with female sexual partners. In 1878, while committing adultery with Laura M. Thorp, their relationship became scandalous. Violence ensued between the couple when Phoenix tried to retrieve letters he had written to Mrs. Thorp, and he was allegedly arrested for assaulting her in her home. To retaliate, he claimed she deceived him and remained in New York after he had paid her $60,000 to leave the country for Europe and not to fight her divorce suit.[9]

According to Laura Thorp's published affidavit in which she sued Phoenix for $5,000, he assaulted her with a poker, chair, and majolica vase. She also swore in court that he pointed a pistol at her.[10]

Phoenix's story was quite different. He said he accidentally broke the vase, thought he was picking up his own pistol to take with him, and that *she* assaulted *him*. By this time he had changed yachts to his well-known *Intrepid*, which carried him through many exciting adventures more safely than his desire led him in affairs with married women.[11]

CHAPTER NINETEEN

Her Checkered Life

*The poor creature resisted for a time and, as she says, left the
marks of her nails on some of the haremites; but finding that they
were determined to strip her . . . she ungracefully yielded.*

—Julian Selby, 1878[1]

In 1878 Ben Holladay brought legal action against Arthur, demanding him to provide his whereabouts, but the railroad king still could not separate the count from his daughter. Tutored privately, Maria continued accompanying Arthur and Marie in their travels.[2]

Marie's life with her count was without major cares and their loving relationship remained nurturing. In her early thirties, Marie was maturing and had succeeded beyond anyone's imagination. She continued to enjoy travel, new acquaintances, and new environments. With her fluency in French—the nineteenth-century international diplomatic language—she dealt with foreign ministers and their wives and associates, and with her support Arthur progressed steadily in his duties.[3]

However, back in Columbia, South Carolina, there were those who continued to resent Marie and her mother for their Northern sympathies, their alleged compensation by the federal government, and Marie's brilliant marriage and happiness after a so-called "checkered life." That label was placed on Marie by a man who was devoted to smearing her name more than any other enemy, Columbia's diehard Rebel, writer, and publisher of the *Phoenix,* Julian A. Selby.

Selby had met Amelia and Marie when they were living in Columbia. He knew of her marriage to the count and that they had been to China. However, despite the passage of years, Selby continued to hold on to a lingering contempt for both Marie and her deceased mother. The women of the Selby family shared his hostility, indicated by the dramatic reaction of one of Selby's female descendants when in the 1950s Elizabeth Boatwright Coker asked if Selby's wife may have owned a photograph of Marie or Amelia. The descendant replied that *"if* her granny had ever been in possession of pictures of either Marie or Amelia . . . she would long ago have burned any likenesses of THOSE WOMEN!"[4]

In 1878 Selby wrote a pamphlet about Marie, printed by the *Phoenix*. Some of Selby's friends tried to dissuade him from publishing it due to its provocative and libelous content, but Selby told them he would use a nom de plume, "One Who Knows."[5]

About 3 percent of Selby's pamphlet was factual, i.e., the church where Marie married Beecher, but the newspaperman fabricated the rest. He was not the first author to conjure up imaginative tales and pass them off as truth. Misogynistic writers had been publishing lies about women in the United States for years—Confederate gossip columnists had done so against Marie as early as 1865. Marie's compatriot, Ada Clare (Ada Agnes Jane McElhenney, born in 1834 in Charleston, South Carolina) wrote in 1860 that she was a victim of "malicious and false statements" written and spoken by men, and declared that: "The taste for exploiting the private lives of those who have rendered themselves in any way famous is becoming more and more confirmed in America. . . . the coarseness and injustice of the personal details appearing in our press have already disgraced us and the civilized world. The belief of men that there is sex in lying;—that is, that when speaking of my sex, truth is of no consequence. To hear some sensible men speaking of women, you might suppose them (the men) to be hopeless lunatics. What confusion of tongues is there; what moral impossibilities . . . what stupendously illogical conclusions!"[6]

Unscrupulous men who weaved elaborate stories about women often remained unchallenged and unpunished. There were no resources to fact-check or rapid communication to quickly discredit the slanderers, and women were easy prey for public wrath because they were deemed inferior to men and incapable of retaliation. Selby also assumed that Marie and the count were occupied in Asia at the time he published his pamphlet. He likely felt confident it would not pose a problem for him but felt little for the consequences to his victim.

The chosen title was *A Checkered Life: Being a Brief History of the Countess Pourtales, formerly Miss Marie Boozer, of Columbia, S.C. Her Birth, Early life, Marriage, Adventures in New York and Europe, Separation from her Husband, Marriage to a French Count, Off to China, Etc., Etc., Etc.* There it was—Marie's full name and where she once lived. There was no Miss B____ or Countess P____ to preserve Victorian conventions of discretion. Selby wanted the world to know exactly whom he libeled.

The title page began "Read this—you'll like it," and many who read it did like the wild adventures. Selby began by extolling the charms of Marie's mother but then confessed that his enchantment with her was matched with repulsion from her purported unsavory character. He recounted Amelia's supposed federal monetary compensation throughout the pamphlet, clearly revealing his irritation over it, but his diatribe chiefly aimed at Marie, whom he called dangerous, depraved, and murderous. He described the Boozer "glass" carriage as "so much more gaudy than elegant." He also stated inaccurately that along with her beauty, Marie's "supposed wealthy" station encouraged attention from the opposite sex and her "independent, even reckless manners secured the avoidance" from the female gender (Marie's admiring schoolmates and close friendship with Buck contradicts this). He cast the aspersion that Marie was seen walking with a Union spy in Columbia, and that en route through North Carolina, Marie married a Union officer named Lieutenant Wilson but selfishly abandoned him at the port for her new life in New York City. This was particularly unkind as Rebels had killed Marie's fiancé, Lieutenant Samuel W. Preston in North Carolina.[7]

Selby then pounced on any scandalous reality in Marie's adult life. For example, he indicated that the "depraved" Marie elicited the affair with Phoenix because of her vanity and desire to mingle with the "fast set" of New York, instead of the other way around. When the romance ended, Selby devised a scenario in which Marie shot Phoenix a second time and then "rushed into a house . . . occupied by a family of South Carolinians, and claimed their protection. . . . She was recognized by one of the ladies." This wicked tale spiced with local interest must have been enjoyed heartily throughout the homes of Columbia.[8]

Selby also concocted that Marie took the train from Paris to Russia with prostitute Cora Pearl and another "female friend" (Hattie Blackford), instead of the truth that Marie journeyed to Saint Petersburg with Ethland. In her memoir, Hattie did not have Marie or Cora Pearl traveling with her from Paris to Russia in November 1871—only Hattie's maid and lapdog "Lloydy" were on the train. And when Cora, according to Selby, was in Russia cavorting with Marie, she was in reality in Paris embroiled in her own scandal regarding the suicide attempt of Alexandre Duval.[9]

Selby fabricated that Cora, Marie, and their other fast friend had been arrested in association with the grand duke's diamond scandal and expelled from Russia. As mentioned, Marie and Ethland had nothing to do with that incident and were not arrested nor expelled from Russia. Official diplomatic correspondence between Russia and United States envoys during the incident do not mention Marie's name, only Hattie Blackford's. Selby again conveniently switched Hattie with Marie in order to label Marie as a notorious prostitute complicit with thievery—retribution for her and her mother's assistance to Yankee prisoners of war and the proposed Senate reimbursement for it—which Selby deemed as a theft by the female traitors.[10]

Selby's false account of the London hotel controversy had Marie traveling again there with Cora Pearl. Of course, Marie and Ethland had in fact journeyed to England together, but in Selby's spurious version, Marie and Cora meet two Cockney men on a train bound for London and become "very sociable" with them. Upon arriving in London, Marie, Cora, and the men get drunk and carry on at their hotel. The police are summoned and Marie and Cora are arrested, thrown in jail, and expelled from England.[11]

An ocean voyage was next on the list of fictional adventures. While Marie may have told Selby of her life-changing marriage to Arthur, her affection for Maria, and the family's voyage from Le Havre to New York aboard the *Klopstock*, Selby morphed an enchanting ocean passage into a salacious transatlantic sex romp with Marie, the captain, and a purser.[12]

One telling allegation in the pamphlet was when Selby purported Marie revealed to him all of her European debauchery, shipboard dalliances, jail time, and expulsion during an intimate nighttime carriage ride in New York City. It is doubtful Selby's romantic fantasy had anything to do with reality.[13]

Selby's twisted narrative continued with Marie traveling to the American West in the company of other "fast women." En route to California, Marie and her circle of loose ladies visit Utah where, after declining to have sex with Brigham Young Jr., she is stripped bare and whipped by a group of Mormon women. According to Selby's sadistic fantasy, these "shriveled hags," part of Young's "harem," seized Marie and forcibly removed her clothing while she fought back but then buckled from exhaustion. Then one of the women brought "several short-lashed whips," which they used on Marie: "At first the blows were only slowly and lightly given, which excited her anger and indignation and she abused all the parties roundly; gradually the broad lashes came down fast and heavy and the torture became so unbearable that she fainted away." To add to her punishment Selby pretended he heard the story from Marie: "You must know . . . that I am very plump, and this lashing made me suffer terribly."[14]

Nell Graydon quoted many parts of Selby's account in the epilogue of her novel primarily about Amelia, and Elizabeth Coker used it heavily for her fictional account of Marie. However, both authors refused to believe or reprint the Utah story that ended with Marie marrying Brigham Young and his son. Graydon confirmed in her epilogue that she had omitted the more tawdry and wild tales from *Checkered Life* because she knew they were falsifications.[15]

Grudgingly acknowledging the legality of Marie's marriage to Pourtalès toward the conclusion of the pamphlet, Selby mislabeled him as a "weak young Frenchman, the Count Pourtales" who "offered his heart, hand, title, and pocket-book."[16] Arthur, in fact, was not weak, not wealthy, and while he was domiciled in Paris and of French ancestry, he was a native of Switzerland.

Selby also falsified that Marie was "distasteful to [Arthur's] friends and relatives." In truth, Marie and Arthur often stayed for months with his mother at Château de Gorgier and spent many, many occasions with Arthur's friends and associates who considered Marie an asset to the count. Selby further invented that Marie's bad reputation caused the count to be repositioned from the United States to a French embassy in China: Arthur made the move "promptly, carrying with him the cause of his troubles."[17] In fact, the China appointment was a promotion in Arthur's career and had nothing to do with Marie. Moreover, Arthur's diplomatic duties often entailed relocation; for example, before his marriage to Marie and his service in Washington, his posts included Darmstadt, Germany, in 1866; Rome in 1868; and Athens in 1869.[18]

Admitting that Marie had "quieted down" since she and the count married, Selby claimed that she was living in China "trying to master a few of the 25,000 characters pertaining to the alphabet of that little known and semi-civilized people."[19] Finally, to add a bit of verisimilitude, he included a bogus letter from Marie dated July 1, 1878, from Shanghai, when Marie was actually in Paris.

Elizabeth Coker reprinted the letter in her novel *La Belle*, believing at the time it was an original. However, after later reading authentic correspondence from Marie, Coker concluded Selby's was a "phony" and realized years after basing much of her novel on the pamphlet, that "The whole book is obvious with errors from start to finish should anybody bother to check them out . . . . Had he published his book as fiction his meanness could have been allowable." Nell Graydon concurred, stating that her research revealed little to confirm *Checkered Life*.[20]

Indeed, when one reads Marie's authentic letter to Tutu (Ethland) from the same year (quoted in chapter eighteen), one realizes the truth. One only needs to compare it with Selby's false text:

> We have traveled a great deal about this God-forsaken, no railroad country (where the men are almond-eyed and the women club-footed and otherwise malformed) . . . the fact is, this a great country for jealous lovers or husbands, as the women are compelled, owing to the laws and the peculiar male population, with their dirty persons and ways (ugh! It makes me shudder now to think of them), to keep much within doors. It's a stupid sort of life we have been leading in China. . . . I hope your "ship will soon come in" so that you can pay me that much talked of visit, when we could knock around and see what Kang-kow, Whang-ton, Ting-re and other delicately spelled places look and smell like—I've been among a few of 'em.[21]

The postscript in the apocryphal letter may be the only hint of reality and is likely what Marie replied when Selby asked her to tell him of her past: "Asking pardon for my non-compliance with your request, I remain, as ever, yours, Marie."[22]

It is not yet known if Marie sued Selby or the *Phoenix* for the pamphlet's 1878 publication. She was still in Europe, which may have prevented her from knowing about it, but interestingly, the *Phoenix* ceased publication by the end of that year and Selby omitted her from his subsequent book about Columbia. Regardless,

Marie was to apparently become aware of *A Checkered Life*. She once had considered Selby a friend, so his pamphlet may have hurt her much more than if it had been written by a stranger or mere acquaintance. The only reaction we know was that Marie implied Selby used quite a bit of his imagination when he wrote it.[23]

The problematic aspect is that Selby's fictional account and the March 1876 *Chronicle* article partially reprinted in it would be relied upon as accurate references and become the basis of several publications by novelists, journalists, historians, and other authors of nonfiction. As a result, there would be an unfortunate deluge of scandalous, false accounts of Marie's life yet to be exposed to the public.

CHAPTER TWENTY

Adoring the Past's Horrors

God has been very good to me . . . my life is very beautiful, and I am very grateful.

—Marie, Countess de Pourtalès-Gorgier,
March 18, 1884[1]

Marie, Arthur, and Maria remained each other's mainstays in a fixed union moving from one exotic destination to the next. On May 8, 1880, Arthur was appointed vice consul at Mostar, a city on the Neretva River accented by an arched, picturesque bridge called Stari Most (Old Bridge) in what is now Bosnia and Herzegovina. Arthur and Marie with Maria and a governess spent the summer there. As a result of Arthur's diplomatic achievements, on September 18, 1880, he was promoted to the first class of his foreign service. After his post ended in Mostar, Arthur and Marie were briefly in Diyarbakir, Turkey, until Arthur became in charge of the management of the French mission at *Foutchéou,* the portal capital of a province of China.[2]

While life grew more fulfilling for Marie, it remained the same for Lloyd Phoenix. In 1880, about a year and a half after his scandal with Laura Thorp, he was named the correspondent in the final divorce judgment involving her and her husband, Gould H. Thorp. After attorneys presented the decree, Phoenix, in keeping with his past behavior, escaped on his yacht and then sailed off to Europe by steamer. Laura Thorp later disclosed an interesting fact about her ex-lover: Phoenix bore three tattoos on his leg with the names of his female conquests—Laura, Hattie, and Marie.[3]

In later years the illustrated Phoenix was included in a book ironically entitled *Men of Affairs in New York*. The publishers, following a glowing biography, asserted that while still a bachelor at the age of sixty-five, Phoenix "is by no means averse to the society of the gentler sex. . . . His celibacy has been for long a vexed problem" and although some women "have tried to solve it, the effort has not so far been attended with any satisfactory results. His manner to women is most deferential and courtly, and his generosity to the sex has been unbounded."[4]

After Marie and Pourtalès left China, he was assigned to Santiago in Cuba where he assumed the role of consul on May 12, 1882. There Marie encountered a historic city with red clay roofs and a cultural mixture of Spanish, African, and French heritages. By April 12, 1883, Pourtalès and his countess were stationed on Java, an island in Indonesia. With Marie's support, Arthur continued to climb the ranks of secretary of the French legation.

Marie's son, Preston, was still raised by his father but boarded at several schools including the Trinity School in New York State; Saint Paul's in Concord, New Hampshire; London's Saint Paul's; and the Lycée Condorcet in Paris. Despite the fact that he hardly saw his father during the school year, Preston loved Beecher and described him as affectionate.[5]

On August 26, 1883, Marie and Arthur were relaxing at home in a fashionable little enclave called Buitenzorg (now Bogor) near the city of Batavia (now Jakarta). They heard a sound of an explosion and rushed to see what had happened, and suddenly they experienced the cataclysmic eruption of the volcano known as Krakatoa. The climate-changing event was one of the most far-reaching catastrophes in history. Thousands of people were killed, the sky turned red in other hemispheres, and the earth's temperature lowered. Some feared Armageddon had arrived. It's been written that it was the first major disaster after the submarine telegraph was invented, and this technological revolution permitted newspapers around the world to report its terrifying details.[6]

Marie later wrote to Ethland, knowing her younger sister had learned of the eruption and had worried about her. She apologized for not writing sooner from "Buitenzorg, March 18th/84, Island of Java, East Indies: Dear 'Tutu,' I am really ashamed not to have answered your letter earlier and I beg you not to think me either forgetful or unkind." She acknowledged that Ethland was "doubtless rather uneasy in reading such exaggerated details" of Krakatoa and described the catastrophe while simultaneously trying to ease Ethland's mind: "Sure it was bad and horrible enough, but we escaped everything! Of course there was a fearful noise like the firing of many and great cannon—at intervals of every 8 minutes. Then the sky was obscured by a thick yellowish cloud—and one could hear the falling of something like very fine soft rain—and by and by one perceived the ground and eaves covered with a grey dust which proved to be the rain of ashes—-I enclose you some—keep them . . . for it is curious. The only effect felt here and at Batavia was the noise and vibration but I assure you although I was not at all alarmed, it was not 'gay.'"[7]

She went on to explain it was true that "thousands of people were destroyed," mostly Chinese and Malays, but only about ten Europeans. "The sea swept over the towns with tremendous force and receded carrying all with it into the main Ocean—it was terrible!!!"[8]

She then changed the subject by describing the lively, neighboring city of Batavia, with a population at the time of around a million comprising native East Indians living with 12,000 Europeans and 80,000 Chinese.[9] Marie pronounced it "one of the prettiest I've ever seen: Every house is a villa surrounded with a large garden and lawns." Buitenzorg, she wrote, was a small jewel and comprised a beautiful palace with gorgeous parks and gardens. The count was a friend of the governor-general so life for Marie among the haut monde was agreeable. For amusements she and Arthur had weekly dinners at the palace and occasional card parties. In Batavia one saw fashionable women and men, and there were "dances, balls, opera dinners, and no end of amusements," but the people in Buitenzorg were far different from Parisians or Batavians and enjoyed their home life instead. She admitted that while Buitenzorg was a "dull little place," the weather was "delicious, a perpetual spring with cool nights," with pure, sweet air.[10]

For the first time in her life, Marie preferred "cool and dullness" to "heat and gaiety." In the past she would have sooner chosen gaiety over moderate weather, but her priorities had noticeably altered. At the age of around thirty-seven, Marie had matured dramatically from her hedonistic behavior as a Parisian *rebelle*. She had learned what long-lasting love between a man and a woman entailed and was grateful for and humbled by that knowledge. As a result, she did her best to keep the relationship a thriving one and would not risk losing it.[11]

No matter where she and Arthur traveled, Marie made their homes attractive and welcoming. She plunged into the Buitenzorg house's decoration and was proud of its appearance. It had an expansive marble veranda—eighteen feet in width—that Marie transformed into a tropical conservatory, replete with palm trees and numerous other types of greenery. She tied hammocks beneath the palms' fronds and placed bamboo and rattan furniture "draped with red plush and fringes" throughout the veranda. She then added plenty of lighting so they could use it for their evening salon as well as a daytime oasis, and felt that she had outdone herself by creating an environment that was "delightful and the effect is very fine." Elegant yet eclectic comfort described the interior of their home. It was, as most of the couple's houses, very large, but as in all their travels to Arthur's diplomatic posts, they left their good furniture in Switzerland. However, in the Java home their windows were accented in opulent drapery, and they brought many of their books, tastefully framed watercolors, and other art objects Marie collected during her courtesan days in Paris. They also had many pieces of decorative needlework, about twelve Turkish carpets, Japanese embroidered "sofa cushions," luxurious table coverings, good china, fine crystal, a "few bibelots," and other "odd pretty things."[12]

The family took scenic drives in the mountains, one 5,000 feet high and the other at 3,000 feet. One was nearby but the other took five hours to reach. On those outings they had carriages—a calèche, and a Victoria—with good horses to pull them. Marie wrote that the horses leading the calèche were from Australia but the Java horses were ponies—"like Hattie's"—but Marie described them as "beautiful little creatures . . . very strong and 'go like the wind.'"[13]

Count and countess hoped to remain in Buitenzorg for a few years to enjoy the lush atmosphere, cool days, and chilly nights. Maria enjoyed the mild climate of Java, played nicely with her friends, and continued with her schooling. Marie still employed the governess to educate the child, just as Amelia had employed Miss Josselyn years before. Marie felt confident in the child's home instruction and thought it was as excellent as in Europe. She loved Maria, and Arthur's daughter worshiped Marie, a devotion Marie had never experienced before. She proudly described Maria as any mother would: "She is so clever, so refined, so well brought up—such a little lady—I am repaid a thousand times in her. She is quite like my own child." Yet Marie later stated, "I have no children [with the count] and regret it, every day of my life."[14]

Marie also commented about her estranged son, whom she missed but realized would never be affectionate to her. Unfortunately, Preston had been groomed to resent his mother. Disappointed from the coolness of Preston's feelings toward her, she had tried to inure herself to further hurt by keeping her affection for him safely stored away with those locks of his hair: "I don't care if Preston loves me or not. His father always swears he does not teach him to forget me but he is a liar. It is natural for a child to forget when separated for years but I don't take it to heart. If I could see him, I should be pleased, but I love my little daughter too well to have room for any heartaches."[15]

Notwithstanding any suppressed heartaches from her son, Marie was finally fulfilled. She confided to Ethland about her marriage, her deep gratitude for a second chance, and her love for the count: "I am heart body and soul devoted to my husband, and my life is very calm, very happy, and very perfect. I regret nothing. I am too happy in my present to even recall the past. . . . God has been very good to me, he has given me a noble refined high souled man—to guide and protect me. He has given me a dear sweet loving child—and my life is very beautiful, and I am very grateful."[16]

It was clear that Marie, in spite of a past encompassed by miserable lows, grasped onto life's positive gifts and put aside the negatives: "I never never think of the grief, I live in the present and for the future.—I had no chance—you had and see how differently we have managed but I pray that God will give you happiness in the end. I am not rich, but I am always living in comfort. I owe all to my husband. . . . I adore the past with all its horrors for it brought me to my blessed husband's protection and my present!!"[17]

She adored her "past with all its horrors." Indeed, after losing her first significant love to a Civil War battle, marrying her mother's choice— not hers—being expelled from that unhealthy marriage due to a heart-wrenching affair with the wrong man, and suppressing her grief by experimenting in risky behavior, Marie had finally found redemption through a brilliant marriage. She had gone from the quickly ignited blaze of fleeting passion between an inexperienced young woman and a duplicitous womanizer to a mature, deep love between two caring people who steadily built upon their feelings. Marie's marriage to the count was on her terms, not her mother's or anyone else's. She also had that adoration and affection from his daughter whom she was raising just as she and Amelia had raised Ethland. This time, Marie was in control and capable of steering her life toward more triumphs.

CHAPTER TWENTY-ONE

A Beautiful Life and Fantastical Death

From Paris they went to Japan, and there the Countess's conduct was . . . similar to what it had been as Mrs. Beecher in New York, and the Count finally abandoned her in disgust.

—"A Woman's Horrible Death,"
New York Times, October 27, 1884

While Marie and the count filled their relationship with mutual love, devotion, travel, and happiness, insulting articles and spurious testaments did not cease. It's as if her success in life after a notorious past could not and would not be rewarded by the printed media. This became most apparent in 1884. That year women continued propounding suffrage and the Lost Cause movement was still actively in force, for which southern women raised money to revere Confederate memory and heroes in stone and bronze.

Marie was a glaring symbol of the ultimate insubordinate female who had spurned the South and the moral standard that men had mapped out for women; yet she had soared ahead. She had not died of tuberculosis in a miserable garret like other adulteresses/courtesans had in reality and literature. Worse yet, what kind of rebellious notions might Marie's success instill in wives and daughters? This was not well handled by those accustomed to maintaining control; therefore, while women journalists and publishers existed in the late nineteenth century, men held most of the power in major cities, and the male-dominated press could not allow a divorced, infamous woman to be a triumph in life. The fact that this rebellious, "loose" woman had not been ruined but thrived after her scandalous breakout to freedom threatened men in general and those southerners of both genders who had many scores to settle. They would not stand for a traitorous hussy to succeed.

Nevertheless, one of the most bizarre legends about Marie was first published in the North. The damaging story appeared on October 26, 1884, in a penny newspaper called the *New York Truth*. Versions of it were soon picked up by the *New York Times,* the *Boston Globe,* and other venerable papers. The tale was purportedly sent from Japan through Paris but clearly had been invented by someone who had known Marie in New York when she was married to Beecher and had also seen her in Europe.[1]

During the 1870s–1890s a succession of hoaxes hoodwinked the American public. One of the most famous of the perpetrators was Joseph Mulhattan, who lived in Louisville and traveled in the Southwest. Mulhattan's hoaxes were generalized, such as the discovery of a talking rock, a stagecoach with thirteen skeletons in it, a giant meteor had struck the earth, or a dreaded disease was spreading throughout the South. The New York perpetrator of Marie's hoax, however, held a motive different from Mulhattan's. Whoever initiated it wished to harm Marie and Arthur.[2]

The *New York Truth's* editor and proprietor, Thomas B. Connery, had in 1874 fabricated a hoax while managing editor of the *New York Herald*—a front-page story that hordes of wild animals had escaped the Central Park Zoo and were rampaging throughout the city. Connery, who edited the *Herald* for many years, worked closely with its publisher, Lloyd Phoenix's good friend, James Gordon Bennett Jr., and had been employed there during the time Marie shot Phoenix. While no direct evidence has been discovered that Connery created the hoax about Marie—it may well have already existed as a subject of Manhattan club gossip—he was the first to put it in print. As had Julian Selby, Connery published Marie's full name and those of others in her life.[3]

The tale was a twisted fantasy portraying Marie as a bed-hopping vixen who had suffered a sadistic death in an extraordinarily gory way.

It began in error by calling Marie a southern beauty from Georgia. While some southern papers reprinted the inaccuracy, Charleston's October 29, 1884, *News and Courier* story made it clear that Marie was actually from Columbia, South Carolina. *The Truth* then recounted Marie's marriage to Beecher and repeated the Lloyd Phoenix affair. As had Phoenix and Selby, the *Truth* blamed Marie entirely for her pursuit of Phoenix instead of the other way around. It then correctly maintained that Marie was well known among the Paris haut monde, but it went on to purport that after she and Arthur married, the count was on the staff of the French legation in Japan, a glaring invention, as in truth the count was in Peking, China, followed by a European hiatus, and then in several locales followed by Java. He and Marie had not been stationed in Japan.[4]

The piece then took an erratic, sensationalist course. It fabricated that Marie flirted with a French officer in Japan and that the jealous Pourtalès discovered her unfaithfulness and, claiming he and Marie were never married, abandoned her and returned to France. It alleged that Marie returned to Paris and began an affair with a French colonel who took her back to Japan as his lover. Marie then supposedly was unfaithful to the Frenchman with those in Japanese political circles, resulting in the colonel also leaving her.[5]

In the *New York Times* version of the hoax, Marie's outrageous behavior "shocked good people of three continents." She became "the mistress of the Japanese prime minister" but she took on yet another lover. Consequently, the prime minister ordered her execution as infidelity in Japan, even by a mistress, was punishable by death.[6]

The Truth reported on October 26 that the form of execution was the guillotine. The following day, however, the paper revised the tale. According to a "friend" of Marie's—a local prominent banker whose name was "familiar as a household word on all the exchanges of Europe"—she had not been beheaded but had been bowstrung to death. *The New York Times* confirmed this drivel: "Two masked men entered the wretched woman's house, seized and bowstrung her, then put her body into a sack and flung it into the river."[7]

Numerous newspapers reprinted the sadistic details of the fantastical incident: "The bow which crossed the back of the neck and the string which came under the chin, were then screwed tighter and tighter, until the countess died in terrible agony. . . . Such was the fate of the woman who had all Paris at her feet, who ruled Japan, and who was the honored guest at the firesides of our best families."[8]

The *New York Times* was more succinct but concluded the tale of wanton sex leading to bowstringing by stating, "The information is undoubtedly true, and it has been known for some time to a number of persons in this city, but has not heretofore gained publication." No doubt the *Times* journalist and editor had trusted more than one source.[9]

In the *Boston Daily Globe* version, the prime minister went to the Mikado and asked him to have Marie decapitated, and that had "actually" occurred. She had been executed because in Japan it was "a heinous offence" for a woman, after she has "smiled upon" one man, to smile upon another.[10]

The tale of Marie's debauchery culminating in her execution quickly created a stir when it reached Japanese diplomatic circles in Washington, DC. The Japanese legation denied the entire story and declared "that life and limb are as safe in Japan as in America . . . and that marital inconstancy there is regarded as no more heinous than here." The assistant secretary consulate of Japan stated that bowstringing was not even a form of execution in that country and added that Japanese officials were "deeply hurt" by the story: "The law there with regard to women of ill-fame is the same as here—a lewd woman, in the case of life or death, being protected by the law as any man."[11]

After the story appeared in the *New York Times,* both that newspaper and the *Truth* heard from Marie's outraged relatives and friends in New York, who stated Marie was living with Count Pourtalès in Switzerland and they have been happy together since their marriage. Friends had Marie's recent letters from Switzerland, and one relative presented a post from Marie dated September 27, 1884, from Marienbad, Bohemia, in which she wrote that "she and her husband were then journeying to Switzerland, where they would remain until January 1885." The relative added *that neither the countess nor count had ever been to Japan.*[12]

The Truth printed a retraction on October 28, 1884, titled, "The Whole Story Denied." A *Truth* reporter claimed that he visited the international banker who told of the bowstringing and explained to him the facts about Marie and Arthur, but the banker oddly contended that the myth was authentic. He stated that of course there would be denials but they weren't worth printing. He also insisted that his "source" was credible and added that bowstringing is "considered a sort of vindication of a Japanese nobleman's honor to pay miserable scoundrels to torture their unfaithful mistresses and toss their bodies to the fishes." Perhaps this financier with European contacts was in fact Marie's longtime ex-lover, "Maurice," who resented her leaving him for the count.

The *Times* printed a small retraction on October 29, 1884, as did a smattering of other papers with titles such as "A Sensation Spoiled." The Elkhart, Indiana, *Daily Review* presumed on October 28, 1884, that it must have been Joe Mulhattan who invented it.[13]

Despite the few retractions, it was too late for the fantasy to die, as a blizzard of nationwide and worldwide newspapers and magazines picked up the spurious articles. They printed eye-grabbing headlines, such as "A Wayward Woman: She meets a Tragic Death in Japan after Startling and Shocking the People of Three Continents."[14]

The decapitation saga stayed in print for years. It didn't help that in 1885 Gilbert and Sullivan's *Mikado* debuted and became internationally celebrated, for in the operetta one of the characters is pardoned from an imminent beheading.

In one of the 1885 articles, the correspondent from Columbia, South Carolina, had an acquaintance with Marie while she was living in the state capital, and he clearly showed lingering contempt for her and her mother. Using local gossip as his source, the correspondent claimed that Peter Burton's "untimely" death had nothing to do with the course of nature, implying that Amelia murdered him, and that David Boozer's suicide occurred just after Amelia "forced" him to make

Fig. 31. *Château de la Corbière, Estavayer le Lac,* Switzerland, courtesy Annie Lise and Philippe Glardon.

a new will. He also insinuated that Marie was "fast" at the age of sixteen: "There was not a college boy in the town who felt that his education was complete unless he had been engaged to Marie Boozer." He then lifted the spurious tales from *Checkered Life* and echoed the beheading incident.[15]

The same year, John S. Beecher resigned from the Union Club for an unstated reason. Perhaps his embarrassment from the articles caused the resignation, but another explanation may have been financial. Beecher's company, not harmed by the economic panic of 1873, failed in 1883, due to the firm's lessening of importing and the change in liquor laws. The company's liabilities were around $500,000 and Beecher's personal debt rose to $81,000 including interest in a Kentucky company and real estate holdings such as several acres of land in New Jersey. As a result, in 1884 Beecher faced the humiliation of giving up many of his assets, coupled with his chagrin from the false, scandalous reports about his ex-wife.[16]

Ironically, while financial difficulty plagued Beecher and antipathy for Amelia and Marie boiled in the printed media, Marie resided in a number of tranquil locales. Arthur's family had sold Château de Gorgier in 1879, but thereafter Arthur's mother began leasing another beautiful castle in Switzerland, Château de la Corbière (fig. 31). In Marie's letter to Ethland on July 1, 1885, from the chateau in *Estavayer le Lac, Canton de Fribourg, Suisse,* she commented, "What long silences there are between us." Once again happily "chez my mother in laws," Marie had been at the chateau for several months. She adored Switzerland, and thought it was the "loveliest country in the world." How could she not be happy, she remarked, when she was in one of her favorite spots in Europe?[17]

Arthur unfortunately had been ailing from liver disease and in September 1884, he and Marie rested at a health spa in Marienbad (just as her relative reported), a scenic resort catering to royalty and luminaries in the arts. The couple partook in the cold mineral water in hopes of improving Arthur's health, and at the end of the month they returned to Switzerland. After traveling to Cartagena, Spain, the following May Marie and Arthur vacationed for five weeks in Carlsbad, Bohemia, another elegant spa resort well known for its healing spring waters. Count and Countess relished the waters of the resort and Marie thought it had improved her health as well as Arthur's. Following their return stay in Switzerland, they planned to head to Paris on July 28.[18]

In her letter to Ethland, Marie revealed some of her aristocratic snobbery. She asked Ethland to forward an enclosed letter to her cousin Mayme, and as much as Marie liked her, she inquired: "I wish you would tell me exactly the style she lives in, how many servants?? Does she live as well as Marie B. of 30 W. 17 used to? I think not. I fancy there are two servants and no style at all. Am I correct?"[19]

She then displayed concern over Arthur's lack of wealth and seemed to share her mother's philosophy regarding poverty: "You know if wishes could make you happy I'd cover you with blessings but alas! Only money can make one happy in this world."[20]

Preston had written to Marie and coolly notified her that he was planning to travel to Europe in the summer. This pleased Marie, but she knew she had to continue to inure herself to his distant behavior toward her. She wrote that she had successfully suppressed lingering emotions for Preston and added, "I am so completely wrapt up in my Arthur and his child that I care very little for anyone else. I've got the best of John there!!"[21]

Fig. 32. Photograph of Marie by Nadar, inscribed by Marie, "Marie, Countess de Pourtalès-Gorgier, Paris, January 1, 1886," courtesy Wilson-Battle-Connell-Park Papers.

After staying on the continent throughout the summer, Marie, Arthur, and Maria journeyed to Newcastle-on-Tyne in northeast England, where Arthur was stationed from October 9, 1885. Any alienation from British society because of Marie's London scandal was not apparent when she accompanied her husband during numerous diplomatic affairs and societal functions in the stately city. But in Newcastle, Marie remained unknown as the notorious Marie Beecher. She instead greeted British and foreign dignitaries as the charming Countess de Pourtalès-Gorgier, the former Marie Adèle de Beauvoir Boozier of New Orleans. As a result of Marie's continued support in her husband's career and Arthur's superb diplomatic conduct, he was promoted to an officer of the academy and premier class consul.

On January 1, 1886, the couple celebrated the New Year in the City of Light when Marie was some thirty-nine years old (fig. 32). Here was a mature, regal countess and wife of a respected diplomat, somewhat thinner but still beautiful.

In 1887, Ethland (who had several babies by then) and her burgeoning family moved from LaGrange to Titusville where they continued to face the challenges of a pioneer community. Concurrently, Arthur and Marie were stationed just off Italy's boot in Sicily. The family lived in Messina in 1887 and then Palermo in 1888. The following year a great milestone occurred—the French government decorated Arthur with the title of *Chevalier de la Legion d'Honneur*, one of the highest honors in Europe.[22]

Despite Arthur's achievements and Marie's success as a diplomat's wife, stepmother, and socialite, she was continually slaughtered in print. The death of Marie by the Mikado's blade was alive and thriving, kept in the limelight by South Carolina historian Yates Snowden, who revived the legend in 1891.

Snowden's father had died during the Civil War when he was a little boy. His mother was a heroine of the Confederacy, supporting the wounded and raising funds to erect monuments to Lost Cause heroes. Snowden and his family escaped to Columbia from Charleston to avoid Sherman's March to the Sea, only to witness the horrific burning of the state capital. He spent his teenage years in Columbia during the challenging Reconstruction period and remained devoted to the memory of the Confederacy.[23]

A University of South Carolina dean later described Snowden: "No man of his generation knew his State more intimately or loved her with more ardent devotion," and Snowden's "calling was the preservation of truth." He possessed a keen mind with historical knowledge and amassed a collection of pamphlets, many of them antebellum.[24]

Snowden's story of Marie's spurious death by beheading first appeared in an article he sent to New Orleans's *Times Picayune* concerning numerous French Huguenot ancestors who settled in South Carolina—in particular Charleston. But the treatise oddly veered off that subject when Snowden inserted Marie into the essay and inaccurately chronicled her later life. He rationalized the inclusion of Marie by deeming her relationship with Count Pourtalès "the most extraordinary and the only disgraceful alliance between a South Carolinian and Frenchman." The *Charleston News and Courier*, where Snowden worked at the time, reprinted the article, retitled as "French Blood Will Tell," on November 3, 1891.[25]

After complimenting Marie on being "lovely" and "accomplished," he rewrote one of the old flawed articles about Marie's philandering and beheading published in other newspapers. One wonders if Snowden, possessed of such historical integrity, at all challenged these reports at that time. Or did he accept the falsities simply based on the newspapers' venerable heritage and seize the excuse to use Marie as a convenient scapegoat for lingering post–Civil War frustrations?

One may wonder why another maelstrom of fiction disguised as fact concerning Marie's melodramatic beheading re-emerged in 1893. The articles, which blatantly used Marie's and the Pourtalès's name, continued to be published from the draw of an audience for sensationalist tales, but they also may have been coupled with a reaction to the further advancement of women. The 1893 World's Columbian Exposition in Chicago took up the feminist cause and sent it skyrocketing. Stunning exhibi-

COUNTESS DE POURTALES, NEE MARY BOOZER.

Fig. 33. Illustration of Marie from "Six Adventuresses," *Sunday Daily Globe*, September 9, 1894, and *Pittsburgh Daily Post*, September 28, 1894, newspapers.com.

tions of women's accomplishments portrayed a progressive approach to their achievements and future. During the time of the fair and shortly after it malicious articles about Marie increased rapidly; yet most were reprints from Yates Snowden's 1891 piece about her published in Charleston's *News and Courier*.[26]

Not to be outdone by the South, northern newspapers invented their own sordid stories of Marie's life and compared her to other bad girls such as Hattie Blackford. It was again as if the press used Marie, Hattie, and other notorious females as scapegoats to maintain male strength. The title of one of these dubious achievements reveals this—"Some Daring Women who have Ruled the Destinies of Weak Men."[27]

The same year, the *National Police Gazette*, a popular men's magazine of the day, published "Two Notorious Women." It also compared Marie with Hattie Blackford, inserted Marie into the Russian jewel scandal (courtesy Julian Selby), and rehashed the Japan beheading.

These never-ending demeaning articles were pointed like swords at Marie. Her son, Preston, who seemed to disdain her when he saw her in Paris in 1893, aimed his disapproving attitude at her as well.[28]

Southern revenge continued the following year. Col. David A. Dickert perpetuated with relish Marie's Selby-initiated, imaginary, lascivious European misadventures with Cora Pearl; the Selby-inspired inclusion of Marie embroiled in the Russian diamond scandal; and the Japanese beheading myth, with Marie paying "the penalty for a wayward and wicked life." Another story by a Columbia, South Carolinian, took liberal swipes at Amelia, such as reiterating the gossip that she murdered Peter Burton.[29]

Yet another tale about the wild and wayward Marie was scattered in the 1890s press. It had her meeting a Turkish pasha in Paris and traveling to Istanbul with him where she became a member of his harem. Unfortunately, the sultry Marie continued her promiscuous bedroom romps, and the pasha discovered her infidelity with visiting Europeans. The pasha consequently threw her in jail where she starved, existing on a meager diet of bread and water. One evening the pasha fed her a grand supper of meats and wine, but it was to be her last meal. A burly Turk brought forth a sword, told her to pray to her "Christian God," and then sliced off her lovely head. This story had been told to a journalist by an ex-Confederate major who was in South Carolina when Sherman tore through the state. Indeed, southern hostility for Marie thrived throughout the United States in the 1890s.[30]

An even more outlandish story of Marie's immoral behavior leading to her violent demise smeared the front page of the Saint Paul *Sunday Daily Globe* on September 9, 1894. In "Six Adventuresses," Marie was one of several women pictured and discussed, but Marie's forlorn image was the largest (see fig. 33). This misogynistic gem declared that Marie had "married several husbands, shot at her husbands, either killing them or making them sue for divorce papers." It related a bizarre fantasy of Arthur de Pourtalès-Gorgier being slain in a duel due to Marie's flirtations, that her execution by the Mikado prompted "rejoicing in the royal palace," and concluded with "Would all countries be better off if their adventuresses could be treated thus?"[31]

In the following years, more accounts of Marie's so-called notorious past were fed to the public, some illustrated by a variety of images of her. They encored the theme of women straying outside of marriage leading to their desolation and/or death. It was yet again sensationalist journalism on steroids serving as a "moral" lesson to women who yearned to be *rebelles* at a time when the female gender was reaching further goals.

Contrary to the fantastical 1890s reports, in actuality, Marie had remained a loyal, loving wife occupied with travel and helping the count in his career. After the family left Sicily, they took a leave of absence and then spent October 1894 to early July 1898 in Tokyo—this time for real—where Arthur was *chargé d'affairs* and secretary to François-Jules Harmand, the plenipotentiary French minister to Japan.[32]

Tokyo not only afforded Marie sights of the beautiful countryside, which appealed to her love of nature; she also enjoyed many dinners, dances, yachting parties, garden parties with Emperor Meiji and his regal empress, lunches with foreign dignitaries, and other events. She participated in "little theatricals" presented to the diplomats and other distinguished guests as well. While Marie and Arthur were popular among both Japanese and foreigners, according to the British minister to Japan, Sir Ernest Satow, the couple felt that François-Jules Harmand and his wife could be quite difficult at times. Marie related to Minister Satow that on one occasion the Harmands took offense from François-Jules not being invited by Satow to meet John Poyntz Spencer (fifth Earl Spencer, great-grand-uncle of Princess Diana, and known for his abundant red beard) along with dignitaries from Germany and Belgium. Satow explained to Marie that it was simply because the other diplomats spoke English. The Harmands were also allegedly known to be unpleasant to the British. As a result, Marie and Arthur were rather apprehensive when hearing the Harmands would be returning to Tokyo after a leave.[33]

Marie also had to deal with the ongoing problem of envy of her good looks and witty personality. It seemed that another couple, Joseph

Roger Herod, secretary at the American Legation, and his wife, did not particularly care for the way people in Tokyo were often centered on Arthur's countess. Herod thought the type of precedence bestowed upon Marie should be instead paid to his wife in accordance with his diplomatic station. However, Satow thought the Herods were being foolish by protesting this mild infringement of protocol.[34]

Aside from socializing with European aristocracy and Japanese royalty, Arthur and Marie had the opportunity to take vacations or leaves from Tokyo. In March 1895, Arthur, Marie, and sixteen-year-old Maria traveled from Yokohama to Le Havre and then onto New York on board *La Champagne* in transit to Vancouver, Canada. Marie's age, which in reality was around forty-eight, was recorded on the passenger list as thirty-six, making it obvious that she continued taking after her mother by counting her years in a creative way.[35]

After they returned to Tokyo, Maria met Baron Antoine de Grubissich-Keresztür, First Secretary of the Austrian Legation. On April 12, 1898, they were married at Tokyo's Roman Catholic Cathedral with Arthur giving the bride away and Marie, in her early fifties, watching intently in the front of the congregation. She may well have been pleased that she raised a polished baroness as expertly and affectionately as she had helped raise Tutu. The audience at the lavish wedding Marie planned comprised many distinguished guests including Ernest Satow, the Herods, and the rest of the foreign diplomats plus their staff; Viscount Aoki, the Japanese ambassador; several ladies-in-waiting to the empress; Baron and Baroness Sannomiya (the baron was the "Grand Master of Ceremonies"); Marquis Nabeshima, attaché to the Japanese legation, and the Marchioness Nabeshima; as well as Viscount Kagawa, "Chief Chamberlain to the Empress." Maria and her new husband honeymooned in the mountain resort of Miyanoshita and Kyoto.[36]

Marie later wrote that she loved yet regretted Tokyo, stemming from the heartache of bidding her stepdaughter adieu on the day of her marriage and having no other young girl as a companion. Also, Arthur's lengthy Japan service from the latter half of 1894 engendered more false reports of Marie's promiscuity leading to an execution by the Mikado, both in print and through babbling mouths. While this occurred outside the diplomatic community, Marie was still sadly affected by the revival of the beheading myth, and Arthur became exceedingly irritated at the assaults against his loving and supportive wife.[37]

After Arthur's diplomatic duty in Japan ended, he and Marie prepared for their return to Europe. The count and countess knew that as they had been so well liked in Tokyo, dignitaries would honor them at a formal farewell ceremony. To avoid "the pain of leave-taking" that accompanies such a demonstration of affection, the couple quietly departed the city on July 6, 1898, without telling their many friends the exact day or time. The *Japanese Weekly Mail* predicted "their loss will be widely felt and regretted in Tokyo."[38]

Marie and Arthur sailed from Yokohama to Europe en route to New York. At some point during their Manhattan stay, Arthur likely contacted a widely syndicated society columnist known as "La Marquise de Fontenoy," the pseudonym of Marguerite Cunliffe-Owen, who with her husband had moved to the United States around 1885 but also frequented Europe. Arthur may well have expressed to her how annoyed he was with the rampant false allegations spread in newspapers and by defamatory chitchat throughout the world, and their discussion produced a column in which Cunliffe-Owen related Arthur's annoyance and disgust. She wrote that the "unpleasant gossip" and "unsavory," "sensational adventures" were due to mistaken identity and that nothing of the kind had happened with Countess Pourtalès in Tokyo. But Cunliffe-Owen soon discarded any allegiance to Pourtalès to apparently sustain incoming dollars through her gossip column's syndication.[39]

In August Arthur and Marie embarked from New York City on *La Bretagne* and headed for Le Havre. After arriving there, they boarded a train en route to Paris with a stop in Rouen where they had planned to spend a few days. Around eleven o'clock at night, the train, traveling around thirty miles per hour, was making its way through a tunnel outside the *Rue Verte* Station at Rouen. Marie rose to wash her hands in the car's bathroom but mistakenly opened not its door but the one leading to the tracks below. She immediately fell onto the footboard of the train and then plunged face-downward onto the tracks, causing a deep gash to her eyebrow and rendering her helpless. The blood gushing into her eyes from the laceration blinded her, and she remained dazed and immobilized, but then realized that by lying prostrate on the tracks she faced imminent death, vulnerable to forthcoming trains certain to crush her. The possible outcome of this bizarre situation mirroring the roller-coaster drama of Marie's earlier gut-wrenching tragedies, flights from convention, and failures ignited her survival instinct. After overcoming her former existence and transforming herself into a vital, diplomatic wife, she simply would not allow herself to die à la Anna Karenina as a literal fallen woman, facedown on a dirty and dark railroad track. Trembling, she managed to crawl to the edge of the tracks where she agonizingly stood and pressed herself against the tunnel's wall.[40]

In the interim, Arthur was gathering their things for the stop in Rouen and hadn't seen the freak accident. As the train neared the station, Arthur looked for Marie and not finding her, became overwhelmed with the horrifying feeling that she had indeed fallen off the train. It was an eerie coincidence as the count's first wife, Jenny, died on a railway trip. As soon as the train stopped at Rouen, Arthur summoned the stationmaster and along with men armed with lanterns, they entered the tunnel and searched for Marie. But when Arthur called out to his wife, she could not respond. The terrifying ordeal had rendered her speechless.[41]

After an excruciating twenty minutes, Arthur finally found Marie still against the wall, bruised, bloody, filthy with the soot from the tunnel's floor, gasping with overwrought emotion, and not able to utter a word. She threw herself into Arthur's arms, and he carried her back to the station.[42]

After arriving at their hotel, Dr. Emile Delabost was summoned and pronounced that Marie's injuries were not life-threatening, but her intense reaction of "nervous excitement" or "shock" was the most problematic. The physician ordered quiet rest for several days and likely administered the frantic Marie a strong sedative. In time she recovered. The event, as others in Marie's life, provoked widespread press coverage. Margaret Cunliffe-Owen, as the Marquise de Fontenoy, reproduced for her readers across the United States a translated article from the French language account in *Le Figaro* describing details of Marie's accident. But she was not quite through with Marie yet.[43]

CHAPTER TWENTY-TWO

The End of the Journey

Of course you know that Florence is one of the loveliest places in the world, and the views we have from our villa are superb.

—Marie, Countess de Pourtalès-Gorgier,
April 15, 1905[1]

Marie and Arthur celebrated the turn of a new century in Central America. Arthur had risen from the position of a secretary of foreign relations to Envoyé Extraordinaire and Plenipotentiary Minister of Foreign Relations in Central America, stationed in Guatemala. He was occupied in many internationally related pursuits, such as obtaining money owed to France by Guatemala and working toward boosting trade between France and Central American countries. Proud of her husband's success, Marie remained devoted to him but she missed her stepdaughter immensely, as shortly after 1900, Maria's husband had become Austria's consul general and the couple was living in Tunis.[2]

Arthur and Marie stayed in Central America until September 1902 when he took another leave of absence. The couple then ventured up the Pacific coast and visited San Francisco before traveling cross-country and sailing back to Europe. They had earned a prolonged rest after so many years of diplomatic service, and moved to a villa in the hills just outside of Florence by the end of 1902. Their "big barn," as Marie called it, was only three miles from the beautiful city and they could see its impressive Duomo from their home. The villa was newly built with the latest conveniences, but Marie admitted it was "much too large" for them. "Just think 25

Fig. 34. Four of Ethland's "chicks" in 1895, top: Leonidas Sees Wilson, twelve; middle left: Jeannette, seven; middle right: Ethel Lorena, five; bottom: (Benjamin) Rush Jr., three, Woodward Photographers, Titusville, courtesy Wilson-Battle-Connell-Park Papers.

rooms—and such a lot of servants to keep it clean." One would think that it cost a significant amount of money to lease but in fact it was only 4,000 francs per year—equivalent to $800 dollars at that time. The expense was in the maintenance of the house, and consequently, Arthur and Marie were looking for a smaller place. They were certain Arthur would soon be sent to yet another post and were in the meantime enjoying their extended stay in Tuscany.[3]

Ethland had given birth to a total of ten babies, called her "chicks" by Marie (see fig. 34). Notwithstanding the constant cares of mothering so many children, Ethland (see fig. 35), like her husband Benjamin (see fig. 36), was active in Brevard County, Florida, civic affairs.

Sadly, only eight of Ethland's children would survive to adulthood. In 1886 Ethland's baby Amelia died in infancy, and daughter Vivian died in 1902 at the age of five. But the rest thrived, including Trezevant DeGraffenried Bartram Wilson, named after both Jacob Feaster's brother and Amelia's aunt, Ann Bartram Carr. Another son's name, Leonidas Sees, also reflected Amelia's family name.

Ethland raised a fine family in the Episcopalian denomination. She insisted that all her children learn to dance, an activity she enjoyed while in Europe with Marie. It especially became the favorite pastime of at least one of Ethland's surviving daughters, Ethel Lorena.[4]

Left, fig. 35. Ethland Feaster Wilson, 1895, courtesy Wilson-Battle-Connell-Park Papers.
Right, fig. 36. Benjamin Rush Wilson, ca. 1896, courtesy Wilson-Battle-Connell-Park Papers.

In the early 1900s, Marie's cousin Sallie Cubbison (d. 1932) had moved in with her niece Florence Feaster (Trezevant and Mary Carr Cubbison Feaster's daughter) in Daytona Beach, some fifty miles from Titusville. Marie asked Ethland how Sallie was in a September 12, 1904, letter, and also about Lizzie, Ethland's former nurse who was still alive and living in Brooklyn. Ethland had remained close to her throughout the years, and Marie had entrusted Lizzie with keeping a full-length portrait she had left in New York. Lizzie had also been storing other family treasures such as silver and jewelry. At one point, Marie asked for Lizzie's address and wrote she would give her a "nice present" if Lizzie would send the painting to her at Arthur's request, but to date, the painting of Marie has remained unidentified and/or unlocated.[5]

Marie commented about Ethland's astounding number of children and assured her that her older sister was just fine. Marie also expressed to Ethland her continued deep affection of Arthur and reiterated his princely qualities, yet revealed his financial situation was not as others supposed: "Yes, I am in good health and am perfectly happy in my husband's

201

love and devotion. And I adore him. He is charming, refined, and distinguished man, and very handsome and above all, he is good, and has every noble trait and a heart of gold but unfortunately for him, not a purse of gold. He is the only one of the family who is not rich."[6]

She went on to explain their financial problems, noting that their only income was from Arthur's position as a minister in the French legation. While prestigious, it was not well paid, but Marie added that she and Arthur had managed by budgeting themselves. The love Marie felt for the count transcended any longings she may have held for her former extravagant lifestyle. She had paid the price in misery during that time and realized this; thus she lived as Arthur wished and followed his plans and advice. Perhaps this is why Marie did not bring legal suits upon all of the perpetrators of countless libelous reports against her. The ramifications of a lawsuit may have stirred up further negative publicity, hurting Marie and perhaps impeding Arthur's diplomatic activities. He also may well have been hesitant to incur exorbitant attorneys' fees as well as the expense, time, and effort entailed in traveling to the United States to testify.

Unfortunately, there were to be no grandchildren for Marie. Preston had no children, nor did Maria, despite her fervent wishes for a baby. The baroness and her husband had departed Florence after staying with the countess and count for two months, and pangs of loneliness engulfed Marie. She longed for the companionship of a little girl and wrote to Ethland: "It is very sad to be alone. . . . I wonder if you would let me have one of your daughters, to live with me for many years. A life in Europe would be a very great advantage in every way. Which one has a taste for languages? And which one has the most quiet sweet disposition—this will be a difficult question to answer, for a mother. We will speak about it later, for I am really in earnest. As I grow older, I feel the want of someone in my daily life as a companion—I doubt that you; or even one of the girls would ever consent to be separated."[7] Marie also invited her second cousin Anna "Annie" McManus (fig. 37), Mayme's daughter, to visit for a lengthy time. Mayme was planning to send Annie to Europe to live with Marie, but Mayme unexpectedly passed away in February 1903, and Annie, left with a disabled sister and elderly grandmother to care for, could not leave her family. Unbeknownst to Marie at the time of her September 1904 letter to Ethland, Annie herself had died in June that year, destroying Marie's hopes to spend any amount of time with her.[8]

Marie then reiterated her devotion to Arthur: "As for my life, it is as near perfect as can be. My husband adores me, and I love him with all my heart and soul . . . and we are so happy together." After sending her love to Ethland and her family, Marie closed the letter.[9]

Fig. 37. Anna "Annie" K. McManus, ca. 1902, Frederick Gutekunst & Co., Philadelphia, Reed family papers, courtesy J. Reed Bradford.

In 1903 a group of southern women published their remembrances of the war years. A chapter by Mrs. Thomas Taylor related what happened to the famous "Boozer" coach after a former slave picked it up from the Elmore house: "Later the car of Venus fell from its high estate, and was used for hauling between the station and home. In after years, the material still reappeared in sundry carts, wagons, etc., till all its usefulness followed its glories into nothingness."[10]

James G. Gibbes helped revitalize southern resentment for Marie and Amelia with the publication of his memoir *Who Burnt Columbia* that falsely accused Amelia of several previously cited crimes. Gibbes repeated the fantasy that Marie was involved in the Russian diamond scandal but he was one of the first defamers to claim that Ethland also participated in it. The Civil War had been over for some thirty-seven years, but evidently, Carolina vengeance had not diminished.[11]

Demeaning literature concerning Marie flourished well into the twentieth century. In 1905, the *Washington Post, Baltimore American,*

New York Tribune, as well as many other newspapers printed the syndicated gossip column by none other than "La Marquise de Fontenoy," a.k.a. Marguerite Cunliffe-Owen. She declared erroneously that Arthur's first wife, Jenny, overdosed on morphine or deliberately poisoned herself on that fateful train ride from Oregon to Chicago. Then the columnist revealed that the European community has always neglected to state that Marie Adèle de Beauvior Boozier from New Orleans was actually the notorious former Mrs. John Beecher who was responsible for shooting "the best known of New York clubmen." Cunliffe-Owen also alluded to Selby's fantasy of Marie's connection with the Russian diamond affair and reported that people in Japan gossiped to "no end" about Marie while she and the count were stationed there, ignoring the fact that they were actually beloved in Japan and no doubt betraying Arthur's confiding in her.[12]

It was evident that Marie and Arthur would never escape the "whips and scorns" lashed against them by the printed media. Due to outside slams against her and the absence of a young companion, Marie, in her late fifties, began to suffer periods of depression, despite her remarkable life. Her feeling of being cornered by the press continued to grate on her nerves and physical health, and there was no relief. The bizarre articles were contaminating what little was left of Marie's shredded reputation. In the early 1900s Dr. James Woods Babcock, director of the state asylum in Columbia, returned home from a tour of Europe and commented he had heard about Marie's depraved life wherever he traveled. He was sadly resigned that their hometown gal had sinned in all languages.[13]

Meanwhile, Preston Beecher, who had spent about six months with his father in France in 1891, had become a Francophile and an oenophile and entered the United States consular service in Bordeaux and Cognac. In 1899 Preston became vice-counsel at Le Havre. He also sent articles about French culture to newspapers, *Harper's*, and other periodicals. It's interesting that Preston, by loving fine wines and all things French, not only reflected his father's interests but also Marie's taste for European culture as well as her paternal French ancestry. The same year Preston began his diplomatic service in Le Havre, John S. Beecher died on March 31 and was buried in Connecticut with his first wife.[14]

By 1905 Preston had married an older woman named Blanche Louise, born in France in 1864. Larger than Preston in height and girth, she was rather unsophisticated, but Marie liked Blanche and treated her well. Preston later apparently remarried as his wife in a 1923 photograph (fig. 38) did not resemble Blanche in the least.[15]

Fig. 38. Preston and his then wife, 1923, indistinctly signed by photographer, inscribed on reverse, J. P. Beecher, #23 Place Gambetta, Havre, France, Reed family papers, courtesy J. Reed Bradford.

Any regard between Marie and Preston, whether cool or mildly cordial, did not last. Preston wrote to Ethland in the summer of 1905, stating he hadn't heard from Marie "for a long time," but he supposed "she was well." He added bitterly that Marie didn't concern herself with him, or "anybody else," an untrue slam displaying deep animosity for his mother. Marie was correct when she told of the resentment being taught to Preston by his father. She described her side of the strained relationship: "As for Preston, I regret to say that he is *very narrow minded,* my husband likes him *for my sake,* but he thinks that *he is narrow minded,* and has *still* the old prejudices his father gave him. I happily can live my life without him. Arthur tells me to do so, and I do!" While Marie was a pragmatic person and adhered to Arthur's advice, she still had that affectionate nature from the time she was young and she still loved Preston. He had hurt her considerably, no matter how she rationalized her feelings.[16]

Marie and Arthur continued living at their villa in Tuscany with occasional side trips. Marie rarely corresponded with anyone by then, becoming more depressed from the constant flow of poisonous attacks upon her and the potential for whispers and frowning glances wherever she went. On April 15, 1905, she wrote to Ethland and concealed the effect of the chipping away of her body and soul by the constant stream of propaganda against her: "My dearest 'Tutu,'

I sincerely know how to find excuses enough for my *seeming* neglect. I only beg you to believe that I *never* forget you, and remember with *pleasure* the days we passed together. Do you remember what a great scribbler I used to be? Well I am now quite the reverse—I have not written a letter to any one, for years. It is for me a positive penance, and *if I am silent do not misunderstand me.* All that you tell me about yourself and your children interests me."[17]

Marie then commented: "And I am sorry that good fortune has not been as great as it should be, for you and yours." As explained, Ethland and her husband, Benjamin Wilson, had lost two of their ten children by then. Additionally, while the Wilsons were highly respected, successful citizens of Brevard County, they were not terribly wealthy, and in pioneer-day Florida, life was not easy. The Florida freezes of 1894–95 did not help in this instance; it devastated Brevard County from the destruction of the citrus crop and damage to the tourist trade. Ethland's daughter Ethel, who was around six at the time, remembered "seeing long thick icicles hanging down from a huge wooden water tank at the Grand View Hotel and hearing . . . stories of the terrible sound, like a gun, when the sap froze in the orange trees and the tree trunks would burst open."[18]

Bravely enduring emotional and economic hardships, Ethland had become a more active civic booster when she had spare time. She was an officer with the Friendship Chapter, No. 6 of the Order of the Eastern Star, as well as "a valued member" of the Progressive Culture Club, a women's group formed around 1900 to meet and exchange books. This became the basis of the Titusville Woman's Club, and along with the Fortnightly Club formed the Titusville Library. She and Dr. Wilson continued to be beloved by their community and added their immeasurable value to the area. There was no doubt Amelia, Jacob, and Marie raised a strong, benevolent, and highly intelligent individual in Ethland.[19]

In 1905 Ethland read again of Marie's longing for a young girl as a companion, due to the absence of her stepdaughter, the death of Annie, and Marie's sadness of being "alone." However, Arthur thought the notion was impractical. Marie wrote: "I only wish that I could have one of your girls to come and spend some years with me, but my husband says that this would be impossible as 'home sickness' would attack them, and as the voyage is expensive I dare not undertake asking one of them. . . . much love to you and yours, believe me always your most affectionate, Sister."[20]

Marie and Arthur had traveled in the past year—one destination included Paris where Arthur fulfilled an obligatory diplomatic appointment concerning the trade agreement between France and Honduras. After visiting Paris, Marie and the count took a side trip to Nice and Monte Carlo, in Arthur's attempt to cheer her by continuing to offer her a gem of a life. He was well aware of her feelings of depression from the insults against her combined with poor health, loneliness for the companionship of a child, and the icy treatment from her son. The trip to the French Riviera, however, helped to ease morose feelings and she managed to enjoy herself. On April 20, 1905, Marie wrote to her younger sister and described her journey to the South of France where she and Ethland had also visited. Marie closed the letter: "I often thought of you and wished you could again be a young girl and with me. . . . I am always with much love, Sister."[21] She added an aside, "Pray excuse blots all the fault of my big sleeves."[22]

That was Marie's last surviving letter to Ethland. In June, Marie and Arthur asked the Swiss courts for a separation of goods to shield Marie from Arthur's financial problems. They remained together, the couple again visiting Paris in 1906 where Marie saw Preston. Their meeting was cool at best, with Preston again appraising her disapprovingly. By that time Marie's illness and sadness had continued to pull her downward, keeping her from adequately nourishing herself, and as a result she was excessively thin. Her once thick, lustrous hair had become sparse and brittle, and she had taken to wearing a hairpiece. She could no longer fight circumstances or fate as she had so often in her turbulent past, and had resigned herself to a dim future.[23]

That year the *Montgomery Tribune,* among numerous other papers continued to wound Marie. They published a widely reprinted, melodramatic, tabloid-style article entitled "Women as Soldiers of Fortune," in which Marie had a leading role. It stated the "black-haired" beauty, Mary Boozer from South Carolina who is now the Countess Pourtalès, watched a duel being fought for her love. When one man died from a bullet in his heart, she laughed derisively (which was illustrated), blew a kiss to the killer, and turned her attentions from the slayer to yet another man whom she enflamed with passion. She then dropped him and married another young fool but the weakling could not hold her back from flirting and dancing with the most handsome man at each party they attended. When the pitiful husband asked that she tone down her behavior, she shot him dead on their living room carpet (also illustrated). And all of that drama supposedly occurred *before* her marriage to John Beecher. After briefly mentioning that failed marriage, it purported an inaccurate account of Marie's unfaithfulness to the count, a duel in which he died, and so on, with her head removed by Japanese blade as the grand finale.[24]

The false accusations and criticisms in print had not only become infused in common knowledge; they were still well known to Marie, and the sheer number and viciousness of them continued to erode her well-being and further damage her physical health. If the callous perpetrators were trying to hurt her, they were doing an excellent job.

Sadly, on January 25, 1908, at around sixty-one years of age, Marie was forced by nature to relinquish her extraordinary life. Preston received a brief telegram that day from a devastated Arthur: "Mother deceased at 1:45 P. M. -Pourtalès." This was followed by a letter dated January 30, in which he explained: "Your dear mother will be buried tomorrow in a Florence cemetery; however her last remains will be moved to another sepulture later on if this is judged necessary. She laid on her death bed during forty eight hours, then was placed in a double coffin and then moved to the chapel of the villa where she still is and where masses are held every day so that her soul will rest in peace. Tomorrow, at 2 o'clock, burial will be held."[25]

He then disclosed the severe impact upon his wife from the damaging press coverage of her largely fictitious past: "She was, more or less, in ill health for the past several years, and I can say that her melancholy and depressed state have contributed much to shorten her days, and as she was hurt deeply by the calumnies and criticism of which she was a victim and, for a long time, in spite of my attempts to cheer up her morale, she aspired to the rest that death only can procure. You know how devoted I was to your mother and you must understand how deep is my sorrow."[26]

Arthur then explained that Maria was too ill to travel to see her stepmother before her death but Maria's husband made the trip. Pourtalès then asked Preston to notify Ethland. In March, the count expressed to Ethland in a letter bordered in black that he was staying with his daughter in Tunis, "after the cruel shock and irreparable loss that I have sustained." He continued: "I am much touched by the expression of your sympathy and by the nice things you say about poor Marie, but I am afraid you were still too young when you left her to have been able to appreciate all

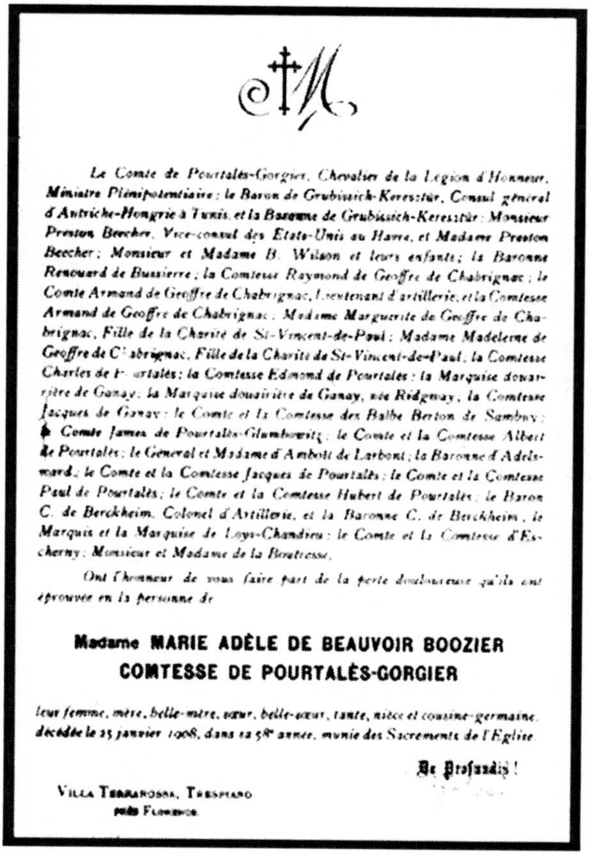

Le Comte de Pourtalès-Gorgier, Chevalier de la Légion d'Honneur, Ministre Plénipotentiaire; le Baron de Grubissich-Keresztür, Consul général d'Autriche-Hongrie à Tunis, et la Baronne de Grubissich-Keresztür; Monsieur Preston Beecher, Vice-consul des Etats-Unis au Havre, et Madame Preston Beecher; Monsieur et Madame B. Wilson et leurs enfants; la Baronne Renouard de Bussierre; la Comtesse Raymond de Geoffre de Chabrignac; le Comte Armand de Geoffre de Chabrignac, Lieutenant d'artillerie, et la Comtesse Armand de Geoffre de Chabrignac; Madame Marguerite de Geoffre de Chabrignac, Fille de la Charité de St-Vincent-de-Paul; Madame Madeleine de Geoffre de Chabrignac, Fille de la Charité de St-Vincent-de-Paul; la Comtesse Charles de Pourtalès; la Comtesse Edmond de Pourtalès; la Marquise douairière de Ganay; la Marquise douairière de Ganay, née Ridgway; la Comtesse Jacques de Ganay; le Comte et la Comtesse des Balbe Berton de Sambuy; le Comte James de Pourtalès-Glumbowitz; le Comte et la Comtesse Albert de Pourtalès; le Général et Madame d'Ambolt de Larbont; la Baronne d'Adelsward; le Comte et la Comtesse Jacques de Pourtalès; le Comte et la Comtesse Paul de Pourtalès; le Comte et la Comtesse Hubert de Pourtalès; le Baron C. de Berckheim, Colonel d'Artillerie, et la Baronne C. de Berckheim; le Marquis et la Marquise de Loys-Chandieu; le Comte et la Comtesse d'Escherny; Monsieur et Madame de la Boutresse,

Ont l'honneur de vous faire part de la perte douloureuse qu'ils ont éprouvée en la personne de

Madame MARIE ADÈLE DE BEAUVOIR BOOZIER
COMTESSE DE POURTALÈS-GORGIER

leur femme, mère, belle-mère, sœur, belle-sœur, tante, nièce et cousine-germaine, décédée le 25 janvier 1908, dans sa 58e année, munie des Sacrements de l'Eglise.

De Profundis!

Villa Terrarossa, Trespiano
près Florence

Fig. 39. Marie's death announcement, Wilson-Battle-Connell-Park Papers.

her great qualities."[27] Of course Marie was then known on the continent as Marie Adèle de Beauvoir Boozier, Comtesse de Pourtalès-Gorgier, born in New Orleans (see fig. 39), and Europeans assumed she was born in 1850 because Marie had concealed her age to Arthur. After Marie died, Ethland, in a letter to the count, shared her inaccurate knowledge of Marie's birth date as February 28, 1848. Marie had obviously provided that birth date as she wanted to be presented as a younger woman but did not want to put the burden of being disingenuous on her sister. When Arthur read of Ethland's assumed date, he questioned her certainty as Marie had previously purported that Jacob Norris Feaster had written the "family bible mentioned she was born on the 2d of February 1850."[28] Of course many records reveal that Marie was clearly born well before 1850 and 1848, including the legal document of her 1848 name change, in which it states Marie was an infant living in Columbia until the 1847 marriage between Amelia and David Boozer; Marie's December 1846 genealogical birth; an 1850 census recording she was three years old; and at least one biographical index. Moreover, Marie was not included in the Andrew Feaster family Bible records. However, Arthur remained devoted and honored Marie's version of her spurious birth date, recorded her age of fifty-eight on her death notice, and forwarded her 1850 birth date to the European noble ranks and genealogical authorities.[29]

Preston wrote to Ethland and claimed to have seen Marie "frequently before her death," but there was a noticeable absence of compassion immediately after she died, coupled with bitterness for Marie not endowing him with money or jewelry. Preston was angry at not having inherited anything of value from his father as well. He conveyed his sour feelings of monetary neglect, stating that while he had loved his father, he resented the fact that Beecher overspent money on himself and his friends as fast as it was earned. Preston also declared that Beecher should have thought of his son's future instead of "having a good time" at his son's expense. He surmised his father could have lived well by spending a quarter of his income instead of all of it every year, and then Preston could have been established in business instead of having to take a job. "But no," Preston wrote, "it all went to the winds."[30]

It is curious that Preston so vigorously disdained John S. Beecher's extravagance and resented his father for not setting him up in business. Beecher had certainly given Preston the best of private education and opportunities for advancement, and Preston's career as a diplomat and journalist afforded him the luxury of living in France and enjoying his hobby as an oenophile. As far as Preston's chastising Marie for not leaving him jewelry, it was merely two months after Marie's death. This was an inappropriate gaffe and certainly not in keeping with his position of diplomacy, as the deceased Marie had no way of defending herself to her sister. Of course, Marie would have left most of her valuables to Arthur and Maria, not Preston, who was estranged from her for so many years and who displeased her with his "narrow minded," disapproving attitude toward her. If Preston had only known about those cherished locks of his hair, he might not have been so harsh.

Marie's son knew very little of family history, including who his grandfather was. Preston revealed this in the same letter to Ethland: "I wish, when you have time, that you would tell me something about my mother's family, who her father was etc. It seems strange that I should not know who my own family were, but I don't."[31]

Ethland complied with Preston's wish, and in 1910 he wrote to Ethland's daughter, Helen, confirming this. Helen scribbled her instructions for Ethland in the corner of Preston's letter: "Mama, keep this letter for me as I'd like to keep it. My suede shoes have a hole in them."[32]

Arthur, who was still an attractive, affectionate man, soon longed for companionship. He evidently found such with his third American wife, thirty-five-year-old Emma-Gabrielle-Caroline O'Collin (a.k.a. Gabrielle-Emma Collin), whom he married on June 23, 1909. Preston wrote in a 1921 letter that he frequently had seen the count, then living in Paris, and at the age of seventy-seven was still "very handsome and distinguished." Preston also remained cordial to the Beechers' former neighbor and friend, Jennie, Lady Randolph Churchill, whom he often visited during the last thirty years of her life.[33]

Arthur de Pourtalès-Gorgier lived the longest of his little family with Marie, and died in 1930 at the age of eighty-six. His daughter, Maria, had succumbed to death at only forty-one on October 19, 1912. She posthumously won a court battle, however, concerning a large amount of West Coast acreage bestowed to her by her grandfather, Ben Holladay, and worth hundreds of thousands of dollars. Apparently, the California and Oregon Railroad claimed the property was theirs, proved by a mislaid piece of paper Holladay signed many years before. But the paper remained elusive and the court of appeals sided with the defendant, Maria, who died in the midst of the case, leading to her estate receiving her rightful inheritance.[34]

Preston's antipathy toward Marie mellowed in later years. In one of the nicer letters he wrote about his mother from the 1920s, when he was in his early fifties but "strong as a bull-dog and as active as a cat," he commented that Marie was lovely until she died. He also expressed the following to a cousin: "She grew very thin and did not eat much, but still remained a coquette . . . and rebelled very hard against growing old."[35]

A Legacy of Rumor

*There once was a glamorous southern woman (originally from
the North) and her equally beautiful daughter. While polite folks
don't repeat the gossip, historical novels do.*

—Pat Brazeel, 1976[1]

Marie had perished but the legacy of printed character and physical
slayings kept her very much alive. Joining the corporation of derogatory articles and books were those Confederate memoirs purporting the
Marie/Kilpatrick myth published from the early 1910s onward.

The most poetic disparagement to Marie and Amelia, however,
came from Yates Snowden, who had become a professor of history at
the University of South Carolina in 1905. He used the metaphor "soiled
doves" to describe mother and daughter in his introduction to the reprint of Selby's *A Checkered Life*, which Snowden helped resurrect in
1915 as *The Countess Pourtales*, printed by one of Selby's sons and James
Gadsden Holmes (1881–1942), a merchant in business in Columbia and
Charleston. Like Selby, Snowden used an alias, concealing the true au-
thorship of the foreword and introduction of *Countess Pourtales* by calling himself "Felix Old Boy," borrowed from the *nom de plume* of John
Flavel Mines.[2]

Snowden sent a copy of the pamphlet to his good friend John Bennett
in Charleston. Aware of a potential bad reaction to Selby's lurid details
from a female, Snowden warned, "Pray God Mrs. Bennett does not look
at it." Snowden obviously thought that the shocking writings could only

be enjoyed by men and would cause his own embarrassment and be too devastating before the delicate eyes of Bennett's spouse, Susan Smythe Bennett.[3]

Snowden's introductory essay of Selby's pamphlet analyzed it in a scholarly fashion by comparing it with other women's depraved behavior in literature, and differed with Selby in some respects. But Snowden believed most of it and deemed it compelling with inaccuracies in only some minor details. However, at least Snowden, who was acquainted with numerous Columbia citizens who knew Marie when she was a girl, defended her concerning the period in which she was living in town, informing the reader that Marie was a young lady, not a teenage slut, thief, or spy. But Snowden disregarded Sherman's actual mention of "Mrs. Feaster and her two beautiful daughters" when the professor wrote "it is safe to assume that no reference to the frail Marie appears in the several biographies and memoirs of Sherman." Snowden added it was amusing for him to think that Sherman and Howard, by providing written affidavits of support for Amelia and Marie in New York, were "hoodwinked by these soiled doves." He also promoted the Kilpatrick myth: "It was generally reported among the South Carolina troops at Fayetteville that Marie had left Columbia under the tender care of General Kilpatrick, and that she was the heroine of the escapade so graphically described."[4]

After John Bennett read *The Countess Pourtales,* he responded from Charleston accusing Snowden of the truth—that being complicit in publishing Selby's pamphlet, he had libeled Marie. Bennett did admit, however, the pamphlet was a popular one, and philosophized that some readers might have found a bit of Marie in themselves. The two friends also discussed the supposed beheading of Marie, with Snowden concluding he really wasn't sure if it was true.[5]

Snowden tried to disassociate himself with the publication and became chagrined when he discovered that Bennett had shown *Countess Pourtales* to a woman they both knew and respected. Snowden not only regretted sending the piece to Bennett but was angry with him for sharing it with such a gentlewoman and sharply admonished his good friend for his behavior. The professor was afraid the woman would think lowly of him for having such lurid taste in literature.[6]

Apparently, neither Ethland nor her children were aware of *The Countess Pourtales*. If Ethland knew of it prior to her death in 1917, she did not share it with her daughters. Ethel and her sister Helen did not know about it until 1959. After reading it Ethel likened "Felix Old Boy" to Denmark's famous weaver of fairy tales.[7]

Marie's legends continued to thrive during the roaring twenties, but the published tales of the countess were not enough for the Marie-obsessed inhabitants of Columbia. A South Carolina matron, whose mother once sat between Buck Preston and Marie in school, related Marie's ultimate fate: It seems that after exiting northward with the Yankees, she found and married a Bagdad caliph who was inordinately jealous of his beautiful conquest. To keep her from growing weary of their relationship and escaping with some other man, he simply severed the Achilles tendons of her heels. She therefore could not walk, grew excessively obese from lying around the palace, and was thereafter lifted upon a huge silk pillow by gigantic Moorish eunuchs who transported her wherever she wanted to go.[8]

Another legend from Columbia was that Marie traveled to Africa where she became part of the Zulu tribe whose members adored her. According to Elizabeth Boatwright Coker in an unpublished essay, the teller of the adventurous tale said that he himself had been to Africa and had "personally seen Marie's shrunken head with all its glory of golden hair on a tribal altar." Yet another rumor was that she reignited her passion with her supposed paramour, General Kilpatrick, in Chile where he was an ambassador.[9]

Then there were at least two published essays about Marie by Robert De Treville Lawrence III, who had been a student at South Carolina College when Marie was a teenager. While he was not acquainted with her, he certainly saw her in the "beauty box" many times. Lawrence described in detail Marie's fantasy divorce from Pourtalès in Paris and her travels to the Far East where she married a high-ranking "Chinaman" before losing her head to the Japanese executioner.[10]

In 1934 Marion Salley, a female Orangeburg correspondent for the *Charleston News and Courier*, wrote an intelligent journalistic piece about

Marie. Salley related reasonable and believable anecdotes told to her by gentlemen who knew Marie in Columbia, and then made it clear that some of the rumors about Marie's later life were false. However, Salley expounded upon Lawrence's bizarre tale. She explained Marie "appears to have left the Russian husband and gone onto China where she captured a Chinaman." At the end of the column Salley added that Marie's head-severing "may be grossly exaggerated for none of those who knew her in her youth could authenticate it. So it is still a matter of conjecture what became of her."[11]

Marie's legendary escapades lingered in 1936 when two scholars' book entitled *Women in the Confederacy* perpetuated the wild tales by reprinting in their endnotes one of Col. Dickert's articles that repeated the diamond scandal and beheading. In 1941 the WPA's *South Carolina: Guide to the Palmetto State* also reiterated Marie's legends.[12]

In the 1950s two talented southern women wrote popular, historical novels with Marie as a character. The first primarily concerned Amelia, and was penned by an upstanding writer and South Carolinian through marriage, Nell Saunders Graydon, her research beginning in 1956. In 1958 the R. L. Bryan & Company of Columbia, whose printing press was established in part by one of Julian Selby's sons, published Graydon's book entitled *Another Jezebel: A Yankee Spy in South Carolina.*[13]

Graydon owned an extensive library of rare books and archival papers, and the novel was well researched from anecdotal sources available at that time. Nevertheless, the fictional account erroneously portrayed Amelia as an ill-bred, lying, greedy, cheating, ruthless Yankee spy. At least one reviewer added the word "murderous" to the list because in the novel Graydon reflected the gossip that Amelia had been complicit in murdering her husband Peter Burton by poisoning him, and it was Amelia's aborting a second child that drove David Boozer to suicide. Furthermore, Graydon had General Kilpatrick pouring onto Amelia's lap expensive jewelry stolen from good Southern women with which the greedy female spy lavishly adorned herself. Marie was largely written as sweet, shy, and bullied by her scandalous mother who embarrassed her when not ignoring her.[14]

Another Jezebel was a stunning success—selling well in both hard-back and paperback. The copies were predicted to sell out by Christmas, and the R. L. Bryan Company wanted to print a second edition. But Graydon declined as she did not feel the book merited it, especially after an embarrassing course of events occurred.[15]

While Graydon wrote her novel mostly concerning Amelia, best-selling author, Elizabeth Boatwright Coker worked on hers primarily about Marie, entitled *La Belle: A Novel Based on the Life of the Notorious Southern Belle, Marie Boozer.* It was largely based on Selby's fantasized *Checkered Life,* the scathing February 20, 1876, *San Francisco Chronicle* article partially reprinted in it, and Gibbes's *Who Burnt Columbia.*

La Belle was published in 1959 by New York's E. P. Dutton Company. Like Graydon, Coker researched well and had help from loyal investigative friends—most notably Julian Bolick. However, Coker let her imaginative novelist's mind lead her and she, like Graydon, portrayed Amelia as envious gossips described her—a depraved, common woman. Coker went a bit further, however. Amelia, who often utters coarse, 1950s expressions, constantly fights with Marie, incessantly smokes thin cigars and plays cards with men, and steals the Witherspoons' silver and tries to blame Marie for the theft. Amelia is also described as a nasty, blatant racist who uses the "n" word, deliberately soils a reverend's tie with remnant ash from her flicked cigar, and after appearing to murder Big Dave with a shotgun, attends his funeral wearing an expensive, gaudy white dress. And it is Amelia who pilfers Willie Capers's timepiece so that he will break off the engagement with Marie.[16]

Marie was written as common, spoiled, and stupid, and at the age of twelve, kissing Willie Capers and discovered by her mother. Amelia thereafter calls her own daughter "Hussy." Furthermore, Marie is expelled from Madame Togno's school for her "fast" behavior and slugs her ruthless mother in the abdomen.[17]

On the way north, the Kilpatrick myth is utilized, and when the deplorable mother and daughter arrive in New York, they behave like cheap con artists instead of heroic Unionists. Among many other made-up scenarios, Amelia states she is a widow (in keeping with the fantasies in *Checkered Life* and *Who Burnt Columbia*), and defrauds the federal government in order to obtain more money from them. Then, Amelia herself is after John Beecher as a husband, claiming that she is a poor, unfortunate widow, thereby acting as a presumptive bigamist until Marie exposes her mother's lies to him.[18]

Of course, later in the book Marie is scandalous in Europe, drunkenly slurring her way in public while picking up men with prostitute Cora Pearl, and apprehended and expelled from Russia in the diamond scandal. Added to this fiction was Marie engaging in a couple of titillating boudoir scenes with Phoenix and a brief yet dramatic description of the shooting.[19]

La Belle was a national best-seller. Four American editions and one United Kingdom version were published. Elizabeth Coker later confessed, "To tell the truth I wrote the entire book without finding out whatever in the world actually happened to Marie Boozer."[20]

Neither of the women authors knew Marie had given birth to a son or that Ethland had a living son as well as two daughters residing in Florida. At least one of them was quite spunky—Ethel Lorena Wilson Battle—who obviously inherited her grandmother and mother's fortitude (fig. 40). After hearing about *La Belle*, Ethel, who was in her late sixties at the time, ordered the novel and established contact with Coker through go-betweens.[21]

Coker wrote to Ethel immediately, explaining, "I was forced to rely heavily on Julian Selby's rather racy version of the *Countess Pourtales* for my information."[22]

Battle countered by educating Mrs.

Fig. 40. Ethel Wilson Battle, courtesy Wilson-Battle-Connell-Park Papers, photographer unknown. Ethel and her husband, Carl, were among the first drivers of school buses in Titusville.

Coker about her aunt and grandmother, as well as their fine family background. Two weeks later Coker, naturally frustrated that she hadn't known about Amelia's living descendants before her book was published, corresponded with Ethel again: "By now you will have read *La Belle* for better or for worse. If I had *known* about you sooner and had known Marie came to good end eventually, rather than a bad end suddenly; that Amelia was not as black as her contemporaries portrayed her, how different I would have planned from the start."[23]

Coker also sent Ethel a copy of *Another Jezebel* as well as *The Countess Pourtales*—the reprint of *A Checkered Life*. Battle thanked her for the copies, but after reading all the publications, Amelia's granddaughter had quite enough. She was exceedingly distressed and disgusted at how Amelia had been portrayed as a common criminal, especially in Coker's book. Ethel wrote to her with a defiant pen, expounding on family history and explaining that her grandmother was not wicked; on the contrary, she held ambition for her children and only wanted the best in life for them. Battle then chastised Coker for leaving out the many true details of her family's life and for barely trying to explore the existence of Amelia's descendants. Finally, in response to Coker's request to borrow the letters and photographs or come see them in Florida, Battle accepted the latter offer and invited Coker to visit her sister to study the family archives.[24]

Mrs. Coker responded but ultimately could not make the visit. She also explained in her defense that she had perused libraries and historical societies, paid for researchers' assistance, and had been assured by Julian Selby's son (Coker's cousin) that *Checkered Life* was accurate and that the Amelia Feaster family had no living descendants. Furthermore, Coker added that she could possibly write a magazine article with photographs from Ethel's archives and might even be able to make revisions in the later editions. After receiving copies of family photos and Marie's letters to Ethland, revealing Marie as not at all how she was portrayed, Coker was most remorseful. She wrote to Ethel, "Let me say that for any unhappiness you have felt I am deeply regretful."[25]

The many letters between these two women flew back and forth with passages ranging from affable to downright contentious. Ethel Battle's annoyance at how Amelia and Marie were portrayed in the novel seemed not to dissipate but increase with time. Battle revealed that *La Belle* harmed her health from the long-lasting emotional hurt she felt after reading such a detrimental portrayal of her grandmother. She then suggested that Coker, while a gifted author, would be more successful by utilizing less crassness in her work, and twice made it clear that she would not allow Coker to quote from her or any of Marie's letters in subsequent editions of such pejorative inaccuracies.[26]

Shortly after reading *Another Jezebel*, Ethel Battle also wrote to Nell Graydon, informing the author that she was Amelia's granddaughter and again describing some of her family's excellent background. Battle firmly let Graydon know that her ancestors were anything but low, common people. "Knowing what a wonderful, intelligent person my mother was," Battle wrote, "I feel that her own mother could never have been the type of person some writers have tried to make her."[27]

Ethel also sent copies of some family archives to Graydon, who felt saddened, humiliated, and filled with regret that she had made such a fine family unhappy. One can imagine her shame and guilt in being introduced to an irate descendant after portraying Amelia as such a heinous character, no matter how subtly written. Graydon confessed to Coker that she had never felt more upset about anything else in her entire life. Coker expressed to Graydon that she also felt badly about the situation stemming from her novel, and that if she had known about Amelia's grandchildren she never would have "dared" it.[28]

Amelia's great-granddaughter, Mary Bradford (Julia Feaster Field's granddaughter and Ethel Field Reed's daughter), also wrote to Nell Graydon after receiving a copy of *Another Jezebel* sent by the author. Bradford expressed politely that while there were indeed errors in the novel, she and her husband thought it was well drafted and pleasing, especially having read it after the other account about her great-grandmother.[29]

Nell Graydon assured Amelia's descendants that she sent reproductions of the photocopied family archives to several important university and public libraries to "help counteract the part I played in writing about

Mrs. Feaster." She added in an apologetic letter to Ethel's niece, "I deeply regret that I wrote *Another Jezebel*. I would not knowingly hurt anyone."[30]

Ethel Battle and her niece accepted Mrs. Graydon's apology, and Battle, who noted Graydon had a "gentle touch" in her book, subsequently became close friends with the author. Battle advised Graydon not to feel so guilt-ridden and added that she was proud of Amelia's courage, even though Columbians abhorred her because of it. However, Amelia's feisty granddaughter was not quite finished with Mrs. Coker. When she learned that there would be a British edition of *La Belle*, she contacted Coker's publisher, Dutton, in New York and informed them the following: "Some time ago we allowed Mrs. Coker to have copies made of pictures and letters of my family, namely my Grandmother and my Aunt. This was solely for her to see that they were not the low class people pictured in her book and was done with the understanding that these Photostats and copies were not to be used here or abroad without our approval and permission, should she have other editions published. I thought it best for me to write you direct so there will be no misunderstanding."[31]

Coker wrote that she did not intend to use them in the reprint of *La Belle* and the discord between novelist and descendant finally ended when Battle apologized for her critique of Coker's writing. Years later at the age of eighty-seven, Ethel philosophically summed up the entire controversy by simply stating, "I guess they figured they had to put a little sex and violence into the books to get them to sell."[32]

By 1966 a woman scholar wrote: "The beautiful Marie has never been forgotten for her escapades . . . and while some stories told have been proved fabrications, those which have been authenticated indicate that her career was bizarre and colorful."[33] Nevertheless, other publications repeated the beheading incident.

In the nineteenth and early twentieth centuries, Yates Snowden and other South Carolina men placed elite women on a pedestal. When Marie fell from this pinnacle of southern womanhood because of baseless rumors, perceived treachery to the Confederate cause, and life choices and circumstances, she became a target of abuse and shame. Julian A.

Selby, James G. Gibbes, and other men created and perpetuated Marie's and Amelia's legends, using mother and daughter as scapegoats in order to soothe hostility and frustration caused by the Confederacy's demise. These men felt immune to any repercussions for their calumnious actions and perceived themselves as entitled and superior. After all, they had kept alive a part of southern heritage and assuaged legions of readers' sore feelings. Yates Snowden also participated in Marie and Amelia's debasement but paradoxically was embarrassed when cultured southern women read his commentary. Scholars and novelists, joined by misogynistic journalists throughout the nation, picked up the myths or wrote their own, and passed the torch of prejudice to future generations.

Perhaps because South Carolinians have remained so resolutely tied to their history, Lost Cause tall tales like the Kilpatrick affair, other imaginative claims, and demeaning innuendos concerning Marie and her mother have survived into the twenty-first century. Many have held firmly to a biased contempt toward the women, and some still believe in it and carry it forward. As a result, some contemporary southern men and women have been equally guilty of stereotyping Marie and Amelia—Marie as the congenital harlot and Amelia as the deceitful black widow. These false assertions purported as truth are a dichotomy of modern feminism and reflect an antiquated perspective soaked with the obsolete lady/Jezebel juxtaposition. While a distorted image of Amelia has remained in libelous publications, it is Marie who has become an enduring legend to be forever fantasized about, mocked, and disdained.

A renowned Civil War scholar and priest, unaware of Marie's volunteerism for the Confederate cause until the end of 1864, once stated: "If she ever performed a noble, selfless act on behalf of her state or its struggle for independence, the deed has escaped historical notice, yet Mary Boozer remains a part of the war-time lore of South Carolina and the Confederacy."[34] She still appears in news reports, making it apparent that people simply cannot get enough of her. Regardless of the blogs, books, newspapers, and broadcasts blasting Marie's legends and decrying her soul, it can be concluded that her life was an extraordinary one. She had more adventures than any ten women and flourished for over thirty years in spite of her former misery and the chronic resentment around her.

Marie Boozer, the Countess de Pourtalès-Gorgier, conveys passion, vulnerability, possibilities, and capabilities of women from any century. Despite anguish and setbacks, she prevailed to attain emotional fulfillment and a destiny far exceeding the ordinary. She proves that the force of love and a woman's will to shine remain constant, and reminds us to hold tightly to the chance for happiness.

NOTES

NOTES TO PREFACE

1. Manly Wade Wellman, "Mary Broke Many Hearts," typewritten essay, 4, Wilson-Battle-Connell-Park Papers.

2. Elizabeth Boatwright Coker, "Sandal or Scandal: Being the True Story of Countess Pourtalès, Formerly Miss Marie Boozer of Columbia, S. C." unpublished essay, 1974, 1–2, Elizabeth Boatwright Coker Papers, box 8, folder 658–9, South Caroliniana Library, University of South Carolina.

3. Coker, "Sandal"; and Yates Snowden, "Study in Scarlet," in Snowden and Julian A. Selby, *Countess Pourtales* (Columbia: S & H Pub. Co., 1915), 15.

NOTES TO INTRODUCTION

1. Thomas Brown, *Civil War Canon: Sites of Confederate Memory in South Carolina* (Chapel Hill: University of North Carolina Press, 2015), e-book, loc. 2107–12, 2305, 2057, 4182; and John Leonard, *Woman's Who's Who of America: A Biographical Dictionary of Contemporary Women of the United States and Canada* (New York: American Commonwealth, 1914–1915), 653.

NOTES TO CHAPTER ONE

1. J. F. Williams, *Old and New Columbia* (Columbia, SC: Epworth Orphanage Press, 1929), 118.

2. Marion Salley, interview with Captain J. M. Moss, former student of Columbia's Arsenal, "Arsenal Students Recall Mary Boozer, Vamp," *News and Courier*, January 7, 1934 (clipping), South Carolina Historical Society; Robert de Treville Lawrence, "The Muchly Married Miss Mary Boozer," *Confederate Veteran* (Nashville: Cunningham), 1921, 23; and "Countess Portallis," [sic] New York letter to the *Florida Times-Union*, reprinted in *Daily Alta California*, May 28, 1885.

3. "Countess Portallis."

4. Wallace Putnam Reed, "Beautiful Miss Boozer," *Chicago Times-Herald*, reprinted in *Ardsleigh Tribune*, January 20, 1897, and *The Journal of the Congress of the Confederate States of America, 1861–1865* (Washington, DC: US Printing Office, 1904), 257.

5. Carr family Bible records, once belonging to Mary Carr Sees's mother, Mary Carr, copied by Henrietta Rosson Morton (Carr Bible spells "Sees"

as "Seese"); Lena Norwood Mitchell (grandniece of Jacob Feaster, cousin of Ethland and Julia, and grandniece of Mary Drucilla, "Aunt Drucie" Feaster Rawls), "Jacob Norris Feaster and His Wife, Amelia Boozer Feaster," typewritten manuscript, Wilson-Battle-Connell-Park Papers; and DAR Genealogical Research System, accessed June 15, 2012, http://services.dar.org/public/dar_research/search/?Tab_ID=1.

6. Ethel Field Reed (Amelia's granddaughter), DAR member number 111231, National Society of the Daughters of the American Revolution, 112:75; and Battle to Coker, September 18, 1959, Coker Papers, box 8, folder 634, South Caroliniana Library, University of South Carolina.

7. "Miscellany," Robert Carr's obituary, *Historical Magazine*, June 1866, 199; "Locust Ward," *Franklin Gazette* (Philadelphia), January 27, 1820; William Bartram Snyder, *Biographical Sketch of Robert Carr*, November 1866, read before the Historical Society of Pennsylvania, 3, 7, 16–17 (Snyder was Carr's nephew and the son of Emily Sees Snyder, Amelia's sister); Emily Sees Snyder, Sees family record, Wilson-Battle-Connell-Park Papers; Carr Family Tree (ancestry.com); "Robert and Ann Bartram Carr, Bartram's Garden," accessed August 7, 2012, http://www.bartramsgarden.org/discover-our-roots/carrs/; Auditor General, Fiscal Year of Pennsylvania, November 30, 1828, 422; Robert Desilver, *Desilver's Philadelphia Directory* and *Stranger's Guide* (Philadelphia: Desilver, 1828), 72; "Patent Law Amendment Act," *Journal of the Society of Arts*, September 19, 1856, 716; "List of Sealed Patents," *Mechanics Magazine*, February 7, 1857, 143; Battle to Graydon in "Living Descendant's Letter Sheds Light," *State*, November 1, 1959; "Act to Incorporate the West Branch Railroad Company," passed February 23, 1871, Acts of the Legislature of West Virginia at its Ninth Session (Charleston, WV: H. S. Walker, 1871), 121; and Last Will and Testament, Emily Sees Snyder, October 5, 1892, Wilson-Battle-Connell-Park Papers.

8. Penny Park, telephone conversation with author, July 9, 2012; Carr family Bible records; and Wilson family Bible, Wilson-Battle-Connell-Park Papers.

9. Desilver, *Desilver's Philadelphia Directory and Stranger's Guide*, 72; Ethel Battle, family history, author's collection; and C. D. M., "A Fair Adventuress," *Atlanta Constitution*, March 16, 1894.

10. Carr Bible records; Helen Cubbison to Ethel Field Reed, June 12, 1909, copied in Mitchell, "Feaster," Wilson-Battle-Connell-Park Papers; Etta Rosson notes, collection of Henrietta Rosson Morton; and "Descendants of Archibald Carr," genealogy compiled by Susan Warren.

11. "The State vs. Peter Burton for the Killing of G. W. Hunt," *Charleston Courier*, November 5, 1839; "Fatal Affray," *Philadelphia Inquirer*, September

5, 1839; "Fatal Encounter," *Southern Patriot*, September 2, 1839; and "Judge Butler, Mr. P. Burton, Mr. G. W. Hunt," *Commercial Advertiser*, November 1, 1839.

12. Ibid.

13. "List of Letters," *Southern Patriot* (Charleston), February 22, 1840, February 27, 1840, and April 16, 1840; "Marriage Notices," *Columbia South Carolinian*, January 21, 1841, from Brent Howard Holcomb, *Marriage and Death Notices from Columbia, South Carolina, Newspapers, 1838–1860* (Columbia, SC, USA: SCMAR, 1988, ancestry.com); and Henry Alexander White, *Southern Presbyterian Leaders* (New York: Neale, 1911), 262.

14. United States District Court, District of South Carolina, filing for bankruptcy in Charleston, August 6, 1842, denied, January 2, 1843, posted in the *Southern Patriot*, August 29, 1842 and March 27, 1843; and Jonathan Daniel Wells, *Origins of the Southern Middle Class, 1800–1861* (Chapel Hill: University of North Carolina Press, 2003), 111, 114.

15. "Petition to change the name of Mary A. P. Burton by her next friend, David Boozer, November 21, 1848," Newberry Equity Records, box 20, Package 34, South Carolina Department of Archives and History (Marie's full name and biological father are recorded); and Amelia Feaster, "Come List Awhile . . . ." poem, Wilson-Battle-Connell-Park Papers. Ethel Battle sent a copy to Coker, Coker papers, box 8, folder 634.

16. "Petition"; United States Federal Census, 1860 (ancestry.com); "Descendants of Archibald Carr"; Wakefield family tree; Ritch-Googe family tree; Anderson family tree; Huber family tree; Claude Clarence Reitzel family tree; Francis (Olson)-Kalar family tree; "Pourtalès, Marie, 1846-1908," *Biography Index: A Cumulative Index to Biographical Material in Books and Magazines*, Vol. 5: September 1958–August 1961 (New York: H. W. Wilson Co., 1962); and 1850 Newberry Census, Publication, M432_856, July 19, 1850, Jim Pinson, South Carolina families, accessed May 23, 2012, http://sc-families.org/tree/I753.html.

17. Julian Bolick, "Notes of Miss Blanche Davidson on Amelia Boozer," Coker papers, box 8, folder 650.

18. John Belton O'Neall, *Annals of Newberry: Part One* (Newberry: Aull and Houseal, 1892), 137.

19. Bolick, "Notes of Davidson"; and South Carolina Temperance Advocate, October 7, 1847, from *Brent Howard Holcomb, Marriage and Death Notices from Columbia, South Carolina Newspapers, 1838–60* (Columbia, SC, USA: SCMAR, 1988: 177, ancestry.com).

20. Thomas H. Pope, *History of Newberry County, South Carolina, 1749–1860*

(Columbia: University of South Carolina Press, 1973, reprint 1992), 102.

21. Bolick, "Notes of Davidson"; and Coker, "Sandal or Scandal," 3.

22. "Petition"; and Victoria E. Bynum, *Unruly Women: The Politics of Social and Sexual Control in the Old South* (Chapel Hill: University of North Carolina Press, 1992), 44.

23. Snowden, "Study in Scarlet," *Countess Pourtales*, 8; and Coker, "Sandal or Scandal," 3.

24. George Leland Summer, *Newberry County, South Carolina: Historical and Genealogical Annals* (Newberry: Summer, 1950, reprint, Baltimore: Genealogy Publishing, 2002), 195; John Belton O'Neall and John Abney Chapman, *Annals of Newberry in Two Parts* (Newberry: Aull and Houseal, 1892), 137–8, 169; and David Boozer's grave marker, public member photographs, accessed June 16, 2012, ancestry.com.

25. "John B O'Neall, Ex'or of David Boozer vs. Amelia Boozer, Columbia, November 1851," J. S. G. Richardson, South Carolina, Court of Appeals, Court of Errors, Appeals in Equity (Columbia: Court of Appeals), 23; Will, David Boozer (copy), Nell Graydon scrapbook, collection of Henrietta Rosson Morton; and United States Federal Census, 1850.

26. Graydon to Patton, ca. October 1, 1959, Nell Graydon Papers, Southern Historical Collection, University of North Carolina and Aveleigh Church minutes, 1850, reproduced in Graydon, *Another Jezebel*, 64–66.

27. Ibid.

28. South Carolina Court of Appeals and James Sanders Guignard Richardson, "O'Neall vs. Boozer," *Report of Cases in Equity: Argued and Determined in the Court of Appeals and Court of Errors, South Carolina, Vol. 4* (Columbia, SC: R. W. Gibbes, 1853), 22–25.

29. Bolick to Coker, July 8, 1958 and Boozer Executor Report copied by Pope in Pope to Bolick, August 27, 1957, Coker Papers, box 8, folder 648.

30. Labeled photograph, ca. 1860, Wilson-Battle-Connell-Park Papers; Park interview with author, July 16, 2012; Feaster to Abraham Lincoln, endorsed by Gen. Oliver Howard, and Gen. Alfred Terry, March 14–15, 1865, handwritten transcription, 6, 278, RG 107, Entry 18: Records of the Secretary of War, Record Series Originating During the Period 1789–1889, Correspondence, Letters Received, Letters Received (Main Series), 1801–89, Re: compensation; Microfilm M 221, Roll 281, Frames 28–33, The Papers of Abraham Lincoln, National Archives; Battle to Graydon in "Living Descendant"; and envelope labeled "daguerreotype of Amelia and Marie," Wilson-Battle-Connell-Park Papers.

31. Feaster, Howard, and Terry to Lincoln; C. D. M., "A Fair Adventuress"; and Wells, *Origins*, 111.

32. Joel Fry, curator, Historic Bartram's Garden, telephone interview with author, August 29, 2012.

33. Andrew Feaster Bible records copied by Henrietta Rosson Morton and Andrew Feaster family Bible in the possession of Lena N. Mitchell, copied by Elberta Feaster Buie, Ethel Battle Papers, North Brevard Historical Society.

34. Ethland's compositions ca. 1873; M. Pourtalès to Wilson, letters, 1878–1905, Wilson-Battle-Connell-Park Papers; "Living Descendant"; William Woodward Dixon, "Mobleys and Their Connections: Descendants of Andrew Feaster," Genealogy Free Pages, accessed July 15, 2012, http://freepages.genealogy. rootsweb.ancestry.com/~mobley/dixon.txt; "Julia C. Feaster," South Carolina Families, accessed July 15, 2012, http://sc-families.org/tree/I850.html; Feaster family Bible; and Andrew Feaster Bible. Julia's middle names were also known as Carry and Caroline. Jakie was also called "Jay" and/or "John."

35. Snowden, "Study in Scarlet"; and *Countess Pourtales*, 8.

36. Jacob Feaster to his father, Andrew, May 27, 1855, in "Papers of the Coleman, Feaster, and Faucette Families, 1787–1943," South Caroliniana Library, University of South Carolina, accessed July 31, 2012, http://library.sc.edu/socar/uscs/1998/colema98.html; and Pinson, South Carolina Families, accessed July 31, 2012, http://sc-families.org/tree/I753.html.

37. Captain David Power Conyngham, *Sherman's March through the South: With Sketches and Incidents of the Campaign* (New York: Sheldon, 1865, reprint Bedford: Applewood Books, 2001), 329; and photographs of Columbia in Graydon, *Tales of Columbia*.

38. Graydon, *Tales of Columbia*, 55.

Notes to Chapter Two

1. R. W. Gibbes, *Columbia, South Carolina Street Directory*, 1859; Graydon, *Tales of Columbia*, 45–46, 66, 245; Alexander Moore, Introduction, *Memoir of James de Veaux of Charleston, S.C.* (Columbia: University of South Carolina Press, 2012), x; and Moore, telephone conversation with author, October 23, 2012.

2. Carr Bible records; Descendants of Archibald Carr; Andrew Feaster Bible records, "Feaster Record"; J. P. Coleman et al, *Robert Coleman* (Kingsport: Kingsport Press, 1965), 306; "Trezevant DeGraffenried Feaster," South Carolina Families, accessed July 13, 2012, http://scfamilies.org/tree/I746.html; Mitchell, "Feaster" (mistakenly calls niece cousin); "Living Descendant"; and United States Federal Census, 1850. Mary Cubbison

Feaster died in 1875 and was buried in Columbia; Margaret died in Columbia in 1883 and was buried in the same plot as Mary.

3. Rev. Daniel Bragg Clayton, "A Sensible Wedding," in *Forty Seven Years in the Universalist Ministry* (Columbia, S.C.: Clayton, 1889), 210–12.

4. United States Federal Census, 1860; and M. Pourtalès to Wilson, September 12, 1904, and April 15, 1905. Some photocopies of the letters were erroneously dated by Coker; however, Marie made the correct years clear by her explanations in her early twentieth-century letters.

5. Margaret Narcissa Feaster, Kathleen Coleman, and Kathryn Scott High (Introduction), eds., *Diary of Margaret Narcissa Feaster, 1860–1865* (privately printed: 1950), January 1, 1865, 58; "Maria Louisa Feaster," South Carolina Families, accessed July 16, 2012, http://sc-families.org/tree/13.html; Columbia Directory, 1859; and "Zimmerman School, Richland County (1336 Pickens St., Columbia)," South Carolina Department of Archives and History, accessed September 18, 2012, http://www.national-register.sc.gov/richland/S10817740054/.

6. Amelia Feaster, *Come List Awhile*. Also quoted in Tom Elmore, *The Scandalous Lives of Carolina Belles Marie Boozer and Amelia Feaster: Flirting with the Enemy* (Charleston: History Press, 2014), 22–23.

7. Ibid.

8. Snyder, Carr, 27; Joel Fry, curator of Bartram's Historical Garden, email message to author, August 29, 2012; and "A Venerable Typo," *Columbia Bulletin*, reprinted in the Charleston Mercury, January 20, 1859.

9. "Venerable."

10. Catalogue, Columbia Female College, 1860, 22; Jane Tuttle, archivist, Edens Library, Columbia College, email message to author, August 28, 2012; and United States Federal Census, 1860.

11. Catalogue, 16; John Frost, ed., *The Class Book of Nature; Comprising Lessons on the Universe, the Three Kingdoms of Nature, and the Form and Structure of the Human Body* (Hartford: Belknap & Hamersley, 1838), 5, 250–6.

12. Bolick to Coker, August 13, 1957, Coker Papers, box 8, folder 648; and Coker, "Sandal or Scandal," 5. From letters a grandmother (Marie's schoolmate) wrote to her daughter, a friend of Julian Bolick's.

13. Ibid., 6, from historian Samuel Gaillard Stoney, whose grandmother sat behind Marie.

14. Snowden, "Study in Scarlet," 5.

15. Col. D. A. Dickert, "Sorceress of the Congaree," *Herald and News*, Newberry, SC, August 6, 1909.

16. Dickert, "Countess Percele: The Famous and Notorious Adventures of a South Carolina Beauty," *Atlanta Constitution*, February 25, 1894; Wells, *Origins*, 10; C. D. M., "Fair Adventuress"; and Snowden, "Study in Scarlet," 8.

17. "Countess Portallis."

18. Ibid.

19. Interview with Marie in "Devoted Woman: How the New Countess de Pourtales Spends her Time," *Sunday Chronicle* (San Francisco), January 30, 1876; "Manhattanville Timeline: The Academy of the Sacred Heart: 1841–1917," Manhattanville College, accessed September 7, 2012, http://www.mville.edu/undergraduate/academics/library/special-collections/manhattanville-timeline.html; Manhattanville College archivist Lauren Ziarko, email message to the author, September 12, 2012; and "Living Descendant's Letter."

20. Snowden, "Study in Scarlet," 9.

21. Feaster, Coleman, and High, *Diary,* July 31, August 1, August 9, August 16, August 17, August 19, August 22, and August 26, 1861, 19–23.

22. Mitchell, "Feaster."

23. Libra Rose Hilde, *Worth a Dozen Men: Women and Nursing in the Civil War South* (Charlottesville: University of Virginia Press, 2012), e-book; Elizabeth Massey, *Bonnet Brigades* (New York: Knopf, 1966), 39–40; Francis Butler Simkins and James Welch Patton, *Women of the Confederacy* (Richmond, VA, and New York: Garrett and Massie, 1936, reprint, St. Claire Shores, MI: Scholarly Press, 1971), 27–28; and Feaster, Coleman, and High, *Diary,* November 12, 1861, 34, November 26, 1861, 40, January 1, 1862, 40.

24. Coker, "Sandal or Scandal," 9; Graydon, *Tales of Columbia*, 125; and Lawrence, "Mary Boozer," 23.

25. Feaster, Howard, and Terry to Lincoln; "Death of Mr. Jacob N. Feaster," *Indian River Advocate*, November 25, 1895, 8; John T. Manning, *The Feaster Family of LaGrange*, unpublished genealogy, 4, Feaster Family Papers, North Brevard Historical Society; Battle to Graydon, October 27, 1959, Graydon Scrapbook; and Battle to Coker, October 9, 1959, Coker Papers, box 8, folder 634.

26. "Local Intelligence Pater Patriae the One Hundred and Twenty-Ninth Anniversary of the Birth of Washington," *Philadelphia Inquirer,* February 23, 1861; Snyder, Carr, 27; "Fourth of July," *Philadelphia Inquirer,* July 5, 1862; and Fry, telephone interview with author, August 29, 2012.

27. Graydon, Tales of Columbia, 125.

28. Mrs. Thomas Taylor, "Two Equipages," Mrs. Thomas Taylor, Mrs. Smythe, Mrs. August Kohn, Miss Poppenheim, and Martha B. Washington, eds., *South Carolina Women of the Confederacy: Records Collected by Mrs. A. T. Smythe, Miss M. B. Poppenheim, and Mrs. Thomas Taylor* (Columbia, SC: State Committee Daughters of the Confederacy, 1903), 251.

29. Ibid.

30. Feaster, Coleman, and High, *Diary*, April 13, 1862, 50.

31. Boozer will; "Devoted Woman"; Ethel Wilson Battle, unpublished essay, Wilson-Battle-Connell-Park papers; and Battle to Graydon in "Living Descendant Sheds Light."

32. Snowden, "Study in Scarlet," 8; Col. James G. Gibbes, "Burning of Columbia," *Philadelphia Weekly Times,* September 4, 1880; and Gibbes, *Who Burnt Columbia?* (Newberry, SC: E. H. Aull, 1902), 20–21.

33. C. D. M., "Fair Adventuress"; Wellman, "Mary"; and "Devoted Woman."

34. Coker, "Sandal or Scandal," 9; Capers to Mrs. Capers, July 3, 1861, Ellison Capers Collection, Citadel Archives and Museum, Charleston, SC; and Confederate Rolls, 437, original record book, South Carolina Digital Library.

35. Graydon, *Tales of Columbia,* 126.

36. Graydon, *Tales of Columbia,* 126–27; Lawrence, "Muchly Married"; and "Miss Mary Boozer," undated essays, Robert de Treville Lawrence III Papers, 1730–1991, Kennesaw State University Archives; "Death of Lieut. Col. William C. Preston, *Charleston Mercury,* July 23, 1864; "Major William Campbell Preston," newsletter, Regimental Courier, South Carolina Confederate Relic Room and Military Museum, accessed August 28, 2012, http://www.state.sc.us/newsletter/crr/2007122059132918.6918. html; Graydon, acknowledgments, for *Jezebel,* 1, thanking the late Dr. Robert W. Gibbes (1872–1956, son of Col. James G. Gibbes), for his information concerning Willie Preston; and R. W. Gibbes to Graydon, October 16, 1956, Graydon scrapbook.

37. "Death"; "Major"; Mary Boykin Miller Chesnut and Ben Ames Williams (ed.), *A Diary from Dixie* (New York: Houghton Mifflin 1949), 1976, reprint Cambridge: Harvard University Press, 1980), July 26, 1864, 315; Graydon, *Tales of Columbia,* 126; and Chesnut and C. Van Woodward (ed.), *Mary Chesnut's Civil War* (New Haven, CT: Yale University Press, 1981), 695.

NOTES TO CHAPTER THREE

1. Edward E. Kendrick Jr., Late Adjutant of the Tenth New Jersey Veteran Volunteers, sworn statement before Congress, June 12, 1865, "Report to Accompany Bill S. No. 434," *Report of the Committees of the Senate of the United States, 1865–66 Congressional Edition* (Washington, DC: Government Printing Office, 1866), 3. Also quoted in Elmore, *Scandalous*, 49.

2. Chesnut and Williams, *Diary,* December 19, 1864, 466; and Feaster, Howard, and Terry to Lincoln.

3. Chesnut and Williams, *Diary,* 466.

4. Mr. Anthony [Senator Henry Bowen], Committee of Claims: "Report to Accompany Bill S. No. 434," The Report of the Committees of the Senate of the United States for the First Session Thirty-ninth Congress, 1865–66 (Washington, DC: Government Printing Office, 1866), 1; and Massey, *Bonnet,* 117.

5. Feaster, Howard, and Terry to Lincoln; Charles O. Hunt, "Our Escape from Camp Sorghum," *War Papers Read before the Commandery of the State of Maine—Military Order of the Loyal Legion of the United States* (Portland: Thurston, 1898), 1:86–92; and W. H. Shelton, "Hard Road to Travel Out of Dixie," Famous Adventures and Prison Escapes of the Civil War (New York: Century, 1885, reprint 1911), 251.

6. Anthony, "Report," 1.

7. Captain Joseph E. Fiske, U. S. V., "An Involuntary Journey Through the Confederacy," in *Civil War Papers: Read Before the Commandery of the State of Massachusetts, Military Order of the Loyal Legion of the United States, Vol. 2* (Boston: Gilson, 1900), 520–21.

8. Joel Tyler Headley, *Farragut, and Our Naval Commanders* (New York: Treat, 1867), 479; Paul Culliton, "A Hero by any Definition: A Canadian sailor's Lasting Legacy," Esprit de Corps, April 1, 2011, The Free Library, 2011, S. R. Taylor Publishing, accessed July 23, 2015, http://www.the-freelibrary.com/ A+hero+by+ any+definition%3a+a+Canadian+sailor%2 7s+ lasting+legacy.-a0254828825; and "The Late Lieutenant, Samuel W. Preston," *Harpers Weekly,* February 4, 1865, 69.

9. DuPont to G. V. Fox, Assistant Secretary of the Navy, August 14, 1862, in United States Naval War Records Office, *Official Records of the Union and Confederate Navies in the War of the Rebellion. / Series I - Volume 13: South Atlantic Blockading Squadron (May 14, 1862–April 7, 1863)* (Washington DC: Government Printing Office, 1901), 255.

10. Chaplain H. Clay Trumbull, U. S. V., "Four Naval Officers Whom I

Knew," in *The United Service: A Quarterly Review of Military and Naval Affairs* (Philadelphia, PA: Hamersly, January 1879), 37–39; and Michael Burlingame, ed., *At Lincoln's Side, John Hay's Civil War* (Carbondale: Southern Illinois Press, 2006), 33, 227.

11. Trumbull, "Four Naval" and James Dunwody Jones, "A Guard at Andersonville," published from his memoir written after the Civil War in *Civil War Times*, January, 1, 1964, reprint in *Andersonville: Penetrating Views from Men Who Were There and from Modern Scholars* (Eastern Acorn Press, 1983), 5. The chaplain disclosed Preston's name; the guard confirmed Marie's name.

12. Trumbull, "Four Naval," 38.

13. Ibid.

14. Chesnut and Woodward, *Chesnut's Civil War*, 695; and Chesnut and Williams, *Diary*, 466.

15. Bynum, *Unruly Women*, 44, affirmed this: "Marriage, of course, provided a white woman's best insurance against the slanderous whims of another."

16. Chesnut and Woodward, *Chesnut's Civil War*, 695.

17. Secretary of War James A. Seddon to General Robert E. Lee, November 17, 1864, Elihu Root, Brigadier General Fred C. Ainsworth, Joseph W. Kirkley, eds., *War of the Rebellion: a Compilation of the Official Records of the Union and Confederate Armies* (Washington DC: Government Printing, 1900), 825; and Chesnut and Williams, *Diary from Dixie*, 466.

18. Anthony, "Report," 1; and "Loyal Woman from South Carolina," Providence Evening Press, May 10, 1865, reprinted from the *Philadelphia Bulletin*.

19. Amelia Feaster, sworn affidavit, June 2, 1865, in *Memorial, Testimony, and Letters of Federal Prisoners: On the Claim of P. F. Frazee, Loyal Citizen of New Jersey, for Property Destroyed at Columbia, S. C., on February 17, 1865 by the Forces of Maj. General Sherman*, ed. C. A. Stevens (Washington, DC: McGill & Witherow, 1866), 25; and Anthony, "Report."

20. Feaster, Howard, and Terry to Lincoln; Anthony and Kendrick Jr., "Report," 1, 3; "Patriotic Southern Woman," *Vermont Journal*, July 28, 1866, "very many prisoners" swore she was arrested twice and threatened with death; "Relief for Southern People," *Springfield [Massachusetts] Republican*, July 19, 1866; Battle to Graydon, October 27, 1959, Graydon scrapbook.

21. Lamson to Commander Alexander C. Rhind, January 16, 1865 in Roswell Hawks Lamson, James M. McPherson, Patricia R. McPherson, eds., *Lamson of the Gettysburg: The Civil War Letters of Lieutenant Roswell H. Lamson, U. S. Navy* (New York: Oxford University Press, 1999), 225;

Eliza Mary Hatch Edwards, *Commander William Barker Cushing, of the United States Navy* (New York: Tennyson Neely, 1898), 190; and Jamie Malanowski, *Commander Will Cushing: Daredevil Hero of the Civil War* (New York: Norton 2014), 219.

22. Lamson to Rhind in Lamson, McPherson and Mcpherson, Lamson, 25; and "Niece Recalls County Man Killed in Civil War and Honored by U. S.," *London* [Ontario, Canada] *Free Press* October 19, 1937. According to Preston's niece, he had been promoted to captain shortly before he died, but she also claimed Preston was engaged to DuPont's daughter at the time of his 1865 death. DuPont had no children.

23. Lamson to Kate Buckingham, January 15, 1865, Roswell Lamson Papers, box 1, folder 7, Rare Books and Special Collections, Princeton University Library; Trumbull, "Four Naval"; and "Lieutenant Samuel W. Preston, USN (1840–65)," U. S. Department of the Navy, accessed July 24, 2016, https://www.ibiblio.org/hyperwar/OnlineLibrary/photos/pers-us/uspers-p/s-prestn.htm.

24. Captain Kidder Randolph Breese, "Lieutenant Samuel W. Preston, USN (1840–65)," in Secretary of the Navy, *Report of the Secretary of the Navy with an Appendix Containing Reports from Officers, December 1865* (Washington DC: Government Printing Office, 1865), 178; and *Harper's Weekly*, February 4, 1865, 69.

25. "Preston," Department of Navy; Chris Eugene Fonvielle, *The Wilmington Campaign: Last Departing Rays of Hope* (Mechanicsburg, Pennsylvania: Stackpole, 2001), 258–59; Trumbull, "Naval Officers" 38; "Preston," Harpers; "USS Preston," Destroyer History Foundation, accessed July 22, 2016, http://destroyerhistory.org/goldplater/index.asp?r=37900&pid=37901; "Devoted Woman"; and M. Pourtalès to Wilson, March 18, 1884, Wilson-Battle-Connell-Park Papers.

26. Feaster, Coleman, and High, *Diary*, January 18, 19, 1865, 65; and Emma Le Conte, Diary 1864–1865, January 18, 1865, 7 (transcript of the manuscript from Southern Historical Collection, University of North Carolina at Chapel Hill, LeConte, Emma Call number 420, Manuscripts Dept., Southern Historical Collection, UNC-CH), 36, electronic edition, *Documenting the American South*, Library of Congress, accessed October 21, 2013, http://docsouth.unc.edu/fpn/leconteemma/leconte.html.

27. Winder to Captain Senn, January 31, 1865, "Prisoners of War and State," *Congressional Series, War of the Rebellion: A Compilation of the Official Records of the Union and Confederate Armies* (Washington, DC: United States Government Printing Office, 1899), 160. Also quoted in Elmore, *Scandalous*, 27.

28. Anthony, "Report," 1; "State Items," *Newark Daily Advertiser*, December 21, 1865; and "Broomsticks to Battlefields" (blog), December 29, 2010, accessed November 19, 2012, http://broomstickstobattlefield.blogspot.com/2010_12_01_archive.html.

29. Kendrick Jr., "Report," 3. Also quoted in Elmore, *Scandalous*, 49.

30. Emlen Carpenter, Captain 6th Pennsylvania Cavalry, sworn statement before Congress dated March 12, 1865, "Report," 2; Burt Froom, "Mt. Airy: Yesterday and Today: The Carpenter Family," March 29, 2012, West Mount Airy Neighbors, Newsworks, WHYY, accessed April 8, 2013, http://www.newsworks.org/index.php/component/flexicontent/items/item/35672-the-carpenter-family; and Eugene Glenn Stackhouse, "Captain Emlen N. Carpenter," Find-a-Grave Memorial, accessed April 8, 2013, http://www.findagrave.com/cgi-bin/fg.cgi?page=gr&GRid=7520625; and Gilbert E. Sabre, *Nineteen Months a Prisoner of War* (New York: American News Company, 1865), 169.

31. "Emlen N. Carpenter," obituary, *New York Times*, March 18, 1891; Carpenter to Col. C. L. Leiper, April 2, 1865; and "Memoriam, Emlen Newbold Carpenter, Military Order of the Loyal Legion of the United States," William Redwood Wright papers, Series 6: Fisher and Wright 1852–1921, box 32, Historical Society of Pennsylvania.

32. Sabre, *Nineteen Months*, 169–71.

33. Sabre, *Nineteen Months*, 171; and Carpenter, "Report," 3.

34. "Loyal South Carolina Lady," *Philadelphia Inquirer*, May 6, 1865; Conyngham, Sherman's March, 328; Oliver Otis Howard, *Autobiography of Oliver Otis Howard, Major-General, United States Army* (New York, Baker & Taylor, 1908), 120; Le Comte, Diary, February 17, 1865, 23; and Simkins and Patton, *Confederacy*, 68.

NOTES TO CHAPTER FOUR

1. Conyngham, *Sherman's March*, 313.

2. Narcissa Feaster, *Diary*, February 16, 1865, 69.

3. Gibbes, *Who Burnt Columbia?* 18–19.

4. William Tecumseh Sherman and Charles Royster, *Memoirs of General William T. Sherman* (Des Moines: Library of America, 1990), 436–37; Moore, *James de Veaux*, xxviii; and Howard, *Autobiography*, 121–22; and C. A. Stevens, *Memorial*, 20–21.

5. Feaster, sworn affidavit, Stevens, Frazee, 20–21; and Howard, *Autobiography*, 121–22.

6. John G. Barrett, *Sherman's March Through the Carolinas* (Chapel Hill: University of North Carolina Press, 1956, reprint 1996), 89.

7. Howard, *Autobiography*, 122; and diary of Major Thomas Osborn, reprinted in Osborn, Richard Harwell and Philip N. Racine, eds., *The Fiery Trail: A Union Officer's Account of Sherman's Last Campaign* (Knoxville: University of Tennessee Press, 1986), 127–32.

8. Conyngham, *Sherman's March*, 328, 331; Howard, *Autobiography*, 121; Marion Brunson Lucas, *Sherman and the Burning of Columbia* (Columbia: University of South Carolina Press, 2000), 108, 158, 161; and Moore, *de Veaux*, xxix.

9. Feaster, sworn affidavit, in Stevens, *Frazee*, 21. Also quoted in Elmore, *Scandalous*, 43.

10. Battle to Graydon in "Living Descendant" and Feaster, Howard, and Terry to Lincoln.

11. "City Affairs," *North American* (Philadelphia), May 6, 1865, 1; "Loyal Woman"; and Feaster sworn affidavit, Stevens, *Frazee*, 20–21. Also quoted in Elmore, *Scandalous*, 43.

12. Feaster, sworn affidavit, Stevens, *Frazee*, 21. Also quoted in Elmore, *Scandalous*, 43.

13. Feaster, Howard, and Terry to Lincoln"; "Loyal Woman"; "City Affairs"; Anthony, "Report," 1, 5; Sabre, *Nineteen Months*, 15; Feaster affidavit, Stevens *Frazee*, 20–21; Lieutenant William H. Mickle of the 20th Corps, Army of Georgia During Sherman's March Through the Carolinas, diary, February 17, 1865, Heritage Auction, lot 49073, ending on April 5, 2016; and Edwin L. Lybarger of the 43rd Ohio Infantry, February 17, 1865, Heritage Auction, lot 49008, ending on April 5, 2016.

14. Gibbes, "Burning of Columbia," 20–21.

15. Sabre, *Nineteen Months*, 15; and Feaster, Howard, and Terry to Lincoln.

16. William Gilmore Simms, *Sack and Destruction of Columbia to which is Added a List of the Property Destroyed* (Columbia: *Phoenix*, 1865), 76; "Sherman in South Carolina: The Occupation and Destruction of Columbia," *South Carolinian*, March 7, 1865; and Gibbes, *Who Burnt Columbia?* 20.

NOTES TO CHAPTER FIVE

1. Le Conte, *Diary*, February 18, 1865, 36.

2. Moore, *de Veaux*, xxix; and several pictures of postconflagration Columbia, Graydon, *Tales of Columbia*.

3. Moore, *de Veaux*, xx, xxx; Richard M. Jellison and Phillip S. Swartz,

"The Scientific Interests of Robert W. Gibbes," *South Carolina Historical Magazine 66* (April 1965): 77–97; and Gibbes, *Who Burnt Columbia?* 20.

4. Osborn, Harwell, and Racine, *Fiery Trail,* 135, entry, February 18, 1865; and Elizabeth Frost-Knappman and Kathryn Cullen-DuPont, *Women's Suffrage in America* (New York: Facts on File, 2005), 159.

5. Ethel Battle, handwritten notes about her mother, Ethland, Wilson-Battle-Connell-Park Papers; "Living Descendant's Letter"; and Mitchell, "Feaster."

6. Amelia Feaster, Philadelphia, Pennsylvania, sworn affidavits, Philadelphia and New York; Feaster, Howard, and Terry to Lincoln; "Emlen N. Carpenter, Captain Sixth Pennsylvania Cavalry," sworn statement, *Report,* Sherman, 448; Howard, *Autobiography,* 120; and Howard to Mrs. Howard, Fayetteville, NC, ca. March 12, 1865, Oliver Otis Howard Papers, Bowdoin College Library, Brunswick, Maine.

7. Feaster, Howard, and Terry to Lincoln; Howard, *Autobiography,* 127; and Brevet Major George Ward Nichols, *The Story of the Great March: From the Diary of a Staff Officer* (New York: Harper, 1865), 209.

8. Gibbes, "Burning of Columbia" and *Who Burnt Columbia?* 20–21.

9. Taylor, "Two Equipages," 252–53.

10. Se De Kay, "Burning and Sacking of Columbia" (Augusta, Georgia) *Daily Constitutionalist,* March 10, 1865.

11. Coker, "Sandal or Scandal," 15.

12. Dickert, "Sorceress of Congaree."

13. Chesnut and Woodward, *Chestnut's Civil War,* March 10, 1865, 753–54; and Chesnut and Williams, *Diary from Dixie,* 502. Also quoted in Elmore, *Scandalous,* 38.

14. De Kay, "Burning and Sacking"; Se De Kay, "On Dit" (Augusta, Georgia) *Daily Constitutionalist,* April 5, 1865; and "Columbia: Miss Boozer," *Macon Telegraph,* April 10, 1865.

15. Trumbull, "Four Naval," 38.

16. Gibbes, "Burning of Columbia" and *Who Burnt Columbia?* 20–21.

17. Howard, Autobiography, 134–135.

18. Janet Zollinger Giele, *Two Paths to Women's Equality: Temperance, Suffrage, and the Origins of Modern Feminism* (New York: Twayne, 1995), 36; and "Women Artists," Southern Review 5, no. 10 (April 1869): 319. Madlyn Millner Kahr also quotes this in "Women as Artists and Women's Art," *Woman's Art Journal* 36, no. 2 (Autumn 1982–Winter 1983): 28.

Notes to Chapter Six

1. Manly Wade Wellman, *The County of Moore, 1847–1947: A North Carolina Region's Second Hundred Years* (Southern Pines, NC, Moore County Historical Association, 1962), 63.

2. Feaster affidavit, Stevens, *Frazee,* 20–21, 25; and "Carpenter, Captain, Sixth Pennsylvania Cavalry," Fayetteville, NC, March 12, 1865, sworn statement, *Report.*

3. Sherman, *Memoir,* 768–70. Emphasis in quote is the author's.

4. Poppenheim, "Experiences with Sherman at Liberty Hill," February 23, 1865, Taylor, et al, *South Carolina Women,* 259; and Coker, "Sandal or Scandal," 17–18.

5. Osborn, Harwell, and Racine, *Fiery Trail,* 144.

6. Feaster, Howard, and Terry to Lincoln; and Howard to Mrs. Howard, ca. March 12, 1865.

7. Edward L. Wells, "Charleston Light Dragoon, A Morning Call on General Kilpatrick," March 1884, in Reverend J. William Jones, ed., Southern Historical Society Papers, Tufts University, accessed September 2, 2012, http://www.perseus.tufts.edu/hopper/text?doc=Perseus%3Atext%3A2001. 05.0269%3Achapter%3D35; Edward L. Wells, *A Sketch of the Charleston Light Dragoons, from the Earliest Formation of the Corps* (Charleston, SC: Lucas, Richardson, & Co., 1888), 88–90; and Edward L. Wells, Hampton and His Cavalry (Richmond: Johnson, 1899), 401–2, 409.

8. 1911 Report by Joseph A. Jones, Birmingham, AL, Company K, 51st Alabama, Partisan Rangers, *Confederate Veteran* 19 (9): 434.

9. J. W. Du Bose, "Fayetteville (NC) Road Fight," *Confederate Veteran* 20, February 1912, 84–86.

10. Lawrence W. Taylor, "Boy Soldiers of the Confederacy," Columbia, SC, July 7, 1916, South Carolina Division, M. C. Butler Chapter, UDC, Columbia, SC, *United Daughters of the Confederacy, Recollections and Reminiscences 1861–65* (1990), 7: 400–406.

11. John G. Barrett, *Sherman's March Through the Carolinas* (Chapel Hill: University of North Carolina Press, 1956, reprint 1996), 93, 128.

12. Burke Davis, *Sherman's March: The First Full-Length Narrative of General William T. Sherman's Devastating March through Georgia and the Carolinas* (New York: Random House, 1980, reprint, Vintage, 1988), 201–19.

13. Osborn, Harwell, and Racine, *Fiery Trail,* 176, note 3.

14. Samuel J. Martin, *Kill-Cavalry: The Life of Union General Hugh Judson*

Kilpatrick (Mechanicsburg: Stackpole, 2000), 217–18.

15. Mark L. Bradley, *This Astounding Close: The Road to Bennett Place* (Chapel Hill: University of North Carolina Press, 2000), 306, note 38; and Eric J. Wittenberg, appendix C, "Who was Judson's Female Companion in March 1865," *Battle of Monroe's Crossroads and the Civil War's Final Campaign* (El Dorado Hills: Savas Beatie, 2005), 254.

16. John A. McGeachy, "In Sherman's Wake: Refugees of the March Through the Carolinas," North Carolina State University, History 546, May 2003, http://www4.ncsu.edu/~jam3/sherman.htm; E. L. Doctorow, *The March: A Novel* (New York: Random House, 2005), 226–38; and Davis, *Sherman's March*, 211–19.

17. James E. Wise, *On Sherman's Trail: The Civil War's North Carolina Climax* (Charleston: History Press, 2008), 61–62.

Notes to Chapter Seven

1. Howard to Mrs. Howard, ca. March 12, 1865, Howard Papers, Bowdoin College; letter reprinted in note 2 in Osborn, Harwell, and Racine, *Fiery Trail*, 181.

2. Ibid.

3. Howard, Autobiography, 127–30, 134; and Osborn, Harwell, and Racine, *Fiery Trail*, 148–54.

4. Howard to Mrs. Howard; and Nichols, *Great March*, 209.

5. Howard to Mrs. Howard; and Howard, *Autobiography*, 127–30, 134.

6. Howard to Mrs. Howard; and Osborn, Harwell, and Racine, *Fiery Trail*, 181.

7. Howard, *Autobiography*, 136; and Pattie Lambert, "She Only Left a Burning Trail," review of *La Belle* (quoting a former Confederate scout's writings), *Rocky Mount Evening Telegram*, September 6, 1959.

8. Sherman, *Memoirs*, 777.

9. Conyngham, March, 359; Osborn, Harwell, and Racine, *Fiery Trail*, 179; and Howard to Mrs. Howard.

10. Conyngham, *March*, 358.

11. Feaster, Howard, and Terry to Lincoln.

12. Sabre, *Nineteen Months*, 172.

13. "Arrivals at the Hotels," *Illustrated New Age*, March 23, 1865.

14. Selby, *Countess Pourtales*, 28.

15. M. Pourtalès to Wilson, July 1, 1885, Wilson-Battle-Connell-Park Papers.

16. "Loyal South Carolina Lady"; "City Affairs"; and Daniel Rolph, "The Plot to Burn Philadelphia to the Ground at the End of the Civil War," Historical Society of Pennsylvania, accessed March 4, 2014, https://hsp.org/blogs/history-hits/the-plot-to-burn-philadelphia-to-the-ground-at-the-end-of-the-civil-war.

17. "Loyal South Carolina Lady"; "City Affairs"; and "Loyal Woman."

18. Ibid.

19. Anthony, "Report," 1; Feaster affidavits, Stevens, *Frazee,* 20; Mitchell, "Feaster"; Reed and Wilson DAR genealogical records, New York City Directory, 1857, 743; and genealogic information, Reed Family Papers, collection of J. Reed Bradford.

NOTES TO CHAPTER EIGHT

1. "Journal of the Senate," June 26, 1866, *Congressional Serial Set* (Washington, DC: Government Printing Office, 1866), 573.

2. Battle to Graydon; "Living Descendant"; and Battle to Coker, November 19, 1959.

3. "Count Pourtales' Wife," *San Francisco Chronicle,* February 20, 1876; "The Corcoran Reception," *New York Times,* August 19, 1862; "About Us: History of the Union League Club," Union League Club Web Site, accessed August 26, 2012, http://www.unionleagueclub.org/Default.aspx?p=DynamicModule&pageid=292355&ssid=172851&vnf=1; Wellman, "Mary"; Anthony, "Report"; and "Thomas Murphy Dead," *New York Tribune,* August 19, 1901.

4. Gibbes, *Who Burnt Columbia?* 21.

5. Gibbes, *Who Burnt Columbia?* 21, "Journal of the Senate," 573, 857, 971; and *Report,* Index, xiii; Selby, in *Checkered Life,* 29, also claims Amelia set herself up as a widow in New York.

6. "Journal," 573; Feaster, Howard, and Terry to Lincoln; and E. M Stanton, Secretary of War, statement before Congress, *Report,* 3. Howard had also presented this plea in Feaster, Howard, and Terry to Lincoln.

7. *Report* and Senate of the United States, Thirty-ninth Congress, First Session, Bill for the relief of Mrs. Amelia Feaster, of Columbia, South Carolina, S. 434, July 16, 1866, Library of Congress, U.S. Congressional Documents and Debates, 1774–1875; and "Relief for Southern People, Report of Senate Hearings," *Springfield Republican,* July 19, 1866.

8. *Journal of the House of Representatives,* December 17, 1866, 94; "Legislative," Daily Eastern Argus (Portland, Maine); and Mitchell, "Feaster." Mitchell lived nearby her cousins Ethland and Julia in Florida.

9. Taylor, "Two Equipages," 253.

10. Yates Snowden and John Bennett, *Two Scholarly Friends: Yates Snowden—John Bennett, Correspondence,* 1902–1932, ed. Mary Crow Anderson (Columbia: University of South Carolina Press, 1993), 355, citing Dr. J. Rion McKissick; and "About The Daily Phoenix," (Columbia, S.C.) 1865–1878," Chronicling America, Library of Congress, accessed July 9, 2012, http://www.loc.gov/index.html.

11. Selby, *Phoenix,* first issue, July 31, 1865.

12. Selby, "Feeding the Prisoners," *Phoenix,* July 22, 1866.

13. Graydon, *Tales of Columbia,* 127.

NOTES TO CHAPTER NINE

1. Trow's *New York City Directory,* 1865, 68; John S. Beecher vs. Marie A. Beecher, Judgment of Divorce, July 18, 1874, Court of Common Pleas, New York; Beecher's passport applications, 1863, 1872, 1891, ancestry. com (signatures match divorce judgment); U.S. IRS Tax Assessment Lists, 1862–1918 for J. S. Beecher, 1863, ancestry.com; "The Income Taxes," *New York World,* January 20, 1865; and "Count Pourtales' Wife."

2. "Devoted Woman."

3. Preston describes his father in P. Beecher to Ethel Field Reed (Julia Feaster Field's daughter), August 17, 1923, courtesy of J. Reed Bradford; John S. Beecher's passport applications wherein he describes himself; "Our Western Department: Edited at Louisville, Kentucky," *Bonfort's Wine and Spirit Circular,* November 10, 1889, 15; and "Devoted Woman."

4. *Trow's New York City Directory,* 1865, obituary; Deposition of Frederick E. Ives, Beecher vs. Beecher, divorce hearing, June 29, 1874, Court of Common Pleas, New York County; "Frederick E. Ives," *New York Times,* June 13, 1894; and "Devoted Woman."

5. Beecher v. Beecher and Matthew Spady, "Audubon Park: A Brief History to 1886," accessed June 29, 2012 and August 23, 2016, http://www.audubonparkny.com/AudubonParkBriefHistory.html#anchor_174.

6. M. Pourtalès to Wilson, March 18, 1884; and "Devoted Woman."

7. Ibid.

8. New York, New York, City Directory, 1872, 80, ancestry.com; M. Pourtales to Wilson, July 1, 1885, Wilson-Battle-Connell-Park Papers; and P. Beecher to Reed, July 17, 1923.

9. "American Jockey Club Races," *New York Herald,* June 7, 1872.

10. Madelin Terrazas, archives assistant, Churchill Archives Centre, Churchill College, email message to author, June 1, 2012; Mitchell, "Feaster," copying a letter from Preston Beecher to Ethel Reed dated September 1, 1921; and P. Beecher to Wilson, March 6, 1908, Wilson-Battle-Connell-Park papers.

11. "Jockey Club Races"; and "Count Pourtales' Wife."

12. P. Beecher to Reed, August 17, 1923; and inscribed packet of Preston's baby hair, Wilson-Battle-Connell-Park Papers.

13. Snyder, Sees family record; Carr Bible record; *Journal of the House,* December 17, 1866, 94; and Mitchell, "Feaster."

14. P. Beecher to Wilson, March 6, 1908, Wilson-Battle-Connell-Park Papers; and Thomas Manning, "Brooklyn Yacht Club" in *Manning's Yachting Annual* (New York: John Filmer, 1875), 53. Beecher's yacht was the *Petrel,* built in 1869.

15. "Living Descendant"; Mitchell, "Feaster"; and undated pamphlet, Academy of the Sacred Heart, Wilson-Battle-Connell-Park Papers.

16. Beecher to Reed, August 17, 1923; and Ziarko, telephone interview with author, September 7, 2012.

17. United States Federal Census Mortality Schedule, 1850–85, ancestry.com; Burial record for Amelia Sees Feaster, Historical Society of Pennsylvania, Daughters of the American Revolution, ancestry.com; Selby, *Countess Pourtales,* 1915, 49; and Woodlands Cemetery records, death certificate issued for Mary Sees, Philadelphia Death Certificates, ancestry.com.

18. Ethel Wilson Battle, "Remembrance of Old Titusville by an Eighty-Four-Year-Old Native," handwritten manuscript, 1973, Wilson-Battle-Connell-Park Papers, and typed manuscript, 1974, Ethel Battle Papers, North Brevard Historical Society; Mitchell, "Feaster"; and Battle to Rosson, March 1, 1960, Etta Rosson Notes.

19. Ibid.

20. James Plemon Coleman, T*he Robert Coleman Family from Virginia to Texas, 1652–1965,* accessed November 12, 2012, http://freepages.genealogy.rootsweb.ancestry.com/~nansemondcolemans/chascity/robtvatx.txt, 298–99; Battle, "Remembrance"; L. C. Crofton, "Speech at LaGrange Church, March 6, 1942," Wilson-Battle-Connell-Park Papers; Scott O'Hara, "School Days," *Star Advocate,* September 24, 1980; United States Federal Census, 1870; obituary, Julia Feaster Coleman, *Star Advocate,* June 13, 1919; and Feaster genealogy and family records, Wilson-Battle-Connell-Park Papers.

21. Superior Court of New York, Abraham B. Clark v. Abraham Bininger, *American Law Register*, 18, No. 5, May 1870 (Philadelphia: University of Pennsylvania Law Review): 304–10 and New York (State) Judiciary Committee, *Proceedings in the Senate on the Investigation of the Charges Preferred against John H. McCunn* (Albany: Reed, Parsons, 1874), 4, 399–458.

22. Ibid.

23. Answer from Marie A. Beecher, John S. Beecher against Marie A. Beecher, filed by Fullerton, Knox, and Crosby, received by the Court of Common Pleas on May 8, 1873, Clerk of New York County.

Notes to Chapter Ten

1. Emily Thornwell, *The Lady's Guide to Perfect Gentility, in Manners, Dress and Conversation* (New York: Derby and Jackson, 1856), 146.

2. "Lloyd Phoenix," *New York Times*, April 1, 1926; and *Important Men of 1913*, database after *Builders of Our Nation: Men of 1913* (Chicago: Men of 1913, 1914), 380, ancestry.com.

3. National Archives and Records Administration, U.S. Military and Naval Academies, Cadet Records and Applications, 1805–1908 Record for Lloyd Phoenix, Vol. 350, 1857–1858, 274, ancestry.com.

4. "Lloyd Phoenix"; and *Important Men*, 380.

5. G. W. Blunt White to Coker, February 15, 1958, Coker papers, box 8, folder 650; and "Lloyd Phoenix," *New York Times*, April 1, 1926.

6. "Yachting Notes," *New York Herald*, June 10, 1872; "New Intrepid Now About Ready," *New York Herald*, April 9, 1893; Pat Schaefer, Collections Access and Research, Mystic Seaport, email message to author, July 21, 2012; and *Important Men*, 380.

7. Melville Elijah Stone II to Coker, November 3, 1957, Coker Papers, box 8, folder 651; *Club Men of New York: Their Occupations, and Business and Home Addresses* (New York: Republic Press, 1893), 79, 362; Wallingsford, "Letter from New York," *Baltimore Bulletin*, May 23, 1874; "Count Pourtales' Wife"; and Horace A. Laffaye, *Polo in the United States: A History* (Jefferson NC: McFarland, 2011), 7.

8. Wallingsford, "Letter"; and Laffaye, *Polo*.

9. Advertisement, "Charity Ball, List of Managers," *Commercial Advertiser*, January 9, 1873.

10. "Count Pourtales' Wife."

11. Eva McDonald, Daniel McDonald, and Harriet Blackford, *Fanny Lear:*

Love and Scandal in Tsarist Russia (Bloomington: IUniverse, 2011), 1.

12. "Phoenix," Hattie Blackford in an interview in Paris, *Augusta Chronicle,* September 27, 1874; and Harriet "Hattie" Ely Blackford, a.k.a. Fanny Lear, *Le Roman d'une Americaine en Russie: Accompagné de Lettres Originales* (Brussels: A. LaCroix, 1875), 118–214.

13. McDonald, McDonald, and Blackford, *Fanny Lear,* 3; Eva McDonald, email message to author, August 19, 2012; and "Fanny Lear, Adventuress," Philadelphia correspondent's letter, May 8, 1886, *New York Sun,* May 18, 1886.

14. McDonald, email, August 19, 2012; "Dangerous Man," *Iowa State Reporter,* March 27, 1886; "Russian Scandal," *Neosho Valley Register,* June 27, 1874; and "An Imperial Liaison," *New York Times,* May 8, 1886.

15. "Phoenix" and Blackford, *Roman,* 16.

16. McDonald, McDonald, and Blackford, *Fanny Lear,* 4.

17. Robert T. Swaine, *Cravath Firm and Its Predecessors, 1819–1947* (New York: Ad Press, 1948), reprint (Clark: Lawbook Exchange, 2006), 1: 294.

18. Answer, Beecher vs. Beecher, and Swaine, *Cravath,* 294.

19. Swaine, *Cravath Firm,* 294. The firm refers to the "only article" they could not suppress—"Female Revenge: A Lady Shoots her Betrayer on Madison Avenue," *Sunday Mercury,* November 9, 1873 (full article also included in author's research).

20. Note by Mary Mitchell Ellington, Lena Norwood Mitchell's daughter, in Mitchell, "Feaster"; Battle to Graydon; "Living Descendant"; Tutu Feaster prayer book, Paris, March 30, 1872; and Tutu's compositions in French, dated 1872 and 1873, Wilson-Battle-Connell-Park Papers.

21. Swaine, *Cravath,* 294; and "Americans Abroad (for the week ending June 3, 1871).

22. Swaine, *Cravath,* 294.

23. Saine, *Cravath,* 295; and "Count Pourtales' Wife."

24. Summons and Complaint, April 9, 1873, folio one, 4, Beecher vs. Beecher; and "Devoted Woman."

25. Deposition of Charles Fleurry, referee's report, July 11, 1874; and Judgment of Divorce, Beecher vs. Beecher.

26. Ibid.

NOTES TO CHAPTER ELEVEN

1. Alexandre Dumas Jr., *Camille (La Dame Aux Camellias)* 1848, reprint (Whitefish: Kessinger, 2004), 65.

2. Summons and Complaint, Answer, May 8, 1873, Reply, May 12, 1873, Beecher vs. Beecher.

3. Ibid.

4. Eli Perkins, a.k.a. Eli Doloroso, a.k.a. Melville De Lancey Landon, letter to the *New York Graphic,* May 15, 1873.

5. "Count Pourtales' Wife"; "Wine and Spirits Trade Society," *New York Herald,* August 8, 1873; "Yachting Notes," *New York Herald,* August 2, 1873; "The Cruise of 73: The New York Yacht Club Squadron at Newport- the Yachtsmen at Divine Service," *New York Herald,* August 18, 1873; "Race of the N. Y. Y. C. Fleet for the Bennett Cup," *New York Herald,* August 22, 1873; and "Female Revenge."

6. Swaine, *Cravath,* 294; and "Female Revenge."

7. "Devoted Woman."

8. Nina Baym, *Woman's Fiction: A Guide to Novels by and About Women in America, 1820–70* (Chicago: University of Illinois Press, 1993) 184, 24–26.

9. Swaine, *Cravath,* 294; and "Female Revenge."

10. Ibid.

11. Swaine, *Cravath,* 294; "Female Revenge"; classified personal ad, *New York Herald,* November 4, 1873; "Count Pourtales' Wife"; and "Way of the World," *Lancaster Intelligencer,* April 14, 1880.

12. Joshua Ruff, curator of the New York City Police Museum, email message to author, May 7, 2012.

13. Swaine, *Cravath,* 294, 296.

14. Ibid.

15. Ibid., 295.

16. Seward to Phoenix, undated letter reprinted in Swaine, *Cravath,* 295.

17. Classified personal advertisement, *New York Herald,* November 4, 1873; and "Count Pourtales' Wife."

18. "Devoted Woman."

19. New York Correspondent, "Two Beautiful Americans," *Pittsburgh Chronicle,* reprinted in *Spirit Lake* (Iowa) *Beacon,* December 6, 1884.

20. Ibid.

21. Tutu (Ethland) Feaster, composition in French dated July 7, 1873, Wilson-Battle-Connell-Park Papers.

22. Feaster composition, invitation for a party at her Paris home, and handwritten invitation to join her literary society, Wilson-Battle-Connell-Park Papers.

Notes to Chapter Twelve

1. Thornwell, *Lady's Guide*, 79.

2. Swaine, *Cravath*, 295.

3. The hotel name differed among the British newspapers.

4. "Police," *London Times*, January 24, 1874, reprinted as "Extraordinary Scandal," *New York Times*, February 7, 1874; and "Highlife in London," *London Daily News*, January 18, 1874.

5. "Devoted Woman."

6. Old Bailey Proceedings Online (PDF), April 1874, Trial of Arthur Foster (30), #231 "Arthur Foster, Breaking Peace, Wounding, 7 April 1874," printed from www.oldbaileyonline.org, accessed June 7, 2012; "Police," January 24, 1874; and "Highlife in London."

7. "Police," *London Times*, February 7, 1874; and "Assault on a Hotel Proprietor," *Morning Post*, January 24, 1874 (London), January 24, 1874.

8. "Extraordinary Scandal" and "Assault on Hotel Proprietor."

9. "Highlife in London"; and "Curious Assault Case," *London Week News*, January 24, 1874.

10. "Extraordinary Scandal"; and "Assault on Hotel Proprietor."

11. "Highlife in London"; "Extraordinary Scandal"; and "Assault on Hotel Proprietor."

12. Ibid.

13. Ibid.

14. Ibid.; Cyril Pearl, *Girl with the Swansdown Seat*, (Indianapolis: Bobbs-Merrill, 1955), 96; and Katie Hickman, *Courtesans: Money, Sex and Fame in the Nineteenth Century* (New York: HarperCollins, 2003), 279.

15. "Police"; "Assault on Hotel Proprietor"; and "Highlife in London."

16. Ibid.

17. "Highlife in London."

18. "Extraordinary Scandal"; and "Assault on Hotel Proprietor."

19. Ibid.

20. Thornwell, *Lady's Guide*, 70, 72; "Extraordinary Scandal"; and "Assault on Hotel Proprietor."

21. "Extraordinary Scandal."

22. 'Assault on Hotel Proprietor."

23. "American Scandal," *New York Sun*, February 6, 1874; "Assault on Hotel Proprietor"; and "Extraordinary Scandal."

24. "Police"; and "Assault on Hotel Proprietor."

25. Ibid.

26. Central Criminal Court, April 7, 1874, Old Bailey Proceedings Online; "Extraordinary Assault on Hotel Keeper," *Manchester Weekly Times*, February 14, 1874 (British Library Board); "Legal Amalgamation," *Central Press* (London), February 16, 1874; and "Extraordinary Case of Assault," *Lloyds Weekly Newspaper*, February 8, 1874.

27. "Police"; and "Extraordinary Assault on Hotel Keeper."

28. Old Bailey Proceedings Online; and *Guardian* (London), April 8, 1874, 11.

29. Swaine, *Cravath*, 295–96.

Notes to Chapter Thirteen

1. Thornwell, *Lady's Guide*, 78.

2. "Beecher, Marie," October 15, 1875, *Répertoire de Personnes, Police des Moeurs*, reprinted in Gabrielle Houbre, *Le Livre des Courtisanes: Archives Secrètes de la Police des Moeurs, 1861–1876* (Paris: Taillandier, 2006), 480, translated by Patrick Morvan.

3. "Mebel Gray" [sic], in Houbre, *Courtisanes*, 120; and J. P. Weatherby et al, eds., *The Racing Calendar for the Year 1874* (London: Weatherby, 1874), 50–51.

4. M. Pourtalès to Wilson, March 18, 1884, Wilson-Battle-Connell-Park Papers; and "Beecher, Marie," in Houbre, *Courtisanes*, 480.

5. Summons and Complaint, Reply, Beecher vs. Beecher; New York Passenger Lists: *Spain*, departing Liverpool, arriving in New York, May 25, 1874, and *Donau*, departing Bremen with a stop in Southampton, arriving in New York, June 10, 1874 and Baltimore, ancestry.com; advertisement, *Baltimore Bulletin*, August 23, 1873; and "Shipping News," *New York Herald*, July 27, 1875.

6. Summons, June 26, 1874, to appear on June 29, 1874, Court of Common Pleas and Judgment of Divorce, Beecher vs. Beecher, July 21, 1874.

7. Ibid.

8. Gould H. Thorp against Laura M. Thorp, Divorce Judgment, January 10, 1880, Superior Court, New York County Clerk; "Creatore v. Creatore," Supreme Court Appellate Division New York (New York, Brown, 1909), 50; and "Thorp Divorce Suit," *New York Times*, December 30, 1880.

9. M. Pourtalès to Wilson, March 18, 1884, Wilson-Battle-Connell-Park Papers. Also quoted in Elmore, *Scandalous*, 53.

10. "Beecher, Marie, Juin 1875," in Houbre, *Courtisanes*, 469–70.

Notes to Chapter Fourteen

1. Ada Clare, "Love," *New York Leader*, reprint *Saturday Evening Post*, May 4, 1861.

2. Mary McAuliffe, *Dawn of the Belle Époque: The Paris of Monet, Zola, Bernhardt, Eiffel, Debussy, Clemenceau, and their Friends* (Lanham, MD: Rowan and Littlefield, 2011), 56, 63, 67, 70, 83, 84, 106.

3. "Beecher, Marie, Juin 1875," fiche 795, Prefecture de Police, Paris; also reprinted in Houbre, *Courtisanes*, 469–70.

4. George Drysdale, *Elements of Social Science or Physical, Sexual, or Natural Religion* (1861, reprint London: E. Truelove, 1877), 241.

5. "Beecher, Marie, Juin 1875"; and Virginia Rounding, *Grandes Horizontales: The Lives and Legends of Four Nineteenth Century Courtesans* (New York: Bloomsbury, 2003), 9–10.

6. Houbre, *Courtisanes*, 36–39; and Hickman, *Courtesans*, 8–12.

7. Rounding, *Grandes Horizontales*, 9–10; Cora Pearl (Emma Crouch), *The Memoirs of Cora Pearl: The English Beauty of the French Empire* (London: Vickers, 1890), 10, 15; "Cruch [sic] Emma, *dite* Cora Pearl," "*Registre de la Police des Moeurs*," in Houbre, *Courtisanes*, 213–22.

8. Houbre, *Courtisanes*, 213, 219–22; Hugh Evelyn Wortham, *Edward VII, Man and King* (Boston: Little Brown, 1931), 116; and Rounding, *Grandes Horizontales*, 292–93.

9. McDonald, McDonald, and Blackford, *Fanny Lear*, 272–73; and Blackford, *Roman*, 312–29.

10. Franzisca, Baroness von Hedemann, *Love Stories of Court Beauties* (New York: Doran, 1917), 63.

11. "Phoenix" and "Blackfort" [sic], January 1874, in Houbre, *Courtisanes*, 370.

12. Franzisca, *Love Stories*, 63.

13. M. Pourtalès to Wilson, March 18, 1884; "Beecher," fiche 795; "Gossip,"

Daily Graphic, November 13, 1875; "A Parisian Scandal," *New York Times,* October 24, 1875; and "Count Portales," interview with Marie, *San Francisco Chronicle,* February 9, 1876 (citing a January 16, 1876 correspondent's report).

14. "Blackfort" [sic], December 21, 1874, 372–73, in Houbre, *Courtisanes*; and McDonald McDonald, and Blackford, *Fanny Lear,* 265.

15. Houbre, *Courtisanes,* 13–14, 45, translated by Leo Mavrovitis.

16. Ibid., 15, 33–34, translated by Mavrovitis and Philippe Brian.

17. Ibid., 12, 41.

18. Houbre, *Courtisanes,* 22; and "Beecher, Marie, *Juin* 1875," in Houbre, *Courtisanes,* 469–470, translated by Morvan.

19. Ibid.

20. "Beecher, Marie," *Octobre* 15, 1875, in Houbre, *Courtisanes,* 479–80, translated by Morvan.

21. Ibid.

22. Houbre, *Courtisanes,* 9–10, translated by Mavrovitis.

23. Joseph Florimond Loubat, ed., *A Yachtsman's Scrap Book: Or, The Ups and Downs of Yacht Racing* (New York: Brentano, 1887), 218; and "Beecher, Marie," *Octobre* 15, 1875, 479–80 in Houbre, *Courtisanes.*

24. Blackford, *Roman,* 275; and "Blackfort," January 1874, Houbre, *Courtisanes,* 372, 374.

25. M. Pourtalès to Wilson, March 18, 1884; and "Beecher, Marie," in Houbre, *Courtisanes,* 479–80.

26. Carol A. Mossman, *Writing with a Vengeance: The Countess de Chabrillan's Rise from Prostitution* (Toronto: University of Toronto Press, 2009), 70; Alfred Ernest Crawley quoting the New English Dictionary (1888) in "The Orgy," in Theodore Besterman, ed., *Studies of Savages and Sex* (New York: Dutton, 1929, reprint Whitefish, MT: Kessinger, 2006), 5, 105.

27. Alastair J. L. Blanshard, *Sex: Vice and Love from Antiquity to Modernity* (Malden, MA: Wiley-Blackwell, 2010), 63.

28. McDonald, McDonald, and Blackford, *Fanny Lear,* 262, 269; Eva McDonald, email message to author, August 20, 2012; and Hickman, *Courtesans,* 275.

29. "Beecher, Marie."

Notes to Chapter Fifteen

1. P. Beecher to Reed, September 1, 1921, copied by Lena Norwood Mitchell in "Feaster."

2. Coker, "Sandal or Scandal," 35; Anne Sebba, *American Jennie: The Remarkable Life of Lady Randolph Churchill* (New York: Norton, 2007), 81–82; Mrs. George Cornwallis-West, *The Reminiscences of Lady Randolph Churchill* (New York: Century, 1909), 6; and "Railroad King: Ungrateful Son-in-Law," *San Francisco Chronicle,* January 30, 1876.

3. Genealogy, Arthur de Pourtalès-Gorgier, *Société Genevoise de Généalogie*, accessed May 3, 2012, http://www.gen-gen.ch/de-POURTALÈS-Arthur de/; Marquis of Ruvigny, *Titled Nobility of Europe* (London: Harrison & Sons, 1914), 1172; Beecher to Reed, September 1, 1921; and M. Pourtalès to Wilson, March 18, 1884, Wilson-Battle-Connell-Park Papers.

4. "Fribourg: *Le château de la Corbière près Estavayer-le-Lac*," Swiss Castles, accessed July 7, 2012, http://www.swisscastles.ch/fribourg/lacorbiere. html; and "Comte James Alexandre de Pourtalès-Gorgier (collector; merchant/financier; French; Male; 1776–1855)," Collections Database, British Museum, accessed July 7, 2012, www.britishmuseum.org.

5. Obituary, Jenny L. Holladay, *London American Register,* June 21, 1873; "Baroness de Bussiere," *New York Tribune,* December 17, 1877; "Devoted Woman"; "Miss Bennett," *London American Register,* August 5, 1876; and Annie Gold, "Manhattanville College and Ophir Farm, accessed March 1, 2014, http://www.mville.edu/images/stories/About/VisitTheCampus/Ophir-Farm-History.pdf.

6. "Fine Arts," *American Annual Cyclopædia and Register of Important Events of 1865* (New York: Appleton, 1866), 5: 353–54.

7. "Marriage a la Mode," *Pittsfield Sun,* January 27, 1870.

8. A. Pourtalès to E. Wilson, March 16, 1908, Wilson-Battle-Connell-Park Papers; "Marriage a la Mode"; "Maria-Pauline Louise De Pourtalès," International Genealogical Index (Asia); United States Court of Appeals, Ninth Circuit, Transcript of Records, no. 2181, Oregon & California Railroad Company vs. Maria de Grubissich; and "Maria de Grubissich, née Maria de Pourtales," *Oregon State Journal,* May 24, 1873.

9. Obituary, Jenny L. Holladay, *Oregon State Journal,* May 24, 1873; "Mrs. Ben Holladay's Will," *San Francisco Bulletin,* January 6, 1874; "Circuit Court Calendar," Oregonian (Portland), June 5, 1874; "Personalities," *Wisconsin State Journal,* May 19. 1873; and Ellis Lucia, *The Saga of Ben Holladay: Giant of the Old West* (New York: Hastings House, 1959), 319.

10. Neuchâtel, Switzerland, "Séance du 14 Mars 1877," *Recours des Citoyens Pourtalès Recueil des Arrêts Rendus par la Cour de Cassation Civile de la Canton De Neuchâtel* (Canton Neuchâtel: Montandon, 1881), 1: 295–300.

11. "Fashionable Entertainments," *Morning Post* (London), May 12, 1875, and July 25, 1875; and "Pourtalès-Gorgier (Arthur, comte de)," *Annuaire diplomatique et consulaire de la République française* (Paris Berger-Levrault, 1886), 8: 202.

12. England and Wales, Free BMD Marriage Index, 1837–1915, Volume 1a, 616, ancestry.com; marriage certificate (certified copy), Marie Adèle Beecher and Count Arthur de Pourtales-Gorgier, number 397, November 4, 1875, General Register's Office, England; "Devoted Woman"; M. Pourtalès to Wilson, March 18, 1884, Wilson-Battle-Connell-Park Papers; "Hotel Arrivals," *New York Herald*, December 12, 1875, and "Railroad King."

13. "Devoted Woman"; and "Railroad King."

14. "Devoted Woman"; and New York passenger lists, *Klopstock*, December 6, 1875, departed from Le Havre, ancestry.com.

15. Craig Stein Esq., Stein and Stein PA, interview with author, October 16, 2012; Beecher vs. Beecher; William Wait, *The Practice at Law: In Equity, and in Special Proceedings, in All the Courts in the State of New York* (Albany: Gould, 1874), 3: 628; "Creatore v. Creatore," 50; and "Devoted Woman."

16. "Railroad King."

17. P. Beecher to Reed, August 17, 1923, Reed Family Papers, collection of J. Reed Bradford; and "Club and Society Gossip," *New York Daily Graphic*, December 24, 1875.

NOTES TO CHAPTER SIXTEEN

1. *Klopstock* passenger list.

2. "Hotel Arrivals"; and "Railroad King."

3. "Club and Society Gossip," *New York Daily Graphic*, November 13, 1875, December 11, 1875; "Railroad King"; and Geoff Wexler, library director, Oregon Historical Society, telephone interview with author, July 5, 2012.

4. "Claim of Ben Holladay, Affidavit of George K. Otis," Congressional Edition, United States, sworn and signed February 12, 1874, Miscellaneous Documents, United States Senate (Washington, DC: Government Printing Office, 1880), 86; and "Burying Ben Holladay's Daughter," undated clipping, Ben Holladay Papers, Mss 893, box 1, folder 6, Oregon Historical Society.

5. "Railroad King." Also quoted in Elmore, *Scandalous*, 57.

6. Interview with Marie in "Count de Pourtales," *San Francisco Chronicle*, February 9, 1876.

7. "Railroad King."

8. "Devoted Woman"; and "Railroad King"

9. "Devoted Woman."

10. Ibid.

11. Ibid.

12. Ibid.

13. Ibid.

14. Ibid.

15. Ibid.

16. "Devoted Woman"; and "Lloyd Phoenix."

17. Joan Perkin, *Victorian Women* (New York: NYU Press, 1995), 98.

18. "Devoted Woman."

19. Ibid.

20. Ibid. A topographical three-volume set of books by George Bernard Depping was sold by Sotheby's London, November 13, 2008, accessed September 27, 2012, http://www.sothebys.com. The provenance was Comtesse Arthur de Pourtalès-Gorgier, Château Gorgier, Switzerland, 1878.

21. "Devoted Woman"; and Alexander Moore, emails to author during editing, March 18–19, 2015.

22. Pourtalès-Gorgier Genealogy, *Société Genevoise; Ruvigny, Titled Nobility*, 1172; and "List of American Women who have Married Foreigners," *Hearings before the Committee on Immigration and Naturalization*, 66th Congress (Washington, DC: United States Congress, 1919), 47; "American Girl Abroad," *Library of Tribune Extras*, July 1889, 93.

23. Packet labeled "Preston's hair, eight years old," conjoined with the packet of baby hair, Wilson-Battle-Connell-Park Papers.

24. "Count de Pourtales."

25. Ibid.

26. "Count de Pourtales"; and "Count Pourtales' Wife."

27. "Count de Pourtales."

28. Ibid.

29. Ibid.

30. "Railroad King"; and *Chicago Times* clipping, February 12, 1876, Ben

Holladay Papers, MSS 893, box 1, folder 6, Oregon Historical Society.

31. "Railroad King"; *Chicago Times* clipping; and "Devoted Woman."

Notes to Chapter Seventeen

1. Samuel Joseph Field, autobiographical manuscript, September 1, 1895, Bradford collection.

2. Mitchell, "Feaster"; and Manning, *Feaster Family of LaGrange*, 4.

3. "Living Descendant's Letter."

4. Battle, manuscript; obituary, Benjamin Rush Wilson MD, *East Coast Advocate*, July 25, 1913; and Mitchell, "Feaster."

5. Field, autobiographical manuscript; Ethel Field Reed, listing in the National Society of the Daughters of the American Revolution, 112:75; and military papers, Reed Family Papers, collection of J. Reed Bradford.

6. Ethel Battle, "Born to Ethland Wilson," handwritten undated genealogy, Wilson-Battle-Connell-Park Papers.

7. A. Pourtalès to E. Wilson, March 16, 1908; Battle, genealogy; and Feaster genealogy.

8. "Count Pourtales' Wife," *San Francisco Chronicle*, February 20, 1876; Chicago Times clipping; James Vincent Frederick, *Ben Holladay: The Stage Coach King* (Glendale, CA: Arthur H. Clark Company, 1940), 135, 196, 198, 261; Selby, *A Checkered Life* (Columbia: Phoenix, 1878), microfiche, 19–23; and Graydon, *Jezebel*, 212.

9. "Count Pourtales' Wife."

10. Ibid.

11. Ibid.

12. "Count Pourtales' Wife"; "Mebel Gray" [sic], in Houbre, *Courtisanes*, 120–21; Blackford, *Roman*, 32–34; and McDonald, McDonald, and Blackford, *Fanny Lear*, 26–31. Several British publications in reporting on Hattie's memoir in 1875 referred to Fanny Lear as "Mrs. B_____."

13. Passenger list, arrivals in New York, April 15, 1874, ancestry.com; and McDonald, McDonald, and Blackford, *Fanny Lear*, 271–293.

14. Donn Piatt, "Miss Blackford," *Decatur Republican*, November 25, 1875.

15. "Count Pourtales' Wife"; Selby, *Checkered Life*, 23; and Selby and Snowden, *Countess Pourtales*, 60.

16. Louis Malzac, *"Branche de Gorgier," Les Pourtalès: Histoire d'une Famille Hugenote des Cevennes, 1500–1860* (Paris: Hatchette, 1914), tableau

VIII; "Count de Pourtales"; Alain Garric, "Essai de Généalogie: Arthur de Pourtalès-Gorgier," accessed June 4, 2012, http://gw.geneanet.org/garri c?lang=fr&p=arthur&n=de+pourtales; M. Pourtalès to Wilson, March 18, 1884, Wilson-Battle-Connell-Park Papers; and Thorp vs. Thorp.

17. "Arrivals at the Hotels," *New York Times,* May 10, 1876; *Cleveland Leader,* May 16, 1876; and "Columbia's Centennial," *Sacramento Daily Union,* May 20, 1876.

18. Sebba, *American Jennie,* 82.

19. State Archives, Pennsylvania Historical Commission and Museum, "Women's Pavilion," *Victorian Ideals of Gender,* (description of) albumen photograph, Centennial Photographic Company, December 1876, The Library Company, Philadelphia; Deborah C. Pollack, *Laura Woodward: The Artist Behind the Innovator Who Developed Palm Beach* (Blue Heron Press with the Historical Society of Palm Beach County, 2009), 16, 35–36; and "Women Working, 1800–1930: Centennial Exhibition in Philadelphia," Harvard University Library Open Collections Program, accessed July 8, 2012, http://ocp.hul.harvard.edu/ww/centennial.html.

20. Master's Report, Gould H. Thorp vs. Laura M. Thorp, January 10, 1880.

NOTES TO CHAPTER EIGHTEEN

1. M. Pourtalès to Wilson, January 18, 1878, Wilson-Battle-Connell-Park Papers. Elmore, *Scandalous,* 58, also quotes from this letter.

2. "Pourtalès-Gorgier (Arthur, comte de)," *Annuaire diplomatique,* 1901, 22: 250; M. Pourtalès to Wilson, January 18, 1878; Ethel Battle, Wilson family genealogy, Wilson-Battle-Connell Park Papers; and letter from Marie's relative in "Countess Pourtalès Not Killed," *New York Times,* October 29, 1884.

3. M. Pourtalès to Wilson.

4. Ibid.

5. Ibid.

6. Ibid.

7. Ibid.

8. Ibid.

9. Master's Report, Thorp vs. Thorp, January 10, 1880; "Phoenix-Thorp Case," reprinted sworn statements, *New York Evening Express,* ca. December 25, 1878 (indistinct date); "Mrs. Thorp's Complaint," (New York) *World,* December 27, 1878; "Highly Scented Scandal," *National Police Gazette,* January 11, 1879; and "Shooting of Mrs. Thorp," *New York Tribune,* March 30, 1884.

10. Ibid.

11. Ibid.

Notes to Chapter Nineteen

1. Selby, *Checkered Life*, reprint, *Countess Pourtales*, 44.

2. "Legislative," *Oregonian*, October 18, 1878.

3. M. Pourtalès to "Maralelle," undated (in French), private collection.

4. Coker, "Sandal or Scandal," 8.

5. John Hunter Selby (Julian Selby's son) to Coker, May 22, 1958, Coker Papers, box 8, folder 651; Snowden, Bennett, and Anderson, *Scholarly Friends*, 83; Lawrence, "Muchly Married"; Selby to Coker, May 22, 1958; and Coker, "Sandal or Scandal," 8.

6. Ada Clare, "Thoughts and Things," *Saturday Press*, April 21 and January 21, 1860; and Gloria Goldblatt, "The Queen of Bohemia Grew up in Charleston," *Carologue*, Autumn 1988, 10.

7. Facsimile of original title page, Selby, *Checkered Life*, 1878, reprinted in *Countess Pourtales*, frontispiece; and Selby and Snowden, *Countess Pourtales*, 19, 22, 27, 28.

8. Selby and Snowden, *Countess Pourtales*, 32–33, 47.

9. Blackford, *Roman*, 16; and "Cruch [sic] Emma, *dite* Cora Pearl," in Houbre, *Courtisanes*, 219–22.

10. Selby, *Countess Pourtales*, 35; Trepoff to the Envoy and Minister of the United States of America, April 16/28, 1874, in McDonald, McDonald, and Blackford, *Fanny Lear*, appendix I, A, 284.

11. "Cruch, Emma," in Houbre, *Courtisanes*, 220–21; and Selby, *Countess Pourtales*, 36, 37.

12. Selby, *Countess Pourtales*, 39–40.

13. Ibid., 51; and Graydon to Bolick, October 21, 1957, Coker Papers, box 8, folder 650.

14. Selby, *Countess Pourtales*, 43–44

15. Graydon, *Jezebel*, 218.

16. Ibid., 49.

17. Ibid.

18. "Pourtalès-Gorgier," *Annuaire diplomatique*, 202.

19. Selby, *Countess Pourtales*, 49.

20. Coker, "Sandal or Scandal," 26 (also partially quoted in Elmore, *Scandalous*,

68); and Graydon, *Jezebel*, 218.

21. Selby, *Countess Pourtales*, 61–62; and Coker, "Scandal or Scandal," 26.

22. Selby, *Countess Pourtales*, 64.

23. Graydon to Bolick, October 21, 1957.

Notes to Chapter Twenty

1. M. Pourtalès to Wilson, March 18, 1884, Wilson-Battle-Connell-Park Papers. Also quoted in Elmore, *Scandalous*, 64.

2. "Pourtalès-Gorgier (Arthur, comte de)," *Annuaire diplomatique*, 202; and *Courrier des Etats-Unis*, November 16, 1880.

3. Master's Report, Thorp vs. Thorp; "Shooting of Mrs. Thorp," correspondent to the *Philadelphia Times;* and "Way of the World: Gotham's Latest Bit of Scandal," *Lancaster Daily Intelligencer*, April 14, 1880.

4. Lewis Randolph Hamersly, *Men of Affairs in New York* (New York: L. R. Hamersly, 1906), 279.

5. "Beecher, John Preston," *Who's Who in New York City and State* (New York: Hamersley, 1904), 47; *Catalogue of Trinity School, Tivoli-on-the-Hudson, and English and Classical Boarding School for Boys*, 1877–78, unpaginated, ancestry.com; and P. Beecher to Wilson, March 6, 1908, Wilson-Battle-Connell-Park Papers.

6. Simon Winchester, *Krakatoa: The Day the World Exploded*, August 27, 1883 (New York: Harper Collins, 2003), 6.

7. M. Pourtalès to Wilson, March 18, 1884, Wilson-Battle-Connell-Park Papers. Also quoted in Elmore, *Scandalous*, 60.

8. Ibid.

9. Winchester, *Krakatoa*, 141.

10. M. Pourtalès to Wilson, March 18, 1884.

11. Ibid.

12. Ibid.

13. Ibid.

14. M. Pourtalès to Wilson, March 18, 1884, and September 12, 1904, Wilson-Battle-Connell-Park Papers.

15. M. Pourtalès to Wilson, March 18, 1884. Also quoted in Elmore, *Scandalous*, 60.

16. Ibid. Also quoted in Elmore, *Scandalous*, 64.

17. Ibid.

NOTES TO CHAPTER TWENTY-ONE

1. "Guillotined," *New York Truth*, October 26, 1884; "Poor Pourtales, Famous Beauty Bowstrung no Beheaded," *New York Truth,* October 27, 1884; "A Woman's Horrible Death," *New York Times*, October 27, 1884; "Poor Pourtales," *Charleston News and Courier,* October 30, 1884; "Beheaded in Japan," *Boston Daily Globe*, October 27, 1884; "Life's Romance," Biddeford (Maine) *Daily Journal,* October 28, 1884; and "Beheaded in Japan," *Wheeling* (West Virginia) *Register.*

2. William Shepard Walsh, *Handy-Book of Literary Curiosities* (Philadelphia: Lippincott, 1892), 473.

3. Michael Farquhar, *A Treasury of Deception: Liars, Misleaders, Hoodwinkers, and the Extraordinary True Stories of History's Greatest Hoaxes, Fakes, and Frauds* (New York: Penguin, 2005), 40; and Thomas Connery, "A Famous Newspaper Hoax," *Harper's Weekly*, June 3, 1893, 534–35.

4. "Beheaded in Japan"; and "Woman's Horrible Death."

5. "Guillotined."

6. "A Woman's Horrible Death,"

7. "Pour Pourtales"; and "Woman's Horrible Death."

8. Ibid.

9. "A Woman's Horrible Death."

10. "Beheaded in Japan."

11. *Macon Telegraph*, November 8, 1884; and "The Whole Story Denied," *Truth*, October 28, 1884.

12. "Countess Pourtalès not Killed"; and "Whole Story."

13. "A Sensation Spoiled," *New York Herald*, October 28, 1884.

14. "A Wayward Woman: She meets a Tragic Death in Japan after Startling and Shocking the People of Three Continents," *Kansas City Times*, October 28, 1884.

15. "Countess Portallis" [sic].

16. Stone to Coker, November 3, 1957; "Local Business Troubles," *New York Times,* March 14, 1883; "Financial Diary, 1883," *Manual of Statistics (New York: Financial News Association,* January 1884), 238; "Ives Beecher & Co. Schedule," April 11, 1883, *New York Times;* and "Mr. Cleveland's Escort," *New York Times*, March 3, 1893.

17. "History of Gorgier," Swiss Castles, accessed July 7, 2012, http://www.swisscastles.ch/neuchatel/gorgier.html; "Fribourg: Le château de La Corbière";

258

and M. Pourtalès to Wilson, July 1, 1885.

18. M. Pourtalès to Wilson, July 1, 1885.

19. Ibid.

20. Ibid.

21. Ibid.

22. Afgan Mehtiyev, "The Language of Diplomacy," *California Linguistic Notes* 35:2 (Spring 2010): 2. PDF supplied by California State University, Fullerton, accessed May 25, 2013, http://hss.fullerton.edu/linguistics/cln/ SP10PDF/MethievLgDplmcy.pdf; "Pourtalès-Gorgier (Arthur, Comte de)," *Annuaire diplomatique*, 250; "American Girl"; and M. Pourtalès to Wilson, September 12, 1904.

23. Snowden, Bennett, and Anderson, *Scholarly Friends*, 5.

24. Leonard T. Baker, *In Memoriam, Yates Snowden, 1858–1933* (Columbia: 1934), quoted in W. K. Wood, "'My Dear Mr. Snowden': U. B. Phillips' Letters to Yates Snowden of South Carolina College 1904–1932," *South Carolina Historical Magazine* 85 (October, 1984): 294

25. Yates Snowden, "South Carolinians," *Times Picayune*, June 14, 1891.

26. "Beautiful Mrs. Beecher," *New York World*, October 1, 1893 and *Atlanta Constitution*, October 29, 1893.

27. "Some Daring Women Who have Ruled the Destinies of Weak Men," *Evansville Courier and Press*, November 12, 1893.

28. "Two Notorious Women," *National Police Gazette*, November 11, 1893, 7; and P. Beecher to Wilson, March 6, 1908.

29. Dickert, "Countess Percele; and C. D. M., "Fair Adventuress."

30. "Beautiful Miss Boozer."

31. Also quoted in Elmore, *Scandalous*, 74.

32. "Pourtales-Gorgier, (Arthur, comte de)," *Annuaire diplomatique*, 1901, 250.

33. Ian Ruxton, editor, and Ernest Mason Satow, *Diaries of Sir Ernest Satow, British Minister in Tokyo (1895–1900): A Diplomat Returns to Japan, April 20, 1896* (Tokyo: Edition Synapse, 2003; paperback edition, Raleigh: LuLu, 2010), 36, 83–84, 234.

34. Ibid., 234.

35. *La Champagne* passenger list, March 25, 1895, ancestry.com.

36. Grubissich-Keresztür visiting card, private collection; Pourtalès-Gorgier, Arthur de, *Société Genevoise de Généalogie*, accessed May 3, 2012, http://www.gen-gen.ch/de-POURTALÈS-BEAUVOIR-BOOSIER/

Marie-Adèle/34314; Satow, Diaries, 266; and *Japan Weekly Mail*, April 16, 1898, 387.

37. M. Pourtalès to Wilson, September 12, 1904 and Marguerite Cunliffe-Owen, "Marquise de Fontenoy's Letter," *Chicago Tribune*, August 27, 1898.

38. "French Legation," *Japanese Weekly Mail*, July 9, 1898.

39. Cunliffe-Owen, "Letter."

40. "Accident de Chemin de Fer" ("Railroad Accident"), *Figaro*, August 10, 1898; and "Countess Pourtales," *Japan Weekly Mail*, September 24, 1898, 323.

41. Ibid.

42. Ibid.

43. Ibid.

NOTES TO CHAPTER TWENTY-TWO

1. M. Pourtalès to Wilson, April 15, 1905. The year is not included, but Marie writes that they have been renting their villa in Florence for three years (having arrived in 1902).

2. M. Pourtalès to Wilson, September 12, 1904; "Honduras," in *Monthly Bulletin of the International Bureau of the American Republics*, July–December 1902 (Washington, DC: Government Printing Office, 1902), 77–78; and Thomas David Schoonover, *The French in Central America: Culture and Commerce, 1820–1930* (Lanham, MD: Rowman and Littlefield, 1999), 104, 106, 112, 114.

3. M. Pourtalès to Wilson, September 12, 1904 and April 20, 1905; *San Francisco Call*, September 19, 1902; and "Personages in the Public Eye," *Salt Lake Telegram*, September 30, 1902.

4. Pat Brazeel, "From Royalty to Roadways" (interview with Ethel Wilson Battle), *Star-Advocate*, Titusville, Florida, December 8, 1976, Ethel Battle Papers, North Brevard Historical Society.

5. M. Pourtalès to Wilson, September 12, 1904; Battle to Coker, November 19, 1959, Coker Papers, box 8, folder 634; and United States Federal Census, 1900, 1910.

6. M. Pourtalès to Wilson, September 12, 1904.

7. Ibid.

8. Woodlands Trust for Historic Preservation, burial plot fact sheet, section C-338, area 87.

9. M. Pourtalès to Wilson, September 12, 1904.

10. Taylor, "Two Equipages," 253.

11. Gibbes, *Who Burnt Columbia?* 21–22.

12. Marquise de Fontenoy (Cunliffe-Owen), "De Pourtales: A Famous Family," *Washington Post*, January 6, 1905; and Fontenoy, "Counts de Pourtales and their American Wives," *Baltimore American*, June 6, 1905.

13. Coker, "Author's Note," *La Belle*, 8; and "What Actually Happened to Marie Boozer," unpublished essay, ca. 1973, box 9, folder 807, Coker Papers, South Caroliniana Library, University of South Carolina.

14. Hamersly, ed., "Beecher, John Preston," 47; and Grove Street Cemetery, New Haven, Connecticut, inscription on John S. Beecher's headstone, *Hale Cemetery Inscriptions, 1629–1934*, ancestry.com.

15. M. Pourtalès to Wilson, April 15, 1905, Wilson-Battle-Connell-Park Papers; and photo, Blanche Louise Beecher and (John) Preston Beecher, passport applications, 1916, ancestry.com.

16. P. Beecher to Wilson, July 5, 1905; and M. Pourtalès to Wilson, April 15, 1905, Wilson-Battle-Connell-Park Papers.

17. Ibid.

18. Battle, "Remembrances."

19. "Mrs. Wilson Passes Away," *East Coast Advocate*, August 10, 1917, "Area Pioneer, Mayor, Judge, Legislator," (Titusville, Florida) *East Coast Advocate*, July 25, 1913; Manning, *Feaster Family*, 19–20, 21; and "Women's Club Opens New Library in Titusville," *Daytona Beach Morning Journal*, February 22, 1950.

20. M. Pourtalès to Wilson, April 15, 1905, Wilson-Battle-Connell-Park Papers.

21. M. Pourtalès to Wilson, April 20, 1905, Wilson-Battle-Connell-Park Papers.

22. Ibid.

23. P. Beecher to Wilson, March 6, 1908; and *"Extrait de la Feuile Officielle" Feuille d'Avis de Neuchâtel*, June 14, 1905, 6.

24. "Women as Soldiers of Fortune," *Montgomery Tribune*, July 10, 1906.

25. A. Pourtalès to P. Beecher, January 25 and 30, 1908, Wilson-Battle-Connell-Park Papers.

26. A Pourtalès to P. Beecher, January 30, 1908. Elmore quotes part of this letter in *Scandalous*, 63.

27. A. Pourtalès to Wilson, March 16, 1908.

28. Ibid.

29. "Petition"; Carr Family Genealogies; Newberry Census, 1850; United States Federal Census, 1860; and "Pourtalès, Marie, 1846–1908," *Biography Index*, BioIn 5, ancestry.com.

30. P. Beecher to Wilson, March 6, 1908.

31. Ibid.

32. Beecher to Helen Wilson, July 15, 1910.

33. Malzac, "*Branche de Gorgier*"; and Beecher to Reed, September 1, 1921.

34. Pourtalès genealogy; United States Court of Appeals, Ninth Circuit, Transcript of Records, no. 2181, Oregon & California Railroad Company vs. Maria de Grubissich, "Maria de Grubissich, nee Maria de Pourtales," filed October 1, 1912; and "Dead Defendant Wins Law Action," *San Francisco Call*, July 18, 1913.

35. P. Beecher to Reed, August 17, 1923; P. Beecher to Reed, September 1, 1921, also quoted in Elmore, *Scandalous*, 62; and Graydon to Patton, ca. October 1, 1959.

Notes to Epilogue

1. Brazeel, "From Royalty to Roadways."

2. Snowden, "Study in Scarlet," *Countess Pourtales*, 7; and Snowden, Bennett, and Anderson, *Scholarly Friends*, 85, 356.

3. Snowden, Bennett, and Anderson, *Scholarly Friends*, 83.

4. Snowden, "Study in Scarlet," *Countess Pourtales*, 7–9, 14; and Sherman and Royster, *Memoirs of Sherman*, 777.

5. Snowden, Bennett, and Anderson, *Scholarly Friends*, 86, 89, 91.

6. Ibid., 180, 196.

7. Battle to Coker, October 21, 1959, box 8, folder 634, Coker Papers.

8. Coker, "What Actually Happened," 2.

9. Coker, "What Actually Happened," 2; and Herman Hattaway, "Shades of Blue and Gray: An Introductory Military History of the Civil War," *Civil War: The Magazine of the Civil War Society*, 1996, 46–47. Elmore, *Scandalous*, also quotes Coker, 86.

10. Lawrence, "Mary Boozer"; and "Muchly Married," 23.

11. Marion Selly, "Recall Mary Boozer, Vamp," *News and Courier, January 7*, 1934.

12. Simkins and Patton, *Confederacy*, 63, 271; and South Carolina Writers' Project and Governor Burnet R. Maybank, *South Carolina: Guide to the*

Palmetto State (Columbia: South Carolina State Department of Education, Works Progress Administration, 1941), 312.

13. Graydon, *Tales of Columbia*, 244.

14. Eugene B. Sloan, "Mrs. Graydon Writes Delightful War Novel," *State* (Columbia, South Carolina), December 7, 1958; Kathleen Lewis, "State's Romantic Past Inspires SC Author," *State*, May 3, 1959; and Graydon, *Another Jezebel*, 4, 60–62, 201.

15. Graydon to Patton, ca. October 1, 1959.

16. Coker, *Belle*, 23, 29, 106–7.

17. Ibid., 35, 37, 52–55, 106–7, 198.

18. Ibid., 190–93, 211–24.

19. Ibid., 241–305.

20. "What Actually Happened," 1.

21. Coker to Battle, September 16, 1959, Wilson-Battle-Connell-Park Papers; and Bolick to Coker, August 17, 1959, Coker Papers, box 8, folder 649, South Caroliniana Library, University of South Carolina.

22. Coker to Battle, September 16, 1959, Wilson-Battle-Connell-Park Papers.

23. Coker to Battle, October 3, 1959, Wilson-Battle-Connell-Park Papers.

24. Battle to Coker, October 9, 1959 and October 14, 1959, Coker Papers, box 8, folder 634.

25. Coker to Battle, October 10, 1959 and November 27, 1959, Wilson-Battle Connell-Park Papers.

26. Battle to Coker, October 21, 1959, November 6, 1959, January 28, 1960, and February 3, 1960, Coker Papers, box 8, folder 634; and Battle to Etta Rosson, March 1, 1960, Graydon Scrapbook and Rosson Papers, collection of Henrietta Rosson Morton.

27. "Living Descendant"; and Brazeel, "Royalty to Roadways."

28. Graydon to Coker, November 7, 1959, Coker Papers, box 8, folder 634; and Coker to Graydon, November 8, 1959, Graydon Scrapbook.

29. Bradford to Graydon, undated, Graydon Scrapbook.

30. Graydon to Park, undated, ca. 1959, Wilson-Battle-Connell-Park Papers.

31. Battle to Graydon, "Living Descendant"; Battle to Graydon, October 27, 1959; and Battle to editor, Dutton & Co., January 31, 1960 (copy), Wilson-Battle-Connell-Park Papers. (Also copied in Coker Papers, box 8, folder 634.)

32. Battle to Coker, February 6, 1960; Coker to Park, February 23, 1960

(copy), Coker Papers, box 8, folder 634; Battle to Rosson, January 22, 1960; and "Royalty to Roadways."

33. Massey, *Bonnet Brigades,* 238.

34. Hattaway, "Blue and Gray," 46–47.

BIBLIOGRAPHY

Andrew, Rod. *Wade Hampton: Confederate Warrior to Southern Redeemer.* Chapel Hill: University of North Carolina Press, 2008.

Anthony, Mr. [Senator Henry Bowen]. Committee of Claims: "Report to Accompany Bill S. No. 434." *The Report of the Committees of the Senate of the United States for the First Session Thirty-ninth Congress, 1865–66,* Washington, DC: Government Printing Office, 1866.

Battle, Ethel Wilson. Family history essay. Author's collection.

———. Family history essay and genealogy. Wilson-Battle-Connell-Park Papers.

———. Papers, North Brevard Historical Society.

———. "Remembrance of Old Titusville by an Eighty-Four-Year-Old Native." Handwritten manuscript, 1973, Wilson-Battle-Connell-Park Papers.

———. "Remembrance of Old Titusville by an Eighty-Four-Year-Old Native" Typed manuscript, 1974, Ethel Battle Papers, North Brevard Historical Society.

Bay, Nina. *Woman's Fiction: A Guide to Novels by and about Women in America, 1820–1870.* Chicago: University of Illinois Press, 1993.

"Beecher, John S." *Club Men of New York: Their Occupations, and Business and Home Addresses.* New York: Republic Press, 1893, 79.

Beecher, John S. vs. Marie A. Beecher. Summons and Complaint, April 9, 1873, Answer, May 8, 1873, Reply, May 12, 1873. Court of Common Pleas, New York County Clerk.

———. Divorce Hearing, June 29, 1874, Referee's Report, July 11, 1874. Court of Common Pleas, New York County Clerk.

———. Judgment of Divorce, July 20, 1874, Court of Common Pleas, New York County Clerk.

Beecher, Marie Adèle and Count Arthur de Pourtales-Gorgier, marriage certificate, certified copy, no. 397, November 4, 1875. England: General Register's Office.

"Beecher, Marie, Juin 1875," *fiche* 795, Prefecture de Police, Paris.

Bernheimer, Charles. *Figures of Ill Repute: Representing Prostitution in Nineteenth-Century France.* Durham, NC: Duke University Press, 1997.

Blackford, Harriet Ely, a.k.a. Fanny Lear. *Le Roman d'une Americaine en Russie: Accompagné de Lettres Originales.* Brussels: A. LaCroix, 1875.

Blanshard, Alastair J. L. *Sex: Vice and Love from Antiquity to Modernity.* Malden, MA: Wiley-Blackwell, 2010.

Bradley, Mark L. *This Astounding Close: The Road to Bennett Place.* Chapel Hill: University of North Carolina Press, 2000.

Breese, Captain Kidder Randolph. "Lieutenant Samuel W. Preston, USN (1840–65)." Secretary of the Navy, *Report of the Secretary of the Navy with an Appendix Containing Reports from Officers, December 1865,* Washington DC: Government Printing Office, 1865.

Brown, Thomas. *Civil War Canon: Sites of Confederate Memory in South Carolina.* Chapel Hill: University of North Carolina Press, 2015.

Browne, Junius Henri. *The Great Metropolis: A Mirror of New York.* Hartford: American Publishing, 1869.

Burlingame Michael, ed. *At Lincoln's Side, John Hay's Civil War.* Carbondale: Southern Illinois Press, 2006.

Bynum, Victoria E. *Unruly Women: The Politics of Social and Sexual Control in the Old South.* Chapel Hill: University of North Carolina Press, 1992.

Capers, Ellison. Papers. Citadel Archives and Museum, Charleston, South Carolina.

Carr, Mary. Family Bible records, provided by Henrietta Rosson Morton.

Chesnut, Mary Boykin Miller. *Mary Chesnut's Civil War.* Edited by C. Van Woodward. New Haven, CT: Yale University Press, 1981.

———. *A Diary from Dixie.* Edited by Ben Ames Williams. New York: Houghton Mifflin 1949, 1976, reprint Cambridge: Harvard University Press, 1980.

Clayton, Rev. Daniel Bragg. "A Sensible Wedding." In *Forty-Seven Years in the Universalist Ministry.* Columbia, SC: Clayton.

Coker, Elizabeth Boatwright. *La Belle: A Novel Based on the Life of the Notorious Southern Belle.* New York: Dutton, 1959.

———. Papers, South Caroliniana Library, University of South Carolina.

———."Sandal or Scandal: Being the True Story of Countess Pourtalès, Formerly Miss Marie Boozer of Columbia, S. C." Unpublished essay, 1974, box 8, folders 658–59, Coker Papers, South Caroliniana Library, University of South Carolina.

———. "What Actually Happened to Marie Boozer." Unpublished essay, ca. 1973, Coker Papers, box 9, folder 807, South Caroliniana Library, University of South Carolina.

Coleman, James Plemon. *The Robert Coleman Family, From Virginia to Texas, 1652–1965.* Accessed November 12, 2012. http://freepages.genealogy.rootsweb.ances-try.com/~nansemondcolemans/chascity/robtvatx.txt.

Connery, Thomas. "A Famous Newspaper Hoax." *Harper's Weekly,* June 3, 1893, 534–35.

Conyngham, David Power. *Sherman's March through the South: With Sketches and*

Incidents of the Campaign. New York: Sheldon, 1865, reprint Bedford: Applewood, 2001.

Cornwallis-West, Mrs. George. *The Reminiscences of Lady Randolph Churchill.* New York: Century, 1909.

Crawley, Arthur Ernest. "The Orgy." In *Studies of Savages and Sex.* Edited by Theodore Besterman. New York: Dutton, 1929, reprint, Whitefish: Kessinger, 2006.

"Creatore v. Creatore." *Supreme Court Appellate Division*, New York. New York: Brown, 1909.

Culliton, Paul. "A Hero by any Definition: A Canadian Sailor's Lasting Legacy." *Esprit de Corps*, April 1, 2011, The Free Library, 2011. S. R. Taylor Publishing. http://www.thefreelibrary.com/A+hero+by+any+definition%3a+a+Canadian+sailor%27s+lasting+legacy.-a0254828825.

Cunningham, Patricia A. *Women's Clothing, 1850–1920.* Kent, OH: Kent State University Press, 2003.

Davis, Burke. *Sherman's March: The First Full-Length Narrative of General William T. Sherman's Devastating March through Georgia and the Carolinas.* New York: Random House, 1980, reprint Vintage, 1988.

De Bow, James Dunwoody Brownson. *De Bow's Commercial Review of the South & West.* New Orleans: Weld, 1849.

Department of Congress and Labor, Bureau of the Census. *Marriage and Divorce, 1867–1906: Summary, Laws, Foreign Statistics.* Washington, DC: Government Printing Office, 1909.

Deratte, Laure. *"Les Insoumises: Un regard sous les dessous du second empire."* July 7, 2008. http://lesinsoumiseslexpositiondarlesenligne.blogspot.fr/2008_08_01_archive.html.

Desilver, Robert. *Desilver's Philadelphia Directory and Stranger's Guide.* Philadelphia: Desilver, 1828.

Dewey, Melville, Bowker, et al, *Library Journal,* 3 (March–December 1878).

Doctorow, E. L. *The March: A Novel.* New York: Random House, 2005.

Drysdale, George. *Elements of Social Science or Physical, Sexual, or Natural Religion.* 1861, reprint London: E. Truelove, 1877.

Dubose, John W. "Fayetteville (N.C.) Road Fight." *Confederate Veteran* 20: 84–86, February 1912.

Edwards, Eliza Mary Hatch. *Commander William Barker Cushing, of the United States Navy.* New York: Tennyson Neely, 1898.

Elmore, Grace Brown. *A Heritage of Woe: The Civil War Diary of Grace Brown Elmore, 1861–1868.* Edited by Marli F. Weiner. Athens: University of Georgia Press, 1997.

Elmore, Tom. T*he Scandalous Lives of Carolina Belles Marie Boozer and Amelia Feaster: Flirting with the Enemy.* Charleston, SC: History Press, 2014.

Emerson, W. Eric and Karen Stokes. *A Confederate Englishman: The Civil War Letters of Henry Wemyss Feilden.* Columbia: University of South Carolina Press, 2013.

England & Wales, Free BMD Marriage Index, 1837–1915. Volume 1a, 616, ancestry. com.

Farnham, Christie Anne. *Education of the Southern Belle: Higher Education and Student Socialization in the Antebellum South.* New York: New York University Press, 1994.

Farquhar, Michael. *A Treasury of Deception: Liars, Misleaders, Hoodwinkers, and the Extraordinary True Stories of History's Greatest Hoaxes, Fakes, and Frauds.* New York: Penguin, 2005.

Feaster, Amelia Sees. "Come List Awhile." Poem manuscript. Wilson-Battle-Connell-Park Papers, and Elizabeth Boatwright Coker Papers, box 8, folder 634, South Caroliniana Library, University of South Carolina.

———. Sworn affidavits, June 2, 1865, and December 16, 1865. C. A. Stevens, ed. *Memorial Testimony and Letters from Prisoners for the Claim of P. F. Frazee, for Property Destroyed at Columbia, South Carolina, February 17, 1865, by the Forces of Major General Sherman.* Washington, DC: McGill & Witherow, 1866.

——— to Abraham Lincoln endorsed by Generals Howard and Terry. Handwritten transcription, 6, 278, RG 107, Entry 18: Records of the Secretary of War, Record Series Originating During The Period 1789–1889, Correspondence, Letters Received, Letters Received (Main Series), 1801–1889, Re: compensation; Microfilm M 221, Roll 281, Frames 28–33, The Papers of Abraham Lincoln, National Archives.

Feaster, Andrew. Bible records. Collection of Henrietta Rosson Morton.

Feaster Family Papers. North Brevard Historical Society.

Feaster, Margaret Narcissa. Kathleen Coleman and Kathryn Scott High, eds. *Diary of Margaret Narcissa Feaster, 1860–1865.* Privately printed: 1950.

Field, Samuel Joseph. Autobiographical manuscript, September 1, 1895. Reed Papers, collection of J. Reed Bradford.

"Financial Diary, 1883." *Manual of Statistics.* New York: Financial News Association, January 1884, 238.

Fiske, U. S. V., Captain Joseph E. "An Involuntary Journey Through the Confederacy," in *Civil War Papers: Read Before the Commandery of the State of Massachusetts, Military Order of the Loyal Legion of the United States,* vol. 2. Boston: Gilson, 1900, 513–29.

Fonvielle, Chris Eugene. *The Wilmington Campaign: Last Departing Rays of Hope.* Mechanicsburg, PA: Stackpole, 2001.

Fox, Tryphena Blanche Holder. *Northern Woman in the Plantation South. Letters of Tryphena Blanche Holder Fox, 1856–1876.* Edited by and Wilma King. Columbia: University of South Carolina Press, 1994.

Frank, Mary Lisa Tendrich, ed. *Women in the American Civil War, Volume 1.* ABC-Clio, 2007.

Frederick, James Vincent. *Ben Holladay: The Stage Coach King.* Glendale, California: Arthur H. Clark Company, 1940.

Freeling, William F. *Prelude to Civil War: The Nullification Controversy in South Carolina, 1816–46.* New York: Oxford University Press, 1992.

Frost, John. *The Class Book of Nature; Comprising Lessons on the Universe, the Three Kingdoms of Nature, and the Form and Structure of the Human Body.* Hartford: Belknap & Hamersley, 1838. Openlibrary.org, Library of Congress.

Frost-Knappman, Elizabeth and Kathryn Cullen-DuPont. *Women's Suffrage in America.* New York: Facts on File, 2005.

Gibbes, James G. *Who Burnt Columbia?* Newberry, SC: E. H. Aull, 1902.

Gibbes, Robert, *Street Guide to Columbia,* 1859.

Giele, Janet Zollinger. *Two Paths to Women's Equality: Temperance, Suffrage, and the Origins of Modern Feminism.* New York: Twayne, 1995.

Goldblatt, Gloria. "The Queen of Bohemia Grew up in Charleston." *Carologue,* Autumn 1988.

Graydon, Nell S. *Another Jezebel: A Yankee Spy in South Carolina.* Columbia, SC: R. L Bryan, 1958.

———. Papers, Southern Historical Collection, University of North Carolina.

———. Scrapbook, collection of Henrietta Rosson Morton.

———. *Tales of Columbia.* Columbia, SC: R. L. Byan, 1964.

Hamersly Lewis Randolph, ed. "Beecher, John Preston," *Who's Who in New York City and State.* New York: Hamersley, 1904, 100.

———. *Men of Affairs in New York.* New York: L. R. Hamersly, 1906.

Harned Family Papers, Historical Society of Pennsylvania.

Hattaway, Herman. "Shades of Blue and Gray: An Introductory Military History of the Civil War." *Civil War: The Magazine of the Civil War Society,* November 1996: 46–57.

Headley, Joel Tyler. *Farragut and Our Naval Commanders.* New York: Treat, 1867.

Hickman, Katie. *Courtesans: Money, Sex and Fame in the Nineteenth Century.* New York: HarperCollins, 2003.

Hilde, Libra Rose. *Worth a Dozen Men: Women and Nursing in the Civil War South.*

Charlottesville: University of Virginia Press, 2012, e-book.

Holcomb, Brent Howard. *Marriage and Death Notices from Columbia, South Carolina, Newspapers, 1838–1860*. Columbia, SC, USA: SCMAR, 1988, ancestry.com.

Holladay, Ben. Papers. MSS 893, box 1, folder 6, Oregon Historical Society.

"Honduras." *Monthly Bulletin of the International Bureau of the American Republics*, July–December 1902. Washington, DC: Government Printing Office, 1902, 77–78.

Houbre, Gabrielle. *Le Livre des Courtisanes: Archives Secrètes de la Police des Moeurs, 1861–1876*. Paris: Tallander, 2006.

Howard, Oliver Otis. *Autobiography of Oliver Otis Howard, Major-General, United States Army*. New York: Baker & Taylor, 1908.

———. Papers, Bowdoin College Library.

Hunt, Charles O. "Our Escape from Camp Sorghum." *War Papers Read before the Commandery of the State of Maine—Military Order of the Loyal Legion of the United States. Portland: Thurston, 1898*, 1: 86–92.

Jellison, Richard M. and Phillip S. Swartz. "The Scientific Interests of Robert W. Gibbes." *South Carolina Historical Magazine* 66 (April 1965): 77–97.

Jones, James Dunwody. "A Guard at Andersonville." *Civil War Times* (January 1, 1964). Reprint, *Andersonville: Penetrating Views from Men Who Were There and from Modern Scholars*. New York: Eastern Acorn Press, 1983, 3–5.

Kahr, Madlyn Millner. "Women as Artists and Women's Art," *Woman's Art Journal* 36, no. 2 (Autumn 1982–Winter 1983): 28–31.

Kane, Harnett T. and Victor Leclerc. *The Scandalous Mrs. Blackford*. New York: Julian Messner, 1951.

Laffaye, Horace A. *Polo in the United States: A History*. Jefferson, NC: McFarland, 2011.

Lawrence, Robert de Treville III. "The Muchly Married Miss Mary Boozer." *Confederate Veteran*, Nashville: Cunningham, 1921.

———. Papers, 1730–1991. Kennesaw State University Archives.

Le Conte, Emma. Diary, 1864–1865. Transcript of the manuscript from Southern Historical Collection, University of North Carolina at Chapel Hill, i.d. LeConte, Emma, Call number 420, Manuscripts Dept., Southern Historical Collection, UNC-CH. Electronic edition, *Documenting the American South*, Library of Congress, accessed October 21, 2013, http://docsouth.unc.edu/fpn/leconteemma/leconte.html.

Leonard, John William. *Woman's Who's Who of America: A Biographical Dictionary of Contemporary Women of the United States and Canada*. New York: American Commonwealth, 1914–1915.

Loubat, Joseph Florimond, ed. *A Yachtsman's Scrap Book: Or, The Ups and Downs of*

Yacht Racing. New York: Brentano, 1887.

Lowry, Thomas Power. *Story the Soldiers Wouldn't Tell: Sex in the Civil War.* Mechanicsburg, PA: Stackpole, 2012.

Lucas, Marion Brunson. *Sherman and the Burning of Columbia.* Columbia: University of South Carolina Press, 2000.

Lucia, Ellis. *The Saga of Ben Holladay: Giant of the Old West.* New York: Hastings House, 1959.

Malanowski, Jamie. *Commander Will Cushing: Daredevil Hero of the Civil War.* New York: Norton 2014.

Malzac, Louis. *"Branche de Gorgier," Les Pourtalès: Histoire d'une Famille Hugenote des Cevennes, 1500–1860.* Paris: Hatchette, 1914.

Manning, John T. T*he Feaster Family of LaGrange.* Unpublished genealogy, Feaster Family Papers, North Brevard Historical Society.

Martin, Samuel J. *Kill-Cavalry: The Life of Union General Hugh Judson Kilpatrick.* Mechanicsburg, PA: Stackpole, 2000.

Massey, Mary Elizabeth. *Bonnet Brigades.* New York: Knopf, 1966.

McAuliffe, Mary. *Dawn of the Belle Époque: The Paris of Monet, Zola, Bernhardt, Eiffel, Debussy, Clemenceau, and their Friends.* Lanham, MD: Rowan and Littlefield, 2011.

McDonald, Eva, Daniel McDonald, and Harriet Blackford. *Fanny Lear: Love and Scandal in Tsarist Russia.* Bloomington: iUniverse, 2011.

McGeachy, John A. "In Sherman's Wake: Refugees of the March Through the Carolinas." North Carolina State University, History 546, May 2003, http://www4.ncsu.edu/~jam3/sherman.htm.

Mehtiyev, Afgan. "The Language of Diplomacy." *California Linguistic Notes* 35:2 (Spring 2010): 1–10. PDF supplied by California State University, Fullerton, accessed May 25, 2013. http://hss.fullerton.edu/linguistics/cln/SP10PDF/MethievLgDplmcy.pdf.

Miller, Edwin Haviland. "Notes and Queries." *American Literature.* Duke University Press, 33, no. 1 (March 1961): 64–68.

Mitchell, Lena Norwood. "Jacob Norris Feaster and His Wife, Amelia Sees Boozer." Unpublished manuscript, Wilson-Battle-Connell-Park Papers.

Moore, Alexander and Robert W. Gibbes. *Memoir of James de Veaux of Charleston, S.C.* Columbia: University of South Carolina Press, 2012.

Mossman, Carol A. *Writing with a Vengeance: The Countess de Chabrillan's Rise from Prostitution.* Toronto: University of Toronto Press, 2009.

Neuchâtel, Switzerland. "Séance du 14 Mars 1877." *Recours des Citoyens Pourtalès*

Recueil des Arrêts Rendus par la Cour de Cassation Civile de la Canton De Neuchâtel. Canton Neuchâtel: Montandon, 1881, 1: 295–300.

Newberry Equity Records, November 21, 1848, box 20, Package, 34, Newberry Public Archives.

New York (State), Judiciary Committee. *Proceedings in the Senate on the Investigation of the Charges preferred against John H. McCunn.* Albany: Reed, Parsons, 1874.

Nichols, Brevet Major George Ward. *The Story of the Great March: From the Diary of a Staff Officer.* New York: Harper, 1865. http://openlibrary.com.

Old Bailey Proceedings Online. PDF, April 1874, Trial of Arthur Foster (30), #231. "Arthur Foster, Breaking Peace, Wounding, 7th April 1874." Accessed June 7, 2012. http://www.oldbaileyonline.org.

O'Neall, John Belton and John Abney Chapman. *Annals of Newberry in Two Parts.* Newberry: Aull and Houseal, 1892.

Osborn, Major Thomas, *The Fiery Trail: A Union Officer's Account of Sherman's Last Campaign.* Edited by Richard Harwell and Philip N. Racine. Knoxville: University of Tennessee Press, 1986.

Pearl, Cora. *Memoirs of Cora Pearl: The English Beauty of the French Empire.* London: Vickers, 1890.

Pearl, Cyril. *The Girl with the Swansdown Seat.* Indianapolis: Bobbs-Merrill, 1955.

Perkin, Joan. *Victorian Women.* New York: NYU Press, 1995.

"Phoenix, Lloyd." *Club Men of New York: Their Occupations, and Business and Home Addresses.* New York: Republic Press, 1893, 316.

Pollack, Deborah C. *Laura Woodward: The Artist Behind the Innovator Who Developed Palm Beach.* Palm Beach: Blue Heron Press with the Historical Society of Palm Beach County, 2009.

Pope, Thomas H. *History of Newberry County, South Carolina, 1749–1860.* Columbia: University of South Carolina Press, 1973, reprint, 1992.

"Pourtalès-Gorgier (Arthur, Comte de)." *Annuaire Diplomatique et Consulaire de la République française.* Paris Berger-Levrault, 1886, 202; 1901, 250.

"Pourtalès-Gorgier, Arthur de." *Société Genevoise de Généalogie.* Accessed May 3, 2012. http:// www.gen-gen.ch/de-POURTALÈS-BEAUVOIR-BOOSIERMarie-Adèle /34314.

Pourtalès, Marie Countess de. Papers. Duke University.

"Pourtalès, Marie, 1846–1908." *Biography Index: A Cumulative Index to Biographical Material in Books and Magazines,* September 1958–August 1961. New York: H. W. Wilson Co., 1962, BioIn 5. ancestry.com.

Reed Family Papers. Collection of J. Reed Bradford.

Richardson, James Sanders Guignard. "John B. O'Neall vs. Amelia Boozer, July 1850." *South Carolina Court of Appeals, Report of Cases in Equity: Argued and Determined in the Court of Appeals and Court of Errors, Vol. IV.* Columbia, SC: R. W. Gibbes, 1851.

Rolph, Daniel. "The Plot to Burn Philadelphia to the Ground at the End of the Civil War." Historical Society of Pennsylvania. Accessed March 4, 2014. https://hsp.org/blogs/history-hitsthe-plot-to-burn-philadelphia-to-the-ground-at-the-end-of-the-civil-war.

Rosson, Etta. Papers, collection of Henrietta Rosson Morton.

Rounding, Virginia. *Grandes Horizontales: The Lives and Legends of Four Nineteenth-Century Courtesans.* New York: Bloomsbury, 2003.

Ruvigny, Marquis de. *Titled Nobility of Europe.* London: Harrison & Sons,1914.

Sabre, Gilbert. *Nineteen Months a Prisoner of War.* New York: American News Company, 1865.

Satow, Ernest Mason Satow. *Diaries of Sir Ernest Satow, British Minister in Tokyo (1895–1900): A Diplomat Returns to Japan, April 20, 1896.* Edited by Ian Ruxton. Tokyo: Edition Synapse, 2003, paperback edition, Raleigh: LuLu, 2010.

Schoonover, Thomas David. *The French in Central America: Culture and Commerce,* 1820–193. Lanham, MD: Rowman and Littlefield, 1999.

Sebba, Anne. American Jennie: *The Remarkable Life of Lady Randolph Churchill.* New York: Norton, 2007.

Selby, Julian. *A Checkered Life: Being a Brief History of the Countess Pourtales, formerly Miss Marie Boozer, of Columbia, S.C.* Columbia, SC: *Phoenix,* 1878 (microfiche).

Selby, Julian and Yates Snowden. *The Countess Pourtales.* Columbia, SC: S & H., 1915.

Shelton, W. H. "Hard Road to Travel Out of Dixie." *Famous Adventures and Prison Escapes of the Civil War.* New York: Century, 1885, reprint 1911, 251.

Sherman, William Tecumseh. *Memoirs of General William Tecumseh Sherman.* Edited by Charles Royster. Des Moines, IA: Library of America, 1990.

Silber, Nina. *Battle Scars: Gender and Sexuality in the American Civil War.* Oxford: Oxford University Press, 2006.

Simkins, Francis Butler and James Welch Patton. *Women of the Confederacy.* Richmond and New York: Garrett and Massie, 1936, reprint St. Claire Shores, Michigan, Scholarly Press, 1971.

Simms, William Gilmore. *Sack and Destruction of Columbia.* Columbia, SC: *Phoenix,* 1865.

Smythe, Mrs., Mrs. Thomas Taylor, Mrs. August Kohn, et al, eds. *South Carolina Women of the Confederacy: Records Collected by Mrs. A. T. Smythe, Miss M. B.*

Poppenheim, and Mrs. Thomas Taylor. Columbia: State Committee Daughters of the Confederacy, 1903.

Snowden, Yates (as Felix Old Boy). "A Study in Scarlet." In *The Countess Pourtales.* Columbia, SC: S & H, 1915, 6–17.

Snowden, Yates and John Bennett. *Two Scholarly Friends, Yates Snowden—John Bennett, Correspondence, 1902–1932.* Edited by Mary Crow Anderson. Columbia: University of South Carolina Press, 1993.

Snyder, Emily. Sees Family Record. Wilson-Battle-Connell-Park Papers.

Snyder, William Bartram. *Biographical Sketch of Robert Carr.* Manuscript, 1866, Historical Society of Pennsylvania.

South Carolina Writers' Project and Governor Burnet R. Maybank. *South Carolina: Guide to the Palmetto State.* Columbia: South Carolina State Department of Education, Works Progress Administration, 1941.

Spady, Matthew. "Audubon Park: A Brief History." Accessed June 29, 2012. http://www.audubonparkny.com/AudubonParkBriefHistory.html#anchor_174.

Stowe, Steven M. "City Country and the Feminine Voice." In Michael O'Brien, and Moltke-Hansen, eds. *Intellectual Life in Antebellum Charleston.* Knoxville: University of Tennessee Press, 1986.

Summer, George Leland. *Newberry County, South Carolina: Historical and Genealogical Annals.* Newberry: Summer, 1950, reprint, Baltimore: Genealogy Publishing, 2002.

Swaine, Robert T. *The Cravath Firm and Its Predecessors, 1819–1947.* New York: Ad Press, 1948, reprint Clark: Lawbook Exchange, 2006, vol. 1.

Taylor, Lawrence W. "Boy Soldiers of the Confederacy." Columbia, S.C., July 7, 1916, South Carolina Division, M. C. Butler Chapter, UDC, Columbia, SC, United Daughters of the Confederacy, Recollections and Reminiscences 1861–1865, 1990.

Thornwell, Emily. *The Lady's Guide to Perfect Gentility, in Manners, Dress and Conversation.* New York: Derby and Jackson, 1856.

Thorp, Gould H. and Laura M. Thorp. Judgment of Divorce, January 10, 1880. Superior Court, New York County Clerk.

Trumbull, Chaplain H. Clay. "Four Naval Officers Whom I Knew." *The United Service: A Quarterly Review of Military and Naval Affairs.* Philadelphia: Hamersly, January 1879, 32–44.

"Two Notorious Women." *National Police Gazette.* November 11, 1893.

United States Naval War Records Office. *Official records of the Union and Confederate Navies in the War of the Rebellion / Series I – Volume 13: South Atlantic Blockading*

Squadron (May 14, 1862–April 7, 1863). Washington, DC: Government Printing Office, 1901.

"USS *Preston*." Destroyer History Foundation. Accessed July 22, 2016. http://destroyerhistory.org/goldplater/index.asp?r=37900&pid=37901,.

Von Hedemann, Franzisca, Baroness. *Love Stories of Court Beauties*. New York: Doran, 1917.

Wait, William. *The Practice at Law: In Equity, and in Special Proceedings, in All the Courts in the State of New York*. Albany: Gould, 1874.

Walsh, William Shepard. *Handy-Book of Literary Curiosities*. Philadelphia: Lippincott, 1892.

Warren, Susan. *Descendants of Archibald Carr*. Historic Bartram's Garden.

Wellman, Manly Wade. "Mary Broke Many Hearts." Typewritten article, Wilson-Battle-Connell-Park Papers.

———. *The County of Moore, 1847–1947: A North Carolina Region's Second Hundred Years*. Southern Pines, NC: Moore County Historical Association, 1962.

Wells, Edward L. *Hampton and His Cavalry*. Richmond: Johnson, 1899.

———. "A Morning Call on General Kilpatrick." March 1884. In Reverend J. William Jones, ed., Southern Historical Society Papers, Tufts University. Accessed September 2, 2012. http://www.perseus.tufts.edu/hopper/text?doc=Perseus%3Atext%3A2001.05.0269%3Achapter%3D35.

———. *A Sketch of the Charleston Light Dragoons, from the Earliest Formation of the Corps*. Charleston, SC: Lucas, Richardson, and Co., 1888.

Wells, Jonathan Daniel. *Origins of the Southern Middle Class, 1800–1861*. Chapel Hill: University of North Carolina Press, 2003.

Williams, J. F. *Old and New Columbia*. Columbia, SC: Epworth Orphanage Press, 1929.

Wilson-Battle-Connell-Park Papers. Collection of Penny Park.

Wilson, Benjamin Rush Papers. North Brevard Historical Society.

Wilson Family Bible Records. Collection of Penny Park.

Wilson, Rufus Rockwell. *New York: Old & New—Its Story, Streets, and Landmarks*. Philadelphia: Lippincott, 1902.

Wilson, Thomas. *The Philadelphia Directory and Stranger's Guide, 1825*. Philadelphia: Wilson, 1825, Philadelphia Museum of Art.

Winchester, Simon. *Krakatoa: The Day the World Exploded, August 27, 1883*. New York: Harper Collins, 2003.

Winship, Kihm. "Skaneateles: Benjamin Porter, Brave to a Fault. Accessed May 15, 2016.

https://kihm6.wordpress.com/2015/11/08/benjamin-porter-brave-to-a-fault/.

Wise, James E. *On Sherman's Trail: The Civil War's North Carolina Climax.* Charleston, SC: History Press, 2008.

Wittenberg, Eric J. *The Battle of Monroe's Crossroads and the Civil War's Final Campaign.* El Dorado Hills: Savas Beatie, 2005.

"Women Artists." *Southern Review* 5, no. 10 (April 1869): 299–321.

Wood, W. K. "'My Dear Mr. Snowden': U. B. Phillips' Letters to Yates Snowden of South Carolina College 1904–1932." *South Carolina Historical Magazine* 85 (October, 1984): 292–304.

Wortham, Hugh Evelyn. *Edward VII, Man and King.* Boston: Little Brown, 1931.

Wright, William Redwood Family Papers. Series 6: Fisher and Wright 1852–1921, box 32, Historical Society of Pennsylvania.

INDEX

CPSIA information can be obtained
at www.ICGtesting.com
Printed in the USA
LVOW11s1334150817
545093LV00002BA/101/P